The
QUOTABLE
THOREAU

The
QUOTABLE
THOREAU

Collected and Edited by Jeffrey S. Cramer

PRINCETON UNIVERSITY PRESS

PRINCETON AND OXFORD

Grateful acknowledgment is made to the following for permission to reproduce
illustrations from their collections:

The Thoreau Society. Established in 1941, the Thoreau Society is the oldest and
largest organization devoted to an American author. The Society has long con-
tributed to the dissemination of knowledge about Thoreau by collecting books,
manuscripts, and artifacts relating to Thoreau and his contemporaries, by encouraging the use of its collections at the Thoreau Institute at Walden Woods,
and by publishing articles in two Society periodicals. For more information about
the Thoreau Society, visit www.thoreausociety.org.

The Thoreau Institute at Walden Woods. Owned and managed by the Walden
Woods Project, which preserves the land, literature and legacy of Henry David
Thoreau to foster an ethic of environmental stewardship and social responsibility,
the Thoreau Institute Library provides the most comprehensive body of Thoreau-
related material available in one place. For more information about the Walden
Woods Project, visit www.walden.org.

Library of Congress Cataloging-in-Publication Data

Thoreau, Henry David, 1817–1862
The quotable Thoreau / collected and edited by Jeffrey S. Cramer.
p.   cm.
Includes bibliographical references and index.
ISBN 978-0-691-13997-5 (acid-free paper)   1. Thoreau, Henry David,
1817–1862—Quotations.   I. Cramer, Jeffrey S., 1955–   II. Title.
PS3042.C69   2011
818'.302—dc22   2010034860

British Library Cataloging-in-Publication Data is available

This book has been composed in Minion Pro
Printed on acid-free paper. ∞
Printed in the United States of America

1 3 5 7 9 10 8 6 4 2

To Julia

*What is the singing of birds, or any natural
sounds, compared with the voice of one we love?*

—Thoreau in his Journal, April 30, 1851

CONTENTS

Thoreau Described by His Contemporaries:

Physical Characteristics—Conduct and Character—Anecdotes—Death—Some Final Assessments

PREFACE

Henry David Thoreau (1817–1862) is one of America's most influential literary figures. His writings on social reform inspired Tolstoy, Gandhi, Martin Luther King, Jr., and protesters against the war in Vietnam. His natural history writings were a great impetus to John Muir and the establishment of national parks, and he is considered by many to be the father of the American environmental movement. His words in support of John Brown or against the Fugitive Slave Law are as courageous and as forthright as any written by our founding fathers, and his embodiment of the man who "hears a different drummer"[1] has helped many readers pursue their own paths with independence and confidence.

The selections in *The Quotable Thoreau* were chosen not only to present the iconic Thoreau—social reformer, civilly disobedient citizen, environmentalist, self-reliant thinker—but also to show the man who thought about such varied topics as food, love, God, attitude, cities, women, and everything else that fell within his scope.

In the collection that follows you will find disparate and contradictory statements on the same theme. Thoreau did not always fall clearly on any one side of a debate. His writings on civil disobedience and his writings supporting John Brown, for example, do not always seem to come from the same pen. As he wrote in his Journal on November 11, 1851, "Today you may write a chapter on the advantages of travelling & to-morrow you may write another chapter on the advantages of not travelling."[2]

During the selection process, several themes coalesced to become the focus of the primary topical arrangement. These major topics are arranged alphabetically. Many other themes emerged for which there were only a dozen or fewer quotations, and these have been gathered, also alphabetically, under the rubric "On Miscellaneous Subjects." I let the quotations themselves dictate the categories. Many quotations easily could have been placed in more than one section, but the index ensures that these may be found according to any of the appropriate themes under whose umbrella they could have fallen. A cursory glance may reveal apparent gaps: civil disobedience, as a theme, for instance, does not appear in the table of contents. However, quotations that touch on that idea are more pertinently found under broader categories such as "Higher Law" or "Government and Politics."

Many books of quotations are arranged in chronological order, either by date of composition or publication, within each topic. Because so many of Thoreau's writings were published posthumously, however, the date of publication often is not an important clue to his development as a writer or philosopher. This book proceeded instead in the spirit of Thoreau, who, when constructing a lecture or essay, would mine his journals and join previously unassociated lines from various periods into an associated whole. Thoreau did not, as he wrote, "always state the facts exactly in the order in which they were observed" but would "select out of my numerous observations extended over a series of years the most important ones, and describe them in a natural order."[3] Such an arrangement allowed for a deliberate positioning of a chosen line as an introductory quotation within a section or, in many cases, an end quotation that gave a sense of conclusion. One example is the section on the seasons, which benefits from a chronological arrangement of month and day, not year, to give a sense of the cycle of the seasons on which Thoreau commented.

In addition to sections in which Thoreau describes both himself and his contemporaries, and one in which he is in turn described by those who knew him, there is a section entitled "Questions," which is unique to this volume. It was inspired by his statement about Emerson's son, Waldo, whose "questions did not admit of an answer; they were the same which you would ask yourself."[4] In his writings, Thoreau posited questions, whether to himself in his Journal or to his readers in his published works, or to both. "There is no delay in answering great questions,"[5] Thoreau wrote in his Journal on March 6, 1840.

No compendium of quotations could satisfy every reader. Each will have his or her own special and personally relevant quotation from Thoreau. I hope that those who may find their favorite missing will discover a new and previously unknown gem to take its place.

On the death of Charles Stearns Wheeler in 1843 Thoreau wrote that although his friend "did not exhibit the highest qualities of the scholar, he possessed in a re-markable degree many of the essential and rarer ones—and his patient industry and energy—his reverent love of letters—and his proverbial accuracy—."[6] A "love of letters" and "accuracy" do not always go hand in hand. Following the release of the 1981 film *On Golden Pond*, Thoreau's classic began to be called *On Walden Pond*.

In these days of quick Internet searches, incorrect quotations as well as quotations misattributed to Tho-reau have proliferated to an irreparable degree. Mis-quotations and misattributions have been picked up by journalists, published in newspapers and magazines, and then quoted from these once-reliable sources in books, creating a sense of legitimacy and authority.

To address this issue, I have included an appendix of misquotations and misattributions. This is only a small sampling of an apocrypha that is growing at an exponential rate and can be addressed only in an up-datable medium. For further examples I recommend the misquotations section on the Walden Woods Proj-ect's Thoreau Institute Web site, www.walden.org.

I would like to thank several individuals, and organiza-tions, who supported this project in various ways.

Elizabeth Witherell, Editor-in-Chief of *The Writ-ings of Henry D. Thoreau*, published by Princeton Uni-versity Press, for her invaluable help in many ways, including interpreting the sometimes daunting cipher of Thoreau's handwriting.

Kathryn Dolan for proofing several quotations against Thoreau's manuscript Journal.

For their help with a few last-minute questions: Robert N. Hudspeth, editor of the forthcoming *The Correspondence of Henry D. Thoreau* for The Writings of Henry D. Thoreau; Sue Hodson, Curator of Literary Manuscripts at the Huntington Library, San Marino, California; Christine Nelson, Drue Heinz Curator of Literary and Historical Manuscripts at The Morgan Library & Museum, New York; Svante Printz of the Kungliga Biblioteket, The National Library of Sweden; and Charles Green of the Department of Rare Books and Special Collections, Princeton University Library.

The Walden Woods Project for permission to quote from the second draft manuscript of Thoreau's essay "Sir Walter Raleigh," and for images from their collections at their Thoreau Institute at Walden Woods, a center for Thoreau studies housing the most comprehensive collection of Thoreau-related material in the world. These collections are an invaluable and unparalleled resource without which this book could not have been completed.

The Thoreau Society, the oldest and largest organization devoted to an American author, for their generous permission in allowing the reproduction of several images, many of which are unique, from their collections housed at the Thoreau Institute at Walden Woods.

Nathaniel T. Wheelwright for permission to publish a photograph of the slug in his private collection with which Thoreau's cousin, George Thatcher, killed a moose.

Helen Bowdoin for her frequent, welcome, and eagerly anticipated e-mails beginning, "Do you have this one?"

Greg Joly for his continued encouragement.

Special thanks to my editor at Princeton University Press, Anne Savarese, for appreciating the need for a volume such as this, and for making the call. And to Lauren Lepow, who masterfully edited the manuscript so I needn't hang my head in embarrassment.

And to my family—my wife, Julia, and our two daughters, Kazia and Zoë: although you may come last in these acknowledgments, know that you are always, *always* first.

Notes

1. *Walden*, p. 326.
2. *Journal*, vol. 4, p. 177.
3. *Faith in a Seed*, p. 104.
4. Ralph Waldo Emerson, *The Journals of Ralph Waldo Emerson: With Annotations*, vol. 6, p. 153.
5. *Journal*, vol. 1, p. 115.
6. *The Correspondence of Henry David Thoreau*, p. 129.

A NOTE ON THE TEXTS

Thoreau's texts have been drawn, whenever possible, from The Writings of Henry D. Thoreau as prepared by the Thoreau Edition for publication by Princeton University Press. In the case of Thoreau's Journal, volume numbers in arabic numerals refer to *Journal* (edited by John C. Broderick et al. [Princeton: Princeton University Press, 1981–]); volume numbers in roman numerals refer to *The Journal of Henry D. Thoreau* (edited by Bradford Torrey and Francis H. Allen [Boston: Houghton Mifflin, 1906]). For a full listing of works cited, see the bibliography.

Texts not yet available in the Thoreau Edition series have been prepared from the standard edition of that text, usually *The Writings of Henry D. Thoreau* as published by Houghton Mifflin in 1906. These texts have been proofed against the manuscript and/or a draft manuscript transcription prepared by the Thoreau Edition when available. In instances where the published text and the manuscript are substantively parallel and do not vary except in the matter of accidentals such as punctuation or spelling, the published text has been allowed to stand. In cases where there is a substantive difference, the printed text has been emended based on the reading of the manuscript. Where an editor of a printed text has added a word or phrase in brackets, those bracketed interpolations, except in three instances, have been removed.

Texts of Thoreau's Journal from the Thoreau Edition are published as genetic texts, texts that stylistically reflect the physical nature of Thoreau's manuscripts. These have been minimally and silently emended in order to present the reader with a reliable reading text unencumbered with obvious misspellings and other minor slips of the pen. Punctuation, including the addition of terminal punctuation where missing from the manuscript text, has been added or emended for clarity, as has the spelling-out of abbreviations, and the removal of many instances of Thoreau's writing tic, the ever-present dash or series of dashes. This editorial principle is supported by the example of Thoreau's own transcription of an August 30, 1841, Journal passage, "What is a day—if the day's work be not done?"[1] in his 1842 Journal as "What is a day if the day's work be not done?"[2]

NOTES

1. *Journal*, vol. 1, p. 325.
2. *Journal*, vol. 1, p. 413.

INTRODUCTION: THOREAU'S GARMENT OF ART

Thoreau was the vegetarian who ate meat; the conservationist who surveyed woodlots in Walden Woods; the pacifist who endorsed violence; the hermit who loved gossip. This is not to support his detractors who label him a hypocrite. It is, instead, to confirm that he was a questioner of the very concepts we have come to associate with his name. Thoreau was a seeker, a seer, a teacher. Being confident, not convinced, he would not complacently let yesterday's answer settle today's discourse. He was faithful, not dogmatic; principled, not sanctimonious; and transcendentally alert and expectant, not experientially adamant and stolid.

Robert Louis Stevenson dismissed Thoreau as one who "could not clothe his opinions in the garment of art, for that was not his talent."[1] Thoreau may have anticipated such a denunciation when he wrote in *Walden*, "I trust that none will stretch the seams in putting on the coat, for it may do good service to him whom it fits."[2] Or as he more bluntly put it, also in *Walden*, "It is not all books that are as dull as their readers."[3]

The time Thoreau lived in and wrote about was a period of ferment in the United States. It was the era that produced Melville's *Moby-Dick*, Whitman's *Leaves of Grass*, and Hawthorne's *The Scarlet Letter*. In the decades bracketing his move to Walden Pond, Brook

Farm and Fruitlands were established, the Indian Removal Act and the Fugitive Slave Act were both made law, the Irish suffered the potato famine and immigrated to New England in unprecedented numbers, banks failed, various movements were giving birth to various reforms, and the country was heading toward Civil War.

EARLY LIFE

Concord, Massachusetts, the town in which Thoreau was born and where he would spend most of his life, had, in the first half of the nineteenth century, a population of about two thousand. It was primarily an agricultural community, although manufacturing was on the increase, as it was everywhere. The train would reach Concord around the same time Thoreau moved to Walden Pond in 1845. Famous for its part in the American Revolution, Concord was the place where, as Emerson put it, "the shot heard round the world"[4] was fired just under forty-one years before Thoreau was born.

And here, on the 12th of May, 1817, David Henry Thoreau was born in his grandmother's house on Virginia Road. He would reorder his name to Henry David Thoreau around the time of his graduation from Harvard. His immediate family consisted of his father, John, and his mother, Cynthia, and his two older siblings,

Helen and John Jr. His younger sister, Sophia, who would be born two years later, was the only one of the four Thoreau children to live beyond forty-four years, the age at which Henry died.

The family worked to send Thoreau, whom they considered more academically inclined than his older brother, to Harvard in 1833. Harvard, in those days, was small and somewhat provincial, and had moved away from its initial Puritan roots toward a more liberal Unitarianism. Thoreau neither excelled nor failed, graduating nineteenth in a class of forty-seven. Before heading back to Concord he participated in the August 30 graduation "conference," "The Commercial Spirit of Modern Times, considered in its Influence on the Political, Moral, and Literary Character of a Nation." The next day Emerson read his "The American Scholar" to the graduating class, although it is not certain whether Thoreau stayed to hear his fellow Concordian.

On returning to his hometown Thoreau began to seek employment. To support himself throughout his life, Thoreau would take on various forms of work. As he later wrote to his Harvard class secretary, Henry Williams, he did not know whether what he did was "a profession, or a trade, or what not. It is not yet learned, and in every instance has been practised before being studied. . . . It is not one but legion. I will give you some of the monster's heads. I am a Schoolmaster—a Private Tutor, a Surveyor—a Gardener, a Farmer—a Painter, I mean a House Painter, a Carpenter, a Mason, a Day-Laborer, a Pencil-Maker, a Glass-paper Maker, a Writer, and sometimes a Poetaster."[5]

But following graduation he pursued one of the options for which his time at Harvard had prepared him: teaching. He searched for a teaching position and had a job in Concord's Center Grammar School by mid-September, resigning within the month because he was unwilling to cane his students. It was a period in which educational reform was in the air, and Thoreau would not accept the old ways when he was able to see that there were alternatives. Bronson Alcott had opened his Temple School in Boston in 1834, teaching through dialogue, rather than rote, and without resorting to corporal punishment. Horace Mann, after being appointed secretary to the Massachusetts Board of Education in 1837, effected change and improvement in the public school system. Elizabeth Peabody would open the first American kindergarten in 1860.

Thoreau searched for a new position while participating in the family pencil business. The business began in 1821 when Thoreau's uncle, Charles Dunbar, discovered a deposit of plumbago (graphite) in New Hampshire. Thoreau's father soon joined in, eventually becoming sole proprietor. Thoreau assisted in the family business, which consisted of pencil making and later the selling of plumbago, for which, owing to the invention of electrotyping, there came to be a high demand.

Thoreau continued to make inquiries about teaching positions in Massachusetts, New York, Maine, and as far away as Virginia and even Kentucky. Unable to secure a teaching job, he opened his own school. Starting with four students in September 1837, by July 1838 he was able to reopen the recently closed Concord

Academy, with his brother, John, soon joining him, and with a full complement of twenty-five students learning experientially, and by conversation and dialogue.

EMERSON

Ralph Waldo Emerson had moved to Concord in 1834. Stories vary slightly as to how and when he and Thoreau became acquainted, but by October 22, 1837, Emerson, who had published his influential book *Nature* the year before, was showing a keen interest in the recent Harvard graduate, asking the questions that prompted the first entry in Thoreau's two-million-word Journal: "What are you doing now? . . . Do you keep a journal?"[6]

Emerson's influence on Thoreau may be deduced from words—inspiring, oracular, and transcendental— uttered in the address he read to Thoreau's class at Harvard: "If the single man plant himself indomitably on his instincts, and there abide, the huge world will come round to him. Patience,—patience;—with the shades of all the good and great for company; and for solace, the perspective of your own infinite life; and for work, the study and the communication of principles, the making those instincts prevalent, the conversion of the world. Is it not the chief disgrace in the world, not to be an unit;—not to be reckoned one character;—not to yield that peculiar fruit which each man was created to bear. . . . We will walk on our own feet; we will work with our own hands; we will speak our own minds."[7]

Thoreau was ready to embrace what Emerson had to offer. As he wrote in his Journal, "We see so much only as we possess,"[8] or, perhaps even more pertinently, "I think we may detect that some sort of preparation and faint expectation preceded every discovery we have made."[9]

Initially their connection was of that of mentor and student, but as Thoreau came into his own, not just as a writer, but as an individual who could not, or would not, be considered merely an Emerson disciple, their relationship suffered a strain that forced them to realign and adjust. The friendship that developed was more equal and respectful. Fifteen years after Thoreau's death Emerson's admiration continued to grow. Writing to George Stewart, Jr., in 1877, Emerson said that "Thoreau was a superior genius. I read his books and manuscripts always with new surprise at the range of his topics and the novelty and depth of his thought. A man of large reading, of quick perception, of great practical courage and ability,—who grew greater every day, &, had his short life been prolonged would have found few equals to the power and wealth of his mind."[10]

LOVE

In July of 1839 the seventeen-year-old Ellen Devereux Sewall came to Concord to visit her brother, Edmund, who was enrolled in the Thoreau brothers' school, and her aunt, Prudence Ward, who was a boarder in the Thoreau family home. Both Thoreau brothers fell in love with her during her two-week visit. There is little in Thoreau's writings that points to his romance, but one line in his Journal that is unquestionably about Ellen expresses his love in all its power and anguish: "There is no remedy for love but to love more."[11]

In September John went to Scituate, Massachusetts, to visit Ellen, and in the summer of 1840 Ellen returned to Concord. After a boating excursion Henry wrote, "The other day I rowed in my boat a free—even lovely young lady—and as I plied the oars she sat in the stern—and there was nothing but she between me and the sky."[12]

When Ellen returned to Scituate, John soon followed with the intention of proposing marriage. Henry described his anxiety during John's visit to Scituate as "an aeon in which a Syrian empire might rise and fall."[13] Although she briefly accepted, the engagement was broken off. By November Henry had written to Ellen, himself proposing marriage. At her father's insistence this time Ellen wrote to Henry on November 10 rejecting his proposal. The following week she wrote to her aunt, Prudence Ward: "I never felt so badly at sending a letter in all my life. I could not bear to think that both those friends whom I have enjoyed so much with would now no longer be able to have the free pleasant intercourse with us as formerly."[14]

Despite Ellen's concerns that their relationship would end, Thoreau remained friends with her, and, after she married Rev. Joseph Osgood, became friends with her husband and family. Twenty-five years later, on his deathbed, when Ellen's name was mentioned in passing, Thoreau said to his sister, "I have always loved her."[15]

DEATHS AND RENEWAL

In April 1841, following a period in which John was ill and weak, the brothers had to close Concord Academy. With the closing of their school, Thoreau again helped out in the family pencil business, writing, on September 8, 1841, "I, who am going to be a pencil-maker tomorrow, can sympathize with God Apollo, who served King Admetus for a while on earth."[16]

On the first day of 1842, John cut his finger while stropping his razor. When the wound became infected, tetanus, then commonly called lockjaw, set in. John died on January 11. So close were the brothers, and so overwhelming was John's death, that Thoreau developed sympathetic lockjaw, showing all the symptoms of the disease.

Just over two weeks later Emerson suffered an equally painful loss. His five-year-old son, Waldo, died of scarlet fever. Emerson was able to express his grief in letters to friends and family. Thoreau was not. He did not write a word in his Journal for six weeks.

In time Thoreau decided to memorialize his brother and perhaps purge some of his inexorable grief over John's death by writing a book based on a boat trip the two brothers had taken in 1839, following Ellen Sewall's first visit. *A Week on the Concord and Merrimack Rivers* was the first book Thoreau would write, but he needed to find a place where he could write it.

WALDEN

In March 1845 Thoreau borrowed an ax and began to construct a small house in which to live at Walden Pond. He built it on land owned by Emerson and was given permission to live there in exchange for some work, such as planting pine trees.

Friends and neighbors were curious as to why he went to Walden to live. It was not the sort of place one would expect a Harvard graduate to make his home. The land was nonarable and was used primarily as woodlots. For a long period, well into the twentieth century, it was considered marginal territory. Not only was it unproductive as farmland, it was a place where productive and welcome members of Concord society would not live. It was the home of the Irish immigrants working on the railroad; it was the home of alcoholics; it had been the home of former slaves; and it was now the home of Henry David Thoreau.

The two-year, two-month, and two-day experience at Walden Pond was negligible compared with what it became in Thoreau's mind. As he wrote in *A Week on the Concord and Merrimack Rivers*, the book he went to Walden to write, "This world is but canvass to our imaginations."[17] As the river served as the thread in his first book on which to arrange his thoughts on various subjects that concerned him, so the pond and his time there served in his second book as the canvas to his imagination. Questions about which Thoreau thought over the years now began to find a place in the work that he was writing about his time at the pond.

It mattered little whether they were reflections of his actual experience there, or ideas that came to him half a dozen years after he left the pond. His thoughts on living deliberately, on how we should live our lives, and on the influence of nature merged into a truly American work at a time when literature in the United States was just beginning to find its voice.

LECTURER

Thoreau gave a lecture entitled "Society" on March 14, 1838, at Masonic Hall as part of the Concord Lyceum. This was his first public lecture, excluding college exercises at Harvard, and the first of twenty-one lectures he delivered at the Concord Lyceum alone, the last of which, "Wild Apples," was delivered on February 8,

1860. In between he is known to have lectured more than fifty other times.

Although he most often lectured locally, and was not as well known or popular as Emerson, his lecturing activities took him outside Massachusetts, to Pennsylvania, Maine, New Jersey, and Connecticut. In 1859 when the famed orator Frederick Douglass—following John Brown's raid on Harper's Ferry and given his association with Brown—decided to go to Canada on the urgent recommendation of friends, Thoreau was asked to give a lecture in Douglass's place.

SLAVERY AND ABOLITION

Although it was too open and there was nowhere to run or hide if slave-catchers came into the woods, some had said, according to Allen French, "that Henry hid slaves in his hut at Walden."[18] Whether or not there were fugitive slaves at Walden, Thoreau did help slaves on their journey to freedom. French wrote that "it was curious that when strange negroes took the west-bound train, Henry Thoreau was very likely to board it with them, buying tickets to Canada but returning too soon to have used them himself."[19]

Moncure Conway described seeing "the singularly tender and lowly devotion of the scholar to the slave. He must be fed, his swollen feet bathed, and he must think of nothing but rest. Again and again this coolest and calmest of men drew near to the trembling negro, and bade him feel at home, and have no fear that any power should again wrong him."[20]

But Thoreau did not want to spend his time as part of the abolition, or any, movement. Finding himself torn between attending to nature and attending to man, Thoreau wrote to his friend H.G.O. Blake, on September 26, 1855, mildly complaining, "I was glad to hear the other day that Higginson and Brown were gone to Ktaadn; it must be so much better to go to than a Woman's Rights or Abolition Convention."[21] By late 1859 it was clear to him that a "man may have other affairs to attend to."[22]

This was not a turning away from emancipation and reform but a turning inward toward self-emancipation and self-reformation. It was not just, as he wrote in "Resistance to Civil Government," that it was "not a man's duty, as a matter of course, to devote himself to the eradication of any, even the most enormous wrong."[23] Still more, he felt that it was through what he referred to as "the unquestionable ability of man to elevate his life by a conscious endeavor" that we can "affect the quality of the day."[24]

THE NIGHT IN JAIL

Almost as famous as his stay at Walden Pond was an incident that occurred when he walked into town from the pond one day in July 1846. Sam Staples, the jailer and tax collector, approached Thoreau requesting his unpaid poll tax. Thoreau refused to pay and Staples put him jail. During the evening while Staples was out, an unidentified person paid the tax to Staples's daughter. When Staples was informed of this by his daughter, he had already removed his boots and was not willing to put them back on, so he did not let Thoreau out until the next morning.

This incident proved to be the impetus for the writing of Thoreau's best-known essay, "Civil Disobedience," originally published as "Resistance to Civil Government," and first presented as a lecture, in February 1848, called "The Rights and Duties of the Individual in Relation to Government."

As with his river excursion or his stay at the pond, the jailing itself was a minor part of the essay. "Under a government which imprisons any unjustly, the true place for a just man is also in prison,"[25] he wrote, but the central theme, as he expressed it in the essay, is this: "Unjust laws exist: shall we be content to obey them, or shall we endeavor to amend them, and obey them until we have succeeded, or shall we transgress them at once?"[26]

Thoreau's action, his refusal to pay his poll tax and the resulting night in jail, had little effect. Had he not written his essay, his protest would be as little known as an earlier effort made by Bronson Alcott, who also did not pay his tax and also had his tax paid for him. The ethic of his essay, however, has had great value, both politically and otherwise, for a minister trying to end racial segregation in the South, or for one man peacefully leading his country to home rule, or for a generation trying to end a war in Vietnam.

WORDS OVER EXPERIENCE

In his description of what makes mythology, Thoreau wrote in *A Week on the Concord and Merrimack Rivers*, "So far from being false or fabulous in the common sense, it contains only enduring and essential truth, the I and you, the here and there, the now and then, being omitted."[27] It is this for which Thoreau strove as a writer.

He was not writing autobiography in the strictest sense, nor was he writing memoir, but something that went beyond the confines of those genres. *Walden* is not a book about a man living in the woods but one about a man living. *Cape Cod* is not a simple travel narrative about the easternmost part of Massachusetts but a record of the discovery of that vantage point from which a person can literally as well as figuratively put all America behind him. And in *A Week on the Concord and Merrimack Rivers* Thoreau launched himself on a river that was "an emblem of all progress, following the same law with the system, with time, and all that is made."[28]

"To read well, that is, to read true books in a true spirit," Thoreau wrote in the "Reading" chapter of

Walden, "is a noble exercise, and one that will task the reader more than any exercise which the customs of the day esteem. It requires a training such as the athletes underwent, the steady intention almost of the whole life to this object. Books must be read as deliberately and reservedly as they were written."[29]

Thoreau's words are paradigmatic of the writer's art. If we are able to read with deliberation, transcendentally, only then are we reading "true books in a true spirit," and only then are we able to see that for which Robert Louis Stevenson did not know to look.

For Thoreau, a mountain was never just a mountain, a river never merely a river; though morning was always a beginning, night was never an end; the sun was always illuminating and the wind was always inspiriting; and for Thoreau, each phenomenon experienced "must stand for the whole world to you—symbolical of all things."[30]

NOTES

1. Robert Louis Stevenson, *Familiar Studies of Men and Books* (New York: Charles Scribner's Sons, 1905), p. 131.

2. *Walden*, p. 4.

3. *Walden*, p. 107.

4. Ralph Waldo Emerson, *Poems* (Boston: Houghton Mifflin, 1884), p. 139.

5. *The Correspondence of Henry David Thoreau*, p. 186.

6. *Journal*, vol. 1, p. 5.

7. Ralph Waldo Emerson, *Nature; Addresses, and Lectures* (Boston: James Munroe, 1849), p. 110.

8. *Journal*, vol. 1, p. 74.

9. *Journal*, vol. IX, p. 53.

10. Ralph Waldo Emerson, *The Letters of Ralph Waldo Emerson*, vol. 6, p. 303.

11. *Journal*, vol. 1, p. 81.

12. *Journal*, vol. 1, p. 132.

13. *Journal*, vol. 1, p. 158.

14. Walter Harding, *The Days of Henry Thoreau*, p. 102.

15. Ibid., p. 104.

16. *The Correspondence of Henry David Thoreau*, p. 47.

17. *A Week on the Concord and Merrimack Rivers*, p. 292.

18. Alan French, *Old Concord* (Boston: Little, Brown, 1915), p. 12.

19. Ibid.

20. Moncure Conway, "Thoreau," p. 192.

21. *The Correspondence of Henry David Thoreau*, p. 384; emended from manuscript letter (Henry David Thoreau Papers, 1835–1956, in the Clifton Waller Barrett Library, Accession #6345 through 6345-k, Special Collections, University of Virginia Library, Charlottesville, Va.)

22. "A Plea for Captain John Brown," in *Reform Papers*, p. 133.

23. "Resistance to Civil Government" in *Reform Papers*, p. 71.

24. *Walden*, p. 90.

25. "Resistance to Civil Government" in *Reform Papers*, p. 76.

26. Ibid., pp. 72–73.

27. *A Week on the Concord and Merrimack Rivers*, p. 60.

28. Ibid., p. 12.

29. *Walden*, pp. 100–101.

30. *Journal*, vol. 5, pp. 412–413.

ON PRONOUNCING THE NAME THOREAU

A name pronounced is the recognition of the individual to whom it belongs. He who can pronounce my name aright, he can call me, and is entitled to my love and service.

—*A Week on the Concord and Merrimack Rivers*

The proper pronunciation of Thoreau's name has long been a question. Over the years there have been many who have asked it and several who have answered it, although often contradicting someone else's answer in the process.

When Calvin Greene visited Concord the year after Thoreau's death, he wrote in his Journal: "Enquired of a man at work there where the Thoreaus' burying place was. He said, 'At the new grounds.' I also asked if I pronounced the name *Thoreau* right."[1] Whether he did or not is a mystery. Greene recorded neither his pronunciation nor whether it was accepted as correct.

In 1880 Thoreau's Aunt Maria received a newspaper clipping written by an unidentified "Classmate." The author of the clipping wrote: "Whoever pronounces Mr. Thoreau's name, 'thorough' pronounces it barbarously. His ancestors were French, but he never pronounced his name as a Frenchman would, omitting the sound of the h, but accenting the last syllable, Thoreau, or Thor-ro."[2]

Thirty years after Thoreau died, the following question was posted to the "literary querist" column in the May 1892 issue of *The Book Buyer*: "533.—How did Henry D. Thoreau pronounce his name? J. K. L." The editor replied, "As if it were spelled Tho-ro; sound th as in 'thin,' and accent the first syllable."[3]

In 1912 Julius W. Abernethy published his compendium, *Correct Pronunciation: A Manual Containing Two Thousand Common Words That Are Frequently Mispronounced, and Eight Hundred Proper Names, with Practical Exercises*. One of the eight hundred names was that of Thoreau. Abernethy, however, was unable to determine the pronunciation and offered two as equally correct: "Thoreau—thō′ro, *or* tho-rō′."[4]

Kate L. Edwards wrote unsatisfactorily in her "Concord Letter" published in the Southbridge (Massachusetts) *Journal* (December 5, 1895), although she did include an often-used pun: "It is interesting to note how thoroughly Thoreau is pronounced by all Concordians. A lady who has lived her life in Concord went the other day to buy one of Thoreau's books. The girl who waited on her looked perplexed, and after a moment's hesitation, said, 'Oh! You mean Thoreau.' She took the book and moved away wondering if after all people know how to pronounce their own names rightly."[5]

By the beginning of the twentieth century the question had found its way into fiction, although with similarly unsatisfactory results. Ralph Henry Barbour similarly left us hanging in his 1903 novel *The Land of Joy* when one character said: "I don't know how to talk about Emerson or Thoreau. I didn't even know he pronounced his name that way—Thoreau, I mean. They'll think I'm an awful fool, won't they?"[6]

Many who had heard his name from Thoreau himself, or were introduced to him by someone who knew him, left a record of the pronunciation by spelling his name not correctly but phonetically. Bronson Alcott, early in his friendship with Thoreau, spelled his name, "Thorow," "Thoro," and "Thorough."[7] Nathaniel Hawthorne wrote in 1842 that "Mr. Thorow dined with us yesterday."[8] Daniel Clark, brother of the James Clark who purchased Thoreau's Walden house from Emerson, wrote that "Mr. Thoro lectured upon Cape Cod" at the lyceum.[9]

Although Isaac Hecker, writing in 1847, addressed a letter to "Henry Thorough, Concord, Massachusetts,"[10] Ralph Waldo Emerson's son, Edward, wrote in 1918 that many in Concord, "careless, as is usual, in their pronunciation, called the family *Thorough*, just like the adjective, shirking the last syllable."[11] His comment, however, is more a criticism of a New Englander's pronunciation of the adjective than an equation of the pronunciation of the adjective and the name.

Mary Mapes Dodge, author of *Hans Brinker*, published a column in *St. Nicholas* magazine called "Jack-in-the-pulpit." In the January 1882 column she referred to a "scientific friend" who had sent her a passage on bees written by Thoreau. Dodge concluded, "I must add a message from my friend's postscript, which says that most people who see the name in print call it

'Tho-ro,' but that the gentleman himself and his personal friends pronounced it almost exactly like the word 'thorough.'"[12]

Thoreau himself would make self-referencing puns in his work that point to the adjective, calling himself a "thorough-bred business man"[13] or a "thoroughfare."[14] In an allusion to the first syllable of his patronymic, Thoreau wrote in his Journal on May 3, 1857, that he was "a descendant of Northmen who worshipped Thor."[15] Even more elaborately punning, he wrote in *Cape Cod*: "But whether Thor-finn saw the mirage here or not, Thor-eau, one of the same family, did; and perchance it was because Leif the Lucky had, in a previous voyage, taken Thor-er and his people off the rock in the middle of the sea, that Thor-eau was born to see it."[16]

Thoreau's New Bedford friend Daniel Ricketson outlined the pronunciation of the two syllables in a short poem:

> My dear old Northman, sitting by the sea,
> Whose azure tint is seen, reflected in the e'e,
> Leave your sharks and your dolphins, and eke the
>   sporting whale,
> And for a little while on milder scenes regale:
> My heart is beating strongly to see your face once more,
> So leave the land of *Thor*, and *row* along our shore![17]

The final word rests, however, with Edward Emerson, who wrote straightforwardly, "We always called my friend Thó-row, the *h* sounded, and accent on the first syllable."[18]

NOTES

1. Henry David Thoreau, *Some Unpublished Letters of Henry D. and Sophia E. Thoreau: A Chapter in the History of a Still-born Book*, ed. Samuel Arthur Jones (Jamaica; Queensborough, NY: Marion Press, 1899), p. 74.

2. "Answer to query 2418," *Boston Evening Transcript*, July 26, 1880, p. 6.

3. *The Book Buyer A Summary of American and Foreign Literature* vol. 9, no. 4 (May 1892): 178.

4. Julius W. Abernethy, *Correct Pronunciation: A Manual Containing Two Thousand Common Words That Are Frequently Mispronounced, and Eight Hundred Proper Names, with Practical Exercises* (New York: Charles E. Merrill, 1912), p. 147.

5. *The New England Writers and the Press: Evaluations in Contemporary Journalism of Emerson, Hawthorne, Thoreau, Alcott, Longfellow, and Others: New Dimensions for Transcendentalism and the American Renaissance*, comp. Kenneth Walter Cameron (Hartford: Transcendental Books, 1980), p. 257.

6. Ralph Henry Barbour, *The Land of Joy* (New York: A. Wessels Co., 1907), p. 145.

7. Bronson Alcott, *The Journals of Bronson Alcott*, ed. Odell Shepard (Boston: Little, Brown, 1938), p. 127, n. 13.

8. Nathaniel Hawthorne, *The American Notebooks*, p. 353.

9. Ruth Robinson Wheeler, *Concord: Climate for Freedom* (Concord, MA: Concord Antiquarian Society, 1967), p. 176.

10. Walter Harding, *The Days of Henry Thoreau*, p. 166.

11. "About Our 'American Diogenes,'" *The Goddard Biblio Log*, Spring 1973, p. 7.

12. *St. Nicholas* vol. 9, no. 3 (January 1882): 254.

13. "Paradise (to be) Regained" in *Reform Papers*, p. 21.

14. "Life without Principle" in *Reform Papers*, p. 172.

15. *Journal*, vol. IX, p. 352.

16. *Cape Cod*, p. 151.

17. Daniel Ricketson, *Daniel Ricketson and His Friends: Letters*, p. 57.

18 "About Our 'American Diogenes,'" p. 7.

A THOREAU CHRONOLOGY

1817   Born, David Henry Thoreau, July 12, third of four
children—Helen (1812–1849), John (1815–1842), and
Sophia (1819–1876)—to John and Cynthia (Dunbar)
Thoreau in Concord, Massachusetts

1818   Family moves to Chelmsford, Massachusetts, where
father opens a grocery store

1821   Grocery store closes; family moves to Boston, where
father works as a schoolteacher

1822   Visits Walden Pond for the first time

1823   Family moves back to Concord, where father begins
making pencils; family takes in boarders

1828   Enrolls in Concord Academy, as does his brother,
John, where they study geography, history, and science, as well as French, Latin, and Greek

1829   Attends lectures at the Concord Lyceum

1833   Enrolls in Harvard College

1835   To earn money, teaches in Canton, Massachusetts,
during winter term

1836   Leaves Harvard temporarily owing to illness

1837   Graduates from Harvard; begins Journal; friendship
with Emerson begins

1838   Goes to Maine for the first time to search for a teaching position; gives first lecture, on "Society," at Concord Lyceum; elected secretary and curator of the Lyceum; opens small private school before taking over
the Concord Academy in September

1839   John joins Thoreau at Concord Academy as a teacher; meets Ellen Sewall, to whom both he and John will propose and by whom both will be rejected; takes boat trip with John on the Concord and Merrimack Rivers to Concord, New Hampshire

1840   The *Dial* first published, for which Thoreau will be a contributor and sometime editor; learns surveying

1841   Concord Academy closes owing to John's poor health

1842   John dies of lockjaw, January 11; meets Hawthorne; climbs Mount Wachusett; publishes "Natural History of Massachusetts" in the *Dial*

1843   Tutors William Emerson's children on Staten Island, New York; publishes "Paradise (To Be) Regained" in the *United States Magazine and Democratic Review*

1844   Accidentally burns three hundred acres of woodland, causing more than two thousand dollars' damage; helps build the family's "Texas" house in the southwest portion of Concord

1845   Builds and moves into small house at Walden Pond, July 4; begins writing *A Week on the Concord and Merrimack Rivers*

1846   Begins writing *Walden*; spends night in jail for nonpayment of poll tax; climbs Katahdin in Maine

1847   Lectures on "A History of Myself," an early draft of *Walden*, at Concord Lyceum; leaves Walden Pond on September 7, moving in with the Emerson family while Emerson is in Europe; collects specimens for Louis Agassiz at Harvard

1848   Publishes "Ktaadn" in Sartain's *Union Magazine*; lectures on "The Relation of the Individual to the State" ("Civil Disobedience")

1849   Publishes *A Week on the Concord and Merrimack Rivers*; publishes "Resistance to Civil Government" ("Civil Disobedience") in Elizabeth Peabody's *Aesthetic Papers*; sister, Helen, dies of tuberculosis; travels to Cape Cod for the first time

1850   Family moves to house on Main Street, Concord, where Thoreau will live for the remainder of his life; goes to Fire Island, New York, at Emerson's request, to search for the remains and papers of Margaret Fuller who died in a shipwreck; travels to Canada

1852   Publishes excerpts from *Walden* in Sartain's *Union Magazine*

1853   Publishes parts of "A Yankee in Canada" in *Putnam's Monthly*; travels to Maine for the experiences that will be the basis for "Chesuncook"

1854   Publishes "Slavery in Massachusetts" in *Anti-Slavery Standard, The Liberator,* and the New York *Tribune*; publishes *Walden, or Life in the Woods*; lectures in Philadelphia

1855   Grows throat beard, also known as Galway whiskers, early in the year; publishes parts of *Cape Cod* in *Putnam's Monthly*; receives gift of forty-four volumes of Asian literature from Thomas Cholmondeley

1856   Surveys in Perth Amboy, New Jersey; meets Walt Whitman in Brooklyn

1857   Meets John Brown; grows full beard; makes final trip to Maine

1858   Publishes "Chesuncook" in *Atlantic Monthly*; travels through the White Mountains and climbs Mount Washington, July 2–19

1859   Father dies; becomes financially responsible for his family; delivers the first public support of John Brown in "A Plea for Captain John Brown"

1860   Reads Charles Darwin's *Origin of Species*; catches a cold that turns into bronchitis, precipitating his tuberculosis

1861   Visits Minnesota for his health in May, returning unimproved in July; visits Walden Pond for the last time in September; begins revising his writings for posthumous publication

1862   Dies, May 6, of tuberculosis; buried, May 9, in New Burying Ground, Concord, and later moved to Sleepy Hollow Cemetery

The
QUOTATIONS

THOREAU DESCRIBES HIMSELF

Fig. 1. Daguerreotype taken at Benjamin D. Maxham's Daguerrean Palace, Worcester, Massachusetts, on June 18, 1856. Reproduced from *The Writings of Henry D. Thoreau*. The Walden Woods Project Collection at the Thoreau Institute at Walden Woods. Courtesy of the Walden Woods Project.

I have never got over my surprise that I should have been born into the most estimable place in all the world, and in the very nick of time, too.

Written December 5, 1856, in his *Journal*, vol. IX, p. 160

I do not propose to write an ode to dejection, but to brag as lustily as chanticleer in the morning, standing on his roost, if only to wake my neighbors up.

Walden, p. 84

It is my own way of living that I complain of as well as yours.

"Huckleberries," p. 30

I should not talk so much about myself if there were any body else whom I knew as well.

Walden, p. 3

One woman whom I visit sometimes thinks I am conceited and yet wonders that I do not visit her oftener.

Written January 31, 1852, in his *Journal*, vol. 4, p. 312

If I am not I, who will be?

A Week on the Concord and Merrimack Rivers, p. 156

I am not thou—Thou art not I.

Written October 10, 1851, in his *Journal*, vol. 4, p. 137

My life hath been the poem I would have writ,
But I could not both live and live to utter it.

Written August 28, 1841, in his *Journal*, vol. 1, p. 324

What have I to do with plows? I cut another furrow than you see.

Written April 7, 1841, in his *Journal*, vol. 1, p. 297

If corn fails, my crop fails not, and what are drought and rain to me?

A Week on the Concord and Merrimack Rivers, p. 54

My profession is to be always on the alert to find God in nature—to know his lurking places. To attend all the oratorios—the operas in nature.

Written September 7, 1851, in his *Journal*, vol. 4, p. 55

My purpose in going to Walden Pond was not to live cheaply nor to live dearly there, but to transact some private business with the fewest obstacles; to be hindered from accomplishing which for want of a little common sense, a little enterprise and business talent, appeared not so sad as foolish.

Walden, pp. 19–20

I go forth to make new demands on life.

Written March 15, 1852, in his *Journal*, vol. 4, p. 390

My greatest skill has been to want but little.

Written July 19, 1851, in his *Journal*, vol. 3, p. 315

I have seen a bunch of violets in a glass vase, tied loosely with a straw, which reminded me of myself.—

I am a parcel of vain strivings tied
　　By a chance bond together,
　Dangling this way and that, their links
　　Were made so loose and wide,
　　　　Methinks,
　　　For milder weather.

A Week on the Concord and Merrimack Rivers, p. 383

I cannot tell you what I am more than a ray of the summer's sun. What I am—I am—and say not. Being is the great explainer.

Written February 26, 1841, in his *Journal*, vol. 1, p. 273

I must confess there is nothing so strange to me as my own body. I love any piece of nature, almost, better.

Written February 21, 1842, in his *Journal*, vol. 1, p. 365

I came into this world, not chiefly to make this a good place to live in, but to live in it, be it good or bad.

"Resistance to Civil Government" in *Reform Papers*, p. 74

From time to time I overlook the promised land but I do not feel that I am travelling toward it.

Written after July 29, 1850, in his *Journal*, vol. 3, p. 97

For years I marched as to a music in comparison with which the military music of the streets is noise & discord. I was daily intoxicated and yet no man could call me intemperate.

Written July 16, 1851, in his *Journal*, vol. 3, p. 306

I would rather sit on a pumpkin and have it all to myself, than be crowded on a velvet cushion.

Walden, p. 37

I am of the nature of Stone. It takes the summer's sun to warm it.

Written December 21, 1851, in his *Journal*, vol. 4, p. 213

My acquaintances sometimes imply that I am too cold but each thing is warm enough for its kind.

Written December 21, 1851, in his *Journal*, vol. 4, p. 213

If my curve is large, why bend it to a smaller circle?

Written July 19, 1851, in his *Journal*, vol. 3, p. 313

It is impossible for me to be interested in what interest men generally. Their pursuits & interests seem to me frivolous. When I am most myself & see the clearest men are least to be seen.

Written April 24, 1852, in his *Journal*, vol. 4, p. 487

Now if there are any who think that I am vain glorious— that I set myself up above others and crow over their low estate—let me tell them that I could tell a pitiful story respecting myself as well as them. If my spirits held out to do it, I could encourage them with a sufficient list of failures & could flow as humbly as the very gutters themselves. I could enumerate a list of as rank offences as ever reached the nostrils of heaven.

Written February 10, 1852, in his *Journal*, vol. 4, p. 340

I was not born to be forced. I will breathe after my own fashion.

"Resistance to Civil Government" in *Reform Papers*, pp. 80–81

I long ago lost a hound, a bay horse, and a turtle-dove, and am still on their trail. Many are the travellers I have spoken concerning them, describing their tracks and what calls they answered to. I have met one or two who have heard the hound, and the tramp of the horse, and even seen the dove disappear behind a cloud, and they seemed as anxious to recover them as if they had lost them themselves.

Walden, p. 17

You shall have your affairs, I will have mine. You will spend this afternoon in setting up your neighbor's stove, and be paid for it; I will spend it in gathering the few berries of the *Vaccinium Oxycoccus* which Nature produces here, before it is too late, and *be paid for it also* after another fashion. I have always reaped unexpected and incalculable advantages from carrying out at last, however tardily, any little enterprise which my genius suggested to me long ago as a thing to be done,—some step to be taken, however slight, out of the usual course.

Written August 30, 1856, in his *Journal*, vol. IX, p. 36

In youth before I lost any of my senses, I can remember that I was all alive and inhabited my body with inexpressible satisfaction, both its weariness & its refreshment were sweet to me. This earth was the most glorious musical instrument, and I was audience to its strains.

Written July 16, 1851, in his *Journal*, vol. 3, pp. 305–306

I went to the woods because I wished to live deliberately, to front only the essential facts of life, and see if I could not learn what it had to teach, and not, when I came to die, discover that I had not lived. I did not wish to live what was not life, living is so dear; nor did I wish to practice resignation, unless it was quite necessary.

Walden, pp. 90–91

My actual life is unspeakably mean, compared with what I know and see that it might be.

Written on Staten Island to Lidian Emerson, June 20, 1843, in *The Correspondence of Henry David Thoreau*, p. 120

My actual life is a fact in view of which I have no occasion to congratulate myself, but for my faith and aspiration I have respect.

To H.G.O. Blake, March 27, 1848, in *The Correspondence of Henry David Thoreau*, p. 216

I did not wish to take a cabin passage, but rather to go before the mast and on the deck of the world, for there I could best see the moonlight amid the mountains.

Walden, p. 323

Methinks my seasons revolve more slowly than those of nature. I am differently timed.

Written July 19, 1851, in his *Journal*, vol. 3, p. 313

It behoves me . . . to speak out of the rarest part of myself.

To H.G.O. Blake, November 20, 1849, in *The Correspondence of Henry David Thoreau*, p. 250

I believe that it is in my power to elevate myself this very hour above the common level of my life.

To H.G.O. Blake, April 10, 1853, in *The Correspondence of Henry David Thoreau*, p. 303

Here I am 34 years old, and yet my life is almost wholly unexpanded. How much is in the germ! There is such an interval between my ideal and the actual in many instances that I may say I am unborn.

Written July 19, 1851, in his *Journal*, vol. 3, p. 313

I have sworn no oath. I have no designs on society—or nature—or God. I am simply what I am, or I begin to be that.

> To H.G.O. Blake, March 27, 1848, in *The Correspondence of Henry David Thoreau*, p. 216

I believe in the forest, and in the meadow, and in the night in which the corn grows.

> "Walking" in *Excursions*, p. 202

I had three chairs in my house; one for solitude, two for friendship, three for society.

> *Walden*, p. 140

I enjoy more drinking water at a clear spring than out of a goblet at a gentleman's table. I like best the bread which I have baked, the garment which I have made, the shelter which I have constructed, the fuel which I have gathered.

> Written October 20, 1855, in his *Journal*, vol. VII, p. 503

I trust that you realize what an exaggerator I am,—that I lay myself out to exaggerate whenever I have an opportunity,—pile Pelion upon Ossa, to reach heaven so. Expect no trivial truth from me, unless I am on the witness-stand. I will come as near to lying as you can drive a coach-and-four.

> To H.G.O. Blake, April 10, 1853, in *The Correspondence of Henry David Thoreau*, p. 304

One young man of my acquaintance, who has inherited some acres, told me that he thought he should live as I did, *if he had the means*. I would not have any one adopt *my* mode of living on any account; for, beside that before he has fairly learned it I may have found out another for myself, I desire that there may be as many different persons in the world as possible; but I would have each one be very careful to find out and pursue *his own* way, and not his father's or his mother's or his neighbor's instead.

 Walden, p. 71

The true harvest of my daily life is somewhat as intangible and indescribable as the tints of morning or evening. It is a little star-dust caught, a segment of the rainbow which I have clutched.

 Walden, pp. 216–217

I wish so to live ever as to derive my satisfactions and inspirations from the commonest events, every-day phenomena, so that what my senses hourly perceive, my daily walk, the conversation of my neighbors, may inspire me, and I may dream of no heaven but that which lies about me.

 Written March 11, 1856, in his *Journal*, vol. VIII, p. 204

I only know myself as a human entity—the scene, so to speak, of thoughts & affections—and am sensible of a certain doubleness by which I stand as remote from myself as from another. However intense my experience I am conscious of the presence & criticism of a part of me which as it were is not a part of me but spectator sharing no experience, but taking note of it, and that is no more I than it is you.

Written August 8, 1852, in his *Journal*, vol. 5, p. 290

I feel that my life is very homely, my pleasures very cheap. Joy and sorrow, success and failure, grandeur and meanness, and indeed most of the words in the English language do not mean for me what they do for my neighbors.

Written October 18, 1856, in his *Journal*, vol. IX, p. 121

For many years I was self appointed inspector of snowstorms & rainstorms and did my duty faithfully— though I never received one cent for it.

Written after February 22, 1846, in his *Journal*, vol. 2, p. 227

I am so wedded to my way of spending a day,—require such broad margins of leisure, and such a complete wardrobe of old clothes,—that I am ill fitted for going abroad. Pleasant is it sometimes to sit at home, on a single egg all day, in your own nest, though it may prove at last to be an egg of chalk.

To Daniel Ricketson, September 27, 1855, in *Familiar Letters*, p. 262

I take all these walks to every point of the compass, and it is always harvest-time with me. I am always gathering my crop from these woods and fields and waters, and no man is in my way or interferes with me. My crop is not their crop. To-day I see them gathering in their beans and corn, and they are a spectacle to me, but are soon out of my sight. I am not gathering beans and corn. Do they think there are no fruits but such as these? I am a reaper; I am not a gleaner.

Written October 14, 1857, in his *Journal*, vol. X, pp. 93–94

I spend the forenoon in my chamber writing or arranging my papers & in the afternoon I walk forth into the fields & woods. I turn aside perchance into some withdrawn untrodden swamp & find there bilberries large & fair awaiting me in inexhaustible abundance— for I have no tame garden.

Written August 9, 1853, in his *Journal*, vol. 6, p. 293

How to live—How to get the most life! as if you were to teach the young hunter how to entrap his game. How to extract its honey from the flower of the world. That is my every day business. I am as busy as a bee about it. I ramble over all fields on that errand and am never so happy as when I feel myself heavy with honey & wax. I am like a bee searching the livelong day for the sweets of nature.

Written September 7, 1851, in his *Journal*, vol. 4, p. 53

I love a broad margin to myself.

Walden, p. 111

I perceive that I am dealt with by superior powers.

Written July 16, 1851, in his *Journal*, vol. 3, p. 306

I feel blessed. I love my life.

Written November 1, 1851, in his *Journal*, vol. 4, p. 159

My life partakes of infinity.

Written March 15, 1852, in his *Journal*, vol. 4, p. 390

QUESTIONS

It would be worth the while to ask ourselves weekly—
Is our life innocent enough? Do we live *inhumanely*
toward man or beast in thought or act?

Written May 28, 1854, in his *Journal*, vol. 8, p. 161

What may a man do and not be ashamed of it?

Written March 5, 1838, in his *Journal*, vol. 1, p. 34

Life! who knows what it is—what it does?

Written July 6, 1845, in his *Journal*, vol. 2, p. 156

What sort of fruit comes of living as if you were a-going
to die?

Written after October 15, 1849, in his *Journal*, vol. 3, p. 30

Will you live or will you be embalmed?

To H.G.O. Blake, April 3, 1850, in *The Correspondence of Henry
David Thoreau*, p. 257; emended from facsimile of manuscript
letter (manuscript location unknown)

Have I no heart—Am I incapable of expansion and
generosity?

Written August 24, 1852, in his *Journal*, vol. 5, p. 310

Who shall say what prospect life offers to another?
Could a greater miracle take place than for us to look
through each other's eyes for an instant?

Walden, p. 10

Are there duties which necessarily interfere with the serene perception of truth?

Written June 22, 1851, in his *Journal*, vol. 3, p. 274

Are our serene moments mere foretastes of heaven, joys gratuitously vouchsafed to us as a consolation or simply a transient realization of what might be the whole tenor of our lives?

Written June 22, 1851, in his *Journal*, vol. 3, p. 274

How many things can you go away from?

Written November 1, 1858, in his *Journal*, vol. XI, p. 275

Why should we live with such hurry and waste of life?

Walden, p. 93

Why should we knock under and go with the stream?

Walden, p. 97

If the bell rings, why should we run?

Walden, p. 97

Why should we be in such desperate haste to succeed, and in such desperate enterprises?

Walden, p. 326

What is a course of history, or philosophy, or poetry, no matter how well selected, or the best society, or the most admirable routine of life, compared with the discipline of looking always at what is to be seen? Will you be a reader, a student merely, or a seer?

Walden, p. 111

What is the use of going to see people whom yet you never see & who never see you?

Written November 14, 1851, in his *Journal*, vol. 4, p. 185

Who knows what sort of life would result if we had attained to purity?

Walden, p. 219

What is a country without rabbits and partridges?

Walden, p. 281

After a still winter night I awoke with the impression that some question had been put to me, which I had been endeavoring in vain to answer in my sleep, as what—how—when—where?

Walden, p. 282

What is man but a mass of thawing clay?

Walden, p. 307

What does Africa, what does the West stand for? Is not our own interior white on the chart?

Walden, p. 321

Is Franklin the only man who is lost, that his wife should be so earnest to find him?

Walden, p. 321

If a man constantly aspires, is he not elevated?

To H.G.O. Blake, March 27, 1848, in *The Correspondence of Henry David Thoreau*, p. 216

Did ever a man try heroism, magnanimity, truth, sincerity, and find that there was no advantage in them?

To H.G.O. Blake, March 27, 1848, in *The Correspondence of Henry David Thoreau*, p. 216

THE THOUGHTS AND WORDS OF
HENRY D. THOREAU

FIG. 2. Crayon portrait (1854) by Samuel Worcester Rowse. Reproduced from *The Writings of Henry D. Thoreau*. The Walden Woods Project Collection at the Thoreau Institute at Walden Woods. Courtesy of the Walden Woods Project.

BEAUTY

You cannot perceive beauty but with a serene mind.

Written November 18, 1857, in his *Journal*, vol. X, p. 188

There is just as much beauty visible to us in the land-scape as we are prepared to appreciate,—not a grain more. The actual objects which one man will see from a particular hill-top are just as different from those which another will see as the beholders are different.

"Autumnal Tints" in *Excursions*, p. 256

The cart before the horse is neither beautiful nor useful. Before we can adorn our houses with beautiful objects the walls must be stripped, and our lives must be stripped, and beautiful housekeeping and beautiful living be laid for a foundation: now, a taste for the beautiful is most cultivated out of doors, where there is no house and no housekeeper.

Walden, p. 38

How much of beauty—of color, as well as form—on which our eyes daily rest goes unperceived by us!

Written August 1, 1860, in his *Journal*, vol. XIV, p. 3

There are meteorologists—but who keeps a record of the fairer sunsets? While men are recording the direction of the wind they neglect to record the beauty of the sunset or the rain bow.

Written June 28, 1852, in his *Journal*, vol. 5, p. 161

Some love beauty, and some love rum.

Written January 22, 1859, in his *Journal*, vol. XI, p. 423

Enough for the season is the beauty thereof. Spring has a beauty of its own which we would not exchange for that of summer.

Written March 23, 1859, in his *Journal*, vol. XII, p. 76

In what book is this world and its beauty described? Who has plotted the steps toward the discovery of beauty?

Written October 4, 1859, in his *Journal*, vol. XII, p. 371

The ears were made, not for such trivial uses as men are wont to suppose, but to hear celestial sounds. The eyes were not made for such grovelling uses as they are now put to and worn out by, but to behold beauty now invisible. May we not *see* God?

A Week on the Concord and Merrimack Rivers, p. 382

All the world reposes in beauty to him who preserves equipoise in his life, and moves serenely on his path without secret violence; as he who sails down a stream, he has only to steer, keeping his bark in the middle, and carry it round the falls.

A Week on the Concord and Merrimack Rivers, p. 317

The forms of beauty fall naturally around the path of him who is in the performance of his proper work; as the curled shavings drop from the plane, and borings cluster round the auger.

A Week on the Concord and Merrimack Rivers, p. 318

I was inclined to think that the truest beauty was that which surrounded us but which we failed to discern, that the forms and colors which adorn our daily life, not seen afar in the horizon, are our fairest jewelry.

Written September 18, 1858, in his *Journal*, vol. XI, p. 166

Always the line of beauty is a curve.

"The Service" in *Reform Papers*, p. 6

Every landscape which is dreary enough has a certain beauty to my eyes.

Cape Cod, p. 25

Why not take more elevated and broader views, walk in the great garden, not skulk in a little "debauched" nook of it? consider the beauty of the forest, and not merely of a few impounded herbs?

"Autumnal Tints" in *Excursions*, p. 256

The beauty of the earth answers exactly to your demand and appreciation.

Written November 2, 1858, in his *Journal*, vol. XI, p. 278

Beauty is where it is perceived.

Written December 16, 1840, in his *Journal*, vol. 1, p. 205

To him who contemplates a trait of natural beauty no harm nor disappointment can come.

"Natural History of Massachusetts" in *Excursions*, p. 5

BRUTE NEIGHBORS: ANIMALS, BIRDS, FISH, AND INSECTS

I spend a considerable portion of my time observing the habits of the wild animals, my brute neighbors. By their various movements and migrations they fetch the year about to me. Very significant are the flight of geese and the migration of suckers, etc., etc. But when I consider that the nobler animals have been exterminated here,—the cougar, panther, lynx, wolverine, wolf, bear, moose, deer, the beaver, the turkey, etc., etc.,—I cannot but feel as if I lived in a tamed, and, as it were, emasculated country. Would not the motions of those larger and wilder animals have been more significant still? Is it not a maimed and imperfect nature that I am conversant with?

Written March 23, 1856, in his *Journal*, vol. VIII, pp. 220–221

The very dogs & cats incline to affection in their relation to man. It often happens that a man is more humanely related to a cat or dog than to any human being. What bond is it relates us to any animal we keep in the house but the bond of affection? In a degree we grow to love one another.

Written April 29, 1851, in his *Journal*, vol. 3, p. 210

I see a fox run across the road in the twilight. . . . I feel a certain respect for him, because, though so large, he still maintains himself free and wild in our midst, and is so original so far as any resemblance to our race is concerned. Perhaps I like him better than his tame cousin the dog for it.

Written November 25, 1857, in his *Journal*, vol. X, p. 206

The fox seems to get his living by industry and perseverance.

Written February 2, 1860, in his Journal, vol. XIII, p. 124

The musk-rat is the beaver of the settled States.

"Natural History of Massachusetts" in Excursions, p. 13

The moose is singularly grotesque and awkward to look at. Why should it stand so high at the shoulders? Why have so long a head? Why have no tail to speak of?

The Maine Woods, p. 115

The bees are on the pistillate flowers of the early willows,—the honey-bee, a smaller fly-like bee with very transparent wings & bright yellow marks on the abdomen, and also a still smaller bee more like the honey bee. They all hum like summer.

Written April 25, 1852, in his Journal, vol. 4, p. 491

Yet what is the character of our gratitude to these squirrels, these planters of forests? We regard them as vermin, and annually shoot and destroy them in great numbers, because—if we have any excuse—they sometimes devour a little of our Indian corn. . . . Would it [not] be far more civilized and humane, not to say god-like, to recognize once in the year by some significant symbolical ceremony the part which the squirrel plays, the great service it performs, in the economy of the universe?

Written October 22, 1860, in his Journal, vol. XIV, p. 166

Every man says his dog will not touch you. Look out nevertheless.

Written July 23, 1852, in his *Journal*, vol. 5, p. 241

The mice which haunted my house were not the common ones. . . . When I was building, one of these had its nest underneath the house, and before I had laid the second floor, and swept out the shavings, would come out regularly at lunch time and pick up the crumbs at my feet. It probably had never seen a man before; and it soon became quite familiar, and would run over my shoes and up my clothes. It could readily ascend the sides of the room by short impulses, like a squirrel, which it resembled in its motions. At length, as I leaned with my elbow on the bench one day, it ran up my clothes, and along my sleeve, and round and round the paper which held my dinner, while I kept the latter close, and dodged and played at bopeep with it; and when at last I held still a piece of cheese between my thumb and finger, it came and nibbled it, sitting in my hand, and afterward cleaned its face and paws, like a fly, and walked away.

Walden, pp. 225–226

I am not offended by the odor of the skunk in passing by sacred places. I am invigorated rather.

Written after April 26, 1850, in his *Journal*, vol. 3, p. 62

Whether a man's work be hard or easy, whether he be happy or unhappy, a bird is appointed to sing to a man while he is at his work.

Written April 15, 1859, in his *Journal*, vol. XII, p. 144

My life at this moment is like a summer morning when birds are singing.

Written February 9, 1841, in his *Journal*, vol. 1, p. 262

Birds are the truest heralds of the seasons, since they appreciate a thousand delicate changes in the atmosphere which is their own element, of which man and the other animals cannot be aware.

Passage omitted from *A Week on the Concord and Merrimack Rivers* as published in Linck C. Johnson, *Thoreau's Complex Weave*, p. 472

Though I live in the woods I am not so attentive an observer of birds as I was once, but am satisfied if I get an occasional night of sound from them.

To Horatio Robinson Storer, February 15, 1847, while living at Walden, in *The Correspondence of Henry David Thoreau*, p. 175

In Boston yesterday an ornithologist said significantly—"if you held the bird in your hand"—but I would rather hold it in my affections.

Written May 10, 1854, in his *Journal*, vol. 8, p. 111

He who cuts down woods beyond a certain limit exterminates birds.

Written May 17, 1853, in his *Journal*, vol. 6, p. 134

The blue bird carries the sky on his back.

Written April 3, 1852, in his *Journal*, vol. 4, p. 423

I once had a sparrow alight upon my shoulder for a moment while I was hoeing in a village garden, and

I felt that I was more distinguished by that circumstance than I should have been by any epaulet I could
have worn.

    Walden, p. 276

I rejoice that there are owls. . . . They represent the
stark twilight and unsatisfied thoughts which all
have.

    Walden, p. 124

I hear an owl hoot. How glad I am to hear him rather
than the most eloquent man of the age!

    Written December 25, 1858, in his *Journal*, vol. XI, p. 378

I heard a robin in the distance, the first I had heard for
many a thousand years, methought, whose note I shall
not forget for many a thousand more,—the same sweet
and powerful song as of yore. O the evening robin, at
the end of a New England summer day!

    Walden, p. 312

The first sparrow of spring! The year beginning with
younger hope than ever! . . . What at such a time are
histories, chronologies, traditions, and all written
revelations?

    Walden, p. 310

I hear part of a phoebe's strain as I go over the railroad
bridge—It is the voice of dying summer.

    Written August 26, 1854, in his *Journal*, vol. 8, p. 295

A man's interest in a single blue-bird, is more than a complete, but dry, list of the fauna & flora of a town.

> To Daniel Ricketson, November 22, 1858, in *The Correspondence of Henry David Thoreau*, p. 528

How much more habitable a few birds make the fields! At the end of winter, when the fields are bare and there is nothing to relieve the monotony of the withered vegetation, our life seems reduced to its lowest terms. But let a bluebird come and warble over them, and what a change!

> Written March 18, 1858, in his *Journal*, vol. X, p. 302

It is surprising that so many birds find hair enough to line their nests with. If I wish for a horse hair for my compass sights I must go to the stable but the hair bird with her sharp eyes goes to the road.

> Written June 24, 1853, in his *Journal*, vol. 6, p. 243

If you would have the song of the sparrow inspire you a thousand years hence, let your life be in harmony with its strain to-day.

> Written May 12, 1857, in his *Journal*, vol. IX, p. 364

As I come over the hill I hear the wood thrush singing his evening lay. This is the only bird whose note affects me like music—affects the flow & tenor of my thought—my fancy & imagination. It lifts and exhilarates me. It is inspiring. It is a medicative draught to my soul. It is an elixir to my eyes & a fountain of youth to all my senses. It changes all hours to an eternal morning.

Written June 22, 1853, in his *Journal*, vol. 6, pp. 235–236

What a perfectly New England sound is this voice of the crow! If you stand perfectly still anywhere in the outskirts of the town and listen, stilling the almost incessant hum of your own personal factory, this is perhaps the sound which you will be most sure to hear rising above all sounds of human industry and leading your thoughts to some far bay in the woods where the crow is venting his disgust. This bird sees the white man come and the Indian withdraw, but it withdraws not. Its untamed voice is still heard above the tinkling of the forge. It sees a race pass away, but it passes not away. It remains to remind us of aboriginal nature.

Written March 4, 1859, in his *Journal*, vol. XII, pp. 11–12

The tinkling notes of gold-finches & bobolinks which we hear now a days are of one character & peculiar to the season. They are not voluminous flowers but rather nuts of sound, ripened seeds of sound.

Written August 10, 1854, in his *Journal*, vol. 8, p. 260

Would it not be well to carry a spy glass in order to watch these shy birds—such as ducks & hawks? In some respects methinks it would be better than a gun. The latter brings them nearer dead, but the former, alive. You can identify the species better by killing the bird because it was a dead specimen that was so minutely described but you can study the habits & appearance best in the living specimen.

Written March 29, 1853, in his *Journal*, vol. 6, p. 48

Saw a tanager in Sleepy hollow. It most takes the eye of any bird. You here have the red-wing reversed—the deepest scarlet of the red-wing spread over the whole body—not on the wing coverts merely while the wings are black. It flies through the green foliage as if it would ignite the leaves.

Written May 20, 1853, in his *Journal*, vol. 6, p. 139

The thrush alone declares the immortal wealth & vigor that is in the forest. . . . Whenever a man hears it he is young & nature is in her spring. . . . He deepens the significance of all things seen in the light of his strain. He sings to make men take higher and truer views of things.

Written July 5, 1852, in his *Journal*, vol. 5, p. 188

The strains of the aeolian harp & of the wood thrush are the truest & loftiest preachers that I know now left on this earth. I know of no missionaries to us heathen comparable to them.

Written December 31, 1853, in his *Journal*, vol. 7, p. 216

Who hears the fishes when they cry?

A Week on the Concord and Merrimack Rivers, p. 37

I am the wiser in respect to all knowledges, and the better qualified for all fortunes, for knowing that there is a minnow in the brook.

"Natural History of Massachusetts" in *Excursions*, p. 17

CHANGE

Go where we will, we discover infinite change in particulars only, not in generals.

A Week on the Concord and Merrimack Rivers, p. 124

We are independent of the change we detect.

A Week on the Concord and Merrimack Rivers, p. 128

I confess, that practically speaking, when I have learned a man's real disposition, I have no hopes of changing it for the better or worse in this state of existence.

Walden, pp. 120–121

When my thoughts are sensible of change, I love to see and sit on rocks which I *have* known, and pry into their moss, and see unchangeableness so established.

A Week on the Concord and Merrimack Rivers, p. 351

All change is a miracle to contemplate; but it is a miracle which is taking place every instant.

Walden, p. 11

I heard that a distinguished wise man and reformer asked him if he did not want the world to be changed; but he answered with a chuckle of surprise in his Canadian accent, not knowing that the question had ever been entertained before, "No, I like it well enough."

> On Alex Therien, the Canadian woodchopper, in *Walden*,
> p. 148

The higher the mountain on which you stand, the less change in the prospect from year to year, from age to age. Above a certain height there is no change.

> To H.G.O. Blake, February 27, 1853, in *Familiar Letters*,
> pp. 210–211

With regard to essentials, I have never had occasion to change my mind.

> To H.G.O. Blake, August 18, 1857, in *The Correspondence of*
> *Henry David Thoreau*, p. 491

To the sick the doctors wisely recommend a change of air and scenery. Who chains me to this dull town?

> "Resistance to Civil Government" in *Reform Papers*, p. 196

In vain I look for change abroad,
   And can no difference find,
Till some new ray of peace uncalled
   Illumes my inmost mind.

> *A Week on the Concord and Merrimack Rivers*, p. 295

Perhaps an instinct survives through the intensest actual love, which prevents entire abandonment and

devotion, and makes the most ardent lover a little reserved. It is the anticipation of change.

"Love" in *Early Essays and Miscellanies*, p. 269

It will be perceived that there are two kinds of change—
that of the race & that of the individual within the limits of the former.

Written June 7, 1851, in his *Journal*, vol. 3, p. 246

Action from principle,—the perception and the performance of right,—changes things and relations; it is
essentially revolutionary, and does not consist wholly
with any thing which was.

"Resistance to Civil Government" in *Reform Papers*, p. 72

So is all change for the better, like birth and death
which convulse the body.

"Resistance to Civil Government" in *Reform Papers*, p. 74

Though the woodchoppers have laid bare first this
shore and then that, and the Irish have built their sties
by it, and the railroad has infringed on its border, and
the ice-men have skimmed it once, it is itself un-
changed, the same water which my youthful eyes fell
on; all the change is in me.

Walden, pp. 192–193

If I could convince myself that I have any right to be
satisfied with men as they are, and to treat them accordingly, and not according, in some respects, to
my requisitions and expectations of what they and I
ought to be, then, like a good Mussulman and fatalist,

I should endeavor to be satisfied with things as they are, and say it is the will of God. And, above all, there is this difference between resisting this and a purely brute or natural force, that I can resist this with some effect; but I cannot expect, like Orpheus, to change the nature of the rocks and trees and beasts.

"Resistance to Civil Government" in *Reform Papers*, p. 85

I know of no more encouraging fact than the unquestionable ability of man to elevate his life by a conscious endeavor. It is something to be able to paint a particular picture, or to carve a statue, and so to make a few objects beautiful; but it is far more glorious to carve and paint the very atmosphere and medium through which we look, which morally we can do. To affect the quality of the day, that is the highest of arts.

Walden, p. 90

Things do not change; we change.

Walden, p. 328

CHARACTER

A man is not to be measured by the virtue of his described actions or the wisdom of his expressed thoughts merely, but by that free character he is, and is felt to be, under all circumstances.

"Sir Walter Raleigh" in *Early Essays and Miscellanies*, p. 216

We falsely attribute to men a determined character—putting together all their yesterdays and averaging them—we presume to know them. Pity the man who has a character to support.

Written April 28, 1841, in his *Journal*, vol. 1, p. 305

The chief want, in every State that I have been into, was a high and earnest purpose in its inhabitants.

"Life without Principle" in *Reform Papers*, p. 177

Of what consequence, though our planet explode, if there is no character involved in the explosion?

"Life without Principle" in *Reform Papers*, p. 170

It is an important difference between two characters that the one is satisfied with a happy but level success but the other as constantly elevates his *aim*. Though my life is low, if my spirit looks upward habitually at an elevated angle it is, as it were, redeemed. When the desire to be better than we are is really sincere we are instantly elevated, and so far better already.

Written after January 10, 1851, in his *Journal*, vol. 3, pp. 177–178

Talent only indicates a depth of character in some direction.

Written February 18, 1841, in his *Journal*, vol. 1, p. 267

Manners are conscious. Character is unconscious.

Written February 16, 1851, in his *Journal*, vol. 3, p. 195

The Gods have given man no constant gift but the power and liberty to act greatly.

"Sir Walter Raleigh" second draft manuscript (Walden Woods Project Collection at the Thoreau Institute at Walden Woods)

We should make our notch every day on our characters as Robinson Crusoe on his stick. We must be at the helm at least once a day—we must feel the tiller rope in our hands, and know that if we sail, we steer.

Written February 22, 1841, in his *Journal*, vol. 1, p. 271

I observe that the New York Herald advertises situations wanted by "respectable young women" by the column—but never by respectable young men—rather "intelligent" and "smart" ones—from which I infer that the public opinion of New York does not require young men to be respectable in the same sense in which it requires young women to be so.

Written April 30, 1851, in his *Journal*, vol. 3, pp. 211–212

Do you not feel the fruit of your spring & summer beginning to ripen, to harden its seed within you—Do not your thoughts begin to acquire consistency as well as flavor & ripeness—How can we expect a harvest of thought who have not had a seed time of character?

Written August 7, 1854, in his *Journal*, vol. 8, pp. 256–257

Men go to a fire for entertainment. When I see how eagerly men will run to a fire whether in warm or in cold weather by day or by night dragging an engine at their heels, I am astonished to perceive how good a purpose the love of excitement is made to serve. What other force pray—what offered pay—what disinterested neighborliness could ever effect so much? . . .

There is no old man or woman dropping into the grave but covets excitement.

Written June 5, 1850, in his *Journal*, vol. 3, p. 81

Most men can be easily transplanted from here there, for they have so little root—no tap root—or their roots penetrate so little way that you can thrust a shovel quite under them and take them up roots and all.

Written May 14, 1852, in his *Journal*, vol. 5, p. 58

To be a philosopher is not merely to have subtle thoughts, nor even to found a school, but so to love wisdom as to live according to its dictates, a life of simplicity, independence, magnanimity, and trust. It is to solve some of the problems of life, not only theoretically, but practically.

Walden, pp. 14–15

How often are we wise as serpents without being harmless as doves.

Written February 9, 1851, in his *Journal*, vol. 3, p. 185

It is not worth the while to let our imperfections disturb us always. The conscience really does not, and ought not to, monopolize the whole of our lives, any more than the heart or the head. It is as liable to disease as any other part. I have seen some whose consciences, owing undoubtedly to former indulgence, had grown to be as irritable as spoilt children, and at length gave them no peace.

A Week on the Concord and Merrimack Rivers, p. 74

The world rests on principles.

To H.G.O. Blake, December 19, 1854, in *The Correspondence of Henry David Thoreau*, p. 355

You may know what a thing costs or is worth to you; you can never know what it costs or is worth to me.

Written December 27, 1858, in his *Journal*, vol. XI, pp. 379–380

In the course of generations, however, men will excuse you for not doing as they do, if you will bring enough to pass in your own way.

Written December 27, 1858, in his *Journal*, vol. XI, p. 380

It is insignificant & a merely negative good-fortune to be provided with thick garments against cold and wet—an unprofitable weak & defensive condition—compared with being able to extract some exhilaration—some warmth even out of cold & wet themselves & to clothe them with our sympathy.

Written November 12, 1853, in his *Journal*, vol. 7, p. 156

CHARITY AND PHILANTHROPY

Today I have had the experience of borrowing money for a poor Irishman who wishes to get his family to this country. One will never know his neighbors till he has carried a subscription paper among them.

Written October 12, 1853, in his *Journal*, vol. 7, p. 102

What is called charity is no charity but the interference of a third person.

Written February 11, 1841, in his *Journal*, vol. 1, p. 264

To be supported by the charity of friends, or a government-pension,—provided you continue to breathe,—by whatever fine synonymes you describe these relations, is to go into the almshouse.

"Life without Principle" in *Reform Papers*, p. 160

Among my deeds of charity I may reckon the picking of a cherry tree for two helpless single ladies who live under the hill—but i' faith it was robbing Peter to pay Paul—for while I was *exalted* in charity towards them, I had no mercy on my own stomach.

To his brother, John, July 8, 1838, in *The Correspondence of Henry David Thoreau*, p. 27

You must have a genius for charity as well as for any thing else.

Walden, p. 73

The town's poor seem to me often to live the most independent lives of any. May be they are simply great enough to receive without misgiving.

Walden, p. 328

I require of a visitor that he be not actually starving, though he may have the very best appetite in the world, however he got it. Objects of charity are not guests.

Walden, p. 152

I tried to help him with my experience, telling him that he was one of my nearest neighbors, and that I too, who came a-fishing here, and looked like a loafer, was getting my living like himself; that I lived in a tight light and clean house, which hardly cost more than the annual rent of such a ruin as his commonly amounts to; and how, if he chose, he might in a month or two build himself a palace of his own; that I did not use tea, nor coffee, nor butter, nor milk, nor fresh meat, and so did not have to work to get them; again, as I did not work hard, I did not have to eat hard, and it cost me but a trifle for my food; but as he began with tea, and coffee, and butter, and milk, and beef, he had to work hard to pay for them, and when he had worked hard he had to eat hard to repair the waste of his system,—and so it was as broad as it was long, indeed it was broader than it was long, for he was discontented and wasted his life into the bargain.

On John Field, Irish laborer, in *Walden*, p. 205

He who gives himself entirely to his fellow-men appears to them useless and selfish; but he who gives himself partially to them is pronounced a benefactor and philanthropist.

"Resistance to Civil Government" in *Reform Papers*, pp. 66–67

I speak for the slave when I say, that I prefer the philanthropy of Captain Brown to that philanthropy which
neither shoots me nor liberates me.

"A Plea for Captain John Brown" in *Reform Papers*, p. 133

There are a thousand hacking at the branches of evil to
one who is striking at the root, and it may be that he
who bestows the largest amount of time and money on
the needy is doing the most by his mode of life to produce that misery which he strives in vain to relieve. It
is the pious slave-breeder devoting the proceeds of
every tenth slave to buy a Sunday's liberty for the rest.

Walden, pp. 75–76

I know some who in their charity give their coffee
grounds to the poor!

To H.G.O. Blake, May 28, 1850, in *The Correspondence of Henry
David Thoreau*, p. 259

Our charitable institutions are an insult to humanity. A
charity which dispenses the crumbs that fall from its
overloaded tables.

Written January 28, 1852, in his *Journal*, vol. 4, p. 299

It is our weakness that so exaggerates the virtues of
philanthropy & charity & makes it the highest human
attribute. The world will sooner or later tire of philanthropy and all religions based on it. They cannot long
sustain my spirit.

Written April 2, 1852, in his *Journal*, vol. 4, p. 419

There are those who have used all their arts to persuade me to undertake the support of some poor family in the town; and if I had nothing to do,—for the devil finds employment for the idle,—I might try my hand at some such pastime as that. However, when I have thought to indulge myself in this respect, and lay their Heaven under an obligation by maintaining certain poor persons in all respects as comfortably as I maintain myself, and have even ventured so far as to make them the offer, they have one and all unhesitatingly preferred to remain poor.

Walden, p. 72

I have been your pensioner for nearly two years, and still left free as under the sky. It has been as free a gift as the sun or the summer, though I have sometimes molested you with my mean acceptance of it.

To Ralph Waldo Emerson, January 24, 1843, in *The Correspondence of Henry David Thoreau*, p. 78

How can I talk of Charity who at last withhold the kindness which alone makes charity desirable?

The poor want nothing less than me myself and I shirk charity by giving rags and meat.

Written March 25, 1842, in his *Journal*, vol. 1, p. 391

I would not subtract any thing from the praise that is due to philanthropy, but merely demand justice for all who by their lives and works are a blessing to mankind.

Walden, p. 76

Shall we be charitable only to the poor?

Written after August 1, 1844, in his *Journal*, vol. 2, p. 117

If you should ever be betrayed into any of these philan-
thropies, do not let your left hand know what your
right hand does, for it is not worth knowing. Rescue
the drowning and tie your shoe-strings.

Walden, p. 78

All the abuses which are the object of reform with the
philanthropist, the statesman, and the housekeeper, are
unconsciously amended in the intercourse of Friends.

A Week on the Concord and Merrimack Rivers, p. 267

CHILDREN

Every child begins the world again.

Walden, p. 28

Children appear to me as raw as the fresh fungi on a
fence rail.

Written November 7, 1839, in his *Journal*, vol. 1, p. 85

Youth wants something to look up to—to look forward to.

Written in the summer of 1845, in his *Journal*, vol. 2, p. 205

How unaccountable the flow of spirits in youth. You
may throw sticks and dirt into the current, and it will

only rise the higher. Dam it up you may, but dry it up you may not, for you cannot reach its source. If you stop up this avenue or that, anon it will come gurgling out where you least expected, and wash away all fixtures. Youth grasps at happiness as an inalienable right.

Written September 16, 1838, in his *Journal*, vol. 1, p. 56

The mother tells her falsehoods to her child, but thank Heaven, the child does not grow up in its parent's shadow.

A Week on the Concord and Merrimack Rivers, p. 77

How few valuable observations can we make in youth.

Written April 2, 1852, in his *Journal*, vol. 4, p. 416

The child may soon stand face to face with the best father.

Written February 12, 1841, in his *Journal*, vol. 1, p. 264

I am struck by the fact that the more slowly trees grow at first, the sounder they are at the core, and I think that the same is true of human beings. We do not wish to see children precocious, making great strides in their early years like sprouts, producing a soft and perishable timber, but better if they expand slowly at first, as if contending with difficulties, and so are solidified and perfected.

Written November 5, 1860, in his *Journal*, vol. XIV, p. 217

The senses of children are unprofaned. Their whole body is one sense. They take a physical pleasure in riding on a rail. They love to teter—so does the unviolated—the unsophisticated mind derive an inexpressible pleasure from the simplest exercises of thoughts.

Written July 7, 1851, in his *Journal*, vol. 3, p. 291

The child plays continually, if you will let it, and all its life is a sort of practical humor of a very pure kind, often of so fine and ethereal a nature, that its parents, its uncles and cousins, can in no wise participate in it, but must stand aloof in silent admiration, and reverence even. The more quiet the more profound it is.

"Thomas Carlyle and His Works" in *Early Essays and Miscellanies*, p. 237

A child loves to strike on a tin pan or other ringing vessel with a stick, because its ears being fresh sound attentive & percipient it detects the finest music in the sound at which all Nature assists. Is not the very cope of the heavens the sounding board of the infant drummer? So clear and unprejudiced ears hear the sweetest & most soul stirring melody in tinkling cow bells & the like (dogs baying the moon) not to be referred to association but intrinsic in the sound itself. Those cheap & simple sounds which men despise because their ears are dull & debauched. Ah that I were so much a child that I could unfailingly draw music from a quart pot. Its little ears tingle with the melody. To it there is music in sound alone.

Written June 9, 1852, in his *Journal*, vol. 5, pp. 82–83

The youth gets together his materials to build a bridge to the moon or perchance a palace or temple on the earth & at length the middle-aged man concludes to build a wood shed with them.

Written July 15, 1852, in his *Journal*, vol. 5, p. 223

I suspect that the child plucks its first flower with an insight into its beauty & significance which the subsequent botanist never retains.

Written February 5, 1852, in his *Journal*, vol. 4, p. 329

The young man is a demigod; the grown man, alas! is commonly a mere mortal.

Written December 19, 1859, in his *Journal*, vol. XIII, p. 35

Though the parents cannot determine whether the child shall be male or female yet methinks it depends on them whether he shall be a worthy addition to the human family.

Written November 23, 1853, in his *Journal*, vol. 5, p. 398

The voices of school children sound like spring.

Written February 9, 1854, in his *Journal*, vol. 7, p. 276

CITIES

Who can see these cities and say that there is any life in them?

Written in New York, September 24, 1843, in his *Journal*, vol. 1, p. 465

Deliver me from a city built on the site of a more ancient city, whose materials are ruins, whose gardens cemeteries.

Walden, p. 264

It is folly to attempt to educate children within a city. The first step must be to remove them out of it.

Written July 25, 1851, in his *Journal*, vol. 3, p. 332

I am more and more convinced that, with reference to any public question, it is more important to know what the country thinks of it, than what the city thinks. The city does not *think* much. On any moral question, I would rather have the opinion of Boxboro than of Boston and New York put together.

"Slavery in Massachusetts" in *Reform Papers*, pp. 98–99

What is the great attraction in cities? It is universally admitted that human beings invariably degenerate there and do not propagate their kind. Yet the prevailing tendency is to the city life, whether we move to Boston or stay in Concord.

Written fall–winter 1845–1846, in his *Journal*, vol. 2, p. 147

The light behind the face of the clock on the state house in Philadelphia extinguished at 11 o'clock PM with punctuality to save oil. Those hours are resigned to a few watchmen in the cities, watching for the disgrace of humanity.

Written February 1, 1852, in his *Journal*, vol. 4, p. 315

Coming out of town—willingly as usual.

> Written July 9, 1851, in his *Journal*, vol. 3, p. 297

I don't like the city better, the more I see of it, but worse. . . . It is a thousand times meaner than I could have imagined. . . . The pigs in the street are the most respectable part of the population. When will the world learn that a million men are of no importance compared with one man?

> Written on Staten Island to Ralph Waldo Emerson, June 8, 1843, in *The Correspondence of Henry David Thoreau*, pp. 111–112; emended from manuscript letter (*The Writings of Henry David Thoreau* Manuscript Edition #247, RAR 137 Da, Kungl Bib-lioteket, National Library of Sweden)

Though the city is no more attractive to me than ever yet I see less difference between a city & and some dismall-est swamp than formerly. It is a swamp too dismal & dreary even for me.

> Written after July 29, 1850, in his *Journal*, vol. 3, p. 97

I can forego the seeming advantages of cities without misgiving.

> Written after August 8, 1851, in his *Journal*, vol. 3, p. 359

Whoever has been down to the end of Long Wharf, and walked through Quincy Market, has seen Boston.

> *Cape Cod*, pp. 210–211

CONSERVATION

It is well known that the chestnut timber of this vicinity has rapidly disappeared within fifteen years, having been used for railroad sleepers, for rails, and for planks, so that there is danger that this part of our forest will become extinct.

Written October 17, 1860, in his *Journal*, vol. XIV, p. 137

The woods I walked in in my youth are cut off. Is it not time that I ceased to sing?

Written March 11, 1852, in his *Journal*, vol. 4, p. 385

I fear that he who walks over these fields a century hence will not know the pleasure of knocking off wild apples. Ah, poor man, there are many pleasures which he will not know!

"Wild Apples" in *Excursions*, p. 288

I find that the rising generation in this town do not know what an oak or a pine is, having seen only inferior specimens. Shall we hire a man to lecture on botany, on oaks for instance, our noblest plants—while we permit others to cut down the few best specimens of these trees that are left? It is like teaching children Latin and Greek while we burn the books printed in those languages.

"Huckleberries," p. 35

For beauty, give me trees with the fur on.

The Maine Woods, p. 125

We seem to think that the earth must go through the ordeal of sheep-pasturage before it is habitable by man.

The Maine Woods, p. 153

I would rather save one of these hawks than have a hundred hens and chickens. It is worth more to see them soar—especially now that they are so rare in the landscape. It is easy to buy eggs but not to buy hen-hawks. My neighbors would not hesitate to shoot the last pair of henhawks in the town to save a few of their chickens! But such economy is narrow & grovelling. It is unnecessarily to sacrifice the greater value to the less. I would rather never taste chicken's meat nor hen's eggs than never to see a hawk sailing through the upper air again. This sight is worth incomparably more than a chicken soup or a boiled egg.

Written June 13, 1853, in his *Journal*, vol. 6, pp. 197–198

By avarice and selfishness, and a grovelling habit, from which none of us is free, of regarding the soil as property, or the means of acquiring property chiefly, the landscape is deformed, husbandry is degraded with us, and the farmer leads the meanest of lives. He knows Nature but as a robber.

Walden, pp. 165–166

Why should not we, who have renounced the king's authority, have our national preserves, where no villages need be destroyed, in which the bear and panther, and some even of the hunter race, may still exist, and not be "civilized off the face of the earth,"—our forests, not to hold the king's game merely, but to hold and preserve the king himself also, the lord of creation,—not for idle sport or food, but for inspiration and our own true recreation?

The Maine Woods, p. 156

The very willow-rows lopped every three years for fuel or powder,—and every sizable pine and oak, or other forest tree, cut down within the memory of man! As if individual speculators were to be allowed to export the clouds out of the sky, or the stars out of the firmament, one by one. We shall be reduced to gnaw the very crust of the earth for nutriment.

The Maine Woods, p. 154

Strange that so few ever come to the woods to see how the pine lives and grows and spires, lifting its evergreen arms to the light,—to see its perfect success, but most are content to behold it in the shape of many broad boards brought to market, and deem *that* its true success! But the pine is no more lumber than man is, and to be made into boards and houses is no more its true and highest use than the truest use of a man is to be cut down and made into manure. There is a higher law affecting our relation to pines as well as to men. A pine cut down, a dead pine, is no more a pine than a dead human carcass is a man.

The Maine Woods, p. 121

Men & boys are learning all kinds of trades but how to make *men* of themselves. They learn to make houses, but they are not so well housed, they are not so contented in their houses, as the woodchucks in their holes. What is the use of a house if you haven't got a tolerable planet to put it on?

To H.G.O. Blake, May 20, 1860, in *The Correspondence of Henry David Thoreau*, pp. 578–579

What are the natural features which make a township handsome? A river, with its waterfalls and meadows, a lake, a hill, a cliff or individual rocks, a forest, and ancient trees standing singly. Such things are beautiful; they have a high use which dollars and cents never represent. If the inhabitants of a town were wise, they would seek to preserve these things, though at a considerable expense; for such things educate far more than any hired teachers or preachers, or any at present recognized system of school education.

Written January 3, 1861, in his *Journal*, vol. XIV, p. 304

Each town should have a park, or rather a primitive forest of five hundred or a thousand acres, where a stick should never be cut for fuel, a common possession forever, for instruction and recreation. We hear of cow-common and ministerial lots, but we want *men*-commons and lay lots, inalienable forever. Let us keep the New World *new*, preserve all the advantages of living in the country. There is meadow and pasture and wood-lot for the town's poor. Why not a forest and huckleberry-field for the town's rich? All Walden Wood might have been preserved for our park forever, with Walden in its midst, and the Easterbrooks Country, an unoccupied area of some four square miles, might have been our huckleberry-field.

Written October 15, 1859, in his *Journal*, vol. XII, p. 387

But most men, it seems to me, do not care for Nature and would sell their share in all her beauty, as long as they may live, for a stated sum—many for a glass of rum. Thank God, men cannot as yet fly, and lay waste the sky as well as the earth! We are safe on that side for the present.

Written January 3, 1861, in his *Journal*, vol. XIV, pp. 306–307

If some are prosecuted for abusing children, others deserve to be prosecuted for maltreating the face of nature committed to their care.

Written September 28, 1857, in his *Journal*, vol. X, p. 51

As some give to Harvard College or another institution, why might not another give a forest or huckleberry-field to Concord? A town is an institution which deserves to be remembered. We boast of our system of education, but why stop at schoolmasters and schoolhouses? We are all schoolmasters, and our schoolhouse is the universe. To attend chiefly to the desk or schoolhouse while we neglect the scenery in which it is placed is to save at the spile and waste at the bung. If we do not look out we shall find our fair schoolhouse standing in a cow-yard at last.

Written October 15, 1859, in his *Journal*, vol. XII, p. 387; emended from manuscript Journal (MA 1302, The Morgan Library & Museum, New York)

It would be worth the while if in each town there were a committee appointed to see that the beauty of the town received no detriment. If we have the largest boulder in the county, then it should not belong to an individual, nor be made into door-steps.

Written January 3, 1861, in his *Journal*, vol. XIV, pp. 304–305

We accuse savages of worshipping only the bad spirit, or devil, though they may distinguish both a good and a bad; but they regard only that one which they fear and worship the devil only. We too are savages in this, doing precisely the same thing. This occurred to me yesterday as I sat in the woods admiring the beauty of a blue butterfly. We are not chiefly interested in birds and insects, for example, as they are ornamental to the earth and cheering to man, but we spare the lives of the former only on condition that they eat more grubs than they do cherries.

Written May 1, 1859, in his *Journal*, vol. XII, p. 170; emended from manuscript Journal (MA 1302, The Morgan Library & Museum, New York)

The catechism says that the chief end of man is to glorify God and enjoy him forever, which of course is applicable mainly to God as seen in his works. Yet the only account of its beautiful insects—butterflies, etc.—

which God has made and set before us which the State ever thinks of spending any money on is the account of those which are injurious to vegetation! This is the way we glorify God and enjoy him forever. Come out here and behold a thousand painted butterflies and other beautiful insects which people the air, then go to the libraries and see what kind of prayer and glorification of God is there recorded. Massachusetts has published her report on "Insects Injurious to Vegetation," and our neighbor the "Noxious Insects of New York." We have attended to the evil and said nothing about the good.

Written May 1, 1859, in his *Journal*, vol. XII, pp. 170–171

Children are attracted by the beauty of butterflies, but their parents and legislators deem it an idle pursuit. The parents remind me of the Devil, not the children of God. Though God may have pronounced his work good, we ask. "Is it not poisonous?"

Written May 1, 1859, in his *Journal*, vol. XII, p. 171; emended from manuscript Journal (MA 1302, The Morgan Library & Museum, New York)

I thought with regret how soon these trees, like the black birches that grew on the hill near by, would be all cut off, and there would be almost nothing of the old Concord left, and we should be reduced to read old deeds in order to be reminded of such things,—deeds, at least, in which some old and revered bound trees are mentioned. These will be the only proof at last that they ever existed.

Written November 8, 1858, in his *Journal*, vol. XI, p. 299

The bream *appreciated* floats in the pond as the centre of the system, another image of God. Its life no man can explain more than he can his own. I want you to perceive the mystery of the bream. I have a contemporary in Walden. It has fins where I have legs and arms. I have a friend among the fishes, at least a new acquaintance. . . . Acquaintance with it is to make my life more rich and eventful.

Written November 30, 1858, in his *Journal*, vol. XI, p. 359; emended from manuscript Journal (MA 1302, The Morgan Library & Museum, New York)

When the question of the protection of birds comes up, the legislatures regard only a low use and never a high use; the best-disposed legislators employ one, perchance, only to examine their crops and see how many gnats or cherries they contain, and never to study their dispositions, or the beauty of their plumage, or listen and report on the sweetness of their song. The legislature will preserve a bird professedly not because it is a beautiful creature, but because it is a good scavenger or the like. This, at least, is the defence setup. It is as if the question were whether some celebrated singer of the human race— some Jenny Lind or another—did more harm or good, should be destroyed, or not, and therefore a committee should be appointed, not to listen to her singing at all, but to examine the contents of her stomach and see if she devoured anything which was injurious to the farmers and gardeners, or which they cannot spare.

Written April 8, 1859, in his *Journal*, vol. XII, pp. 124–125; emended from manuscript Journal (MA 1302, The Morgan Library & Museum, New York)

In my boating of late I have several times scared up a couple of summer ducks of this year, bred in our meadows. They allowed me to come quite near, and helped to people the river. I have not seen them for some days. Would you know the end of our intercourse? Goodwin shot them, and Mrs. ——, who never sailed on the river *ate* them. Of course, she knows not what she did. . . . They belonged to me, as much as to anyone, when they were alive, but it was considered of more importance that Mrs. —— should taste the flavor of them dead than that I should enjoy the beauty of them alive.

Written August 16, 1858, in his *Journal*, vol. XI, p. 107; emended from manuscript Journal (MA 1302, The Morgan Library & Museum, New York)

We have heard much of the wonderful intelligence of the beaver, but that regard for the beaver is all a pretense, and we would give more for a beaver hat than to preserve the intelligence of the whole race of beavers.

Written April 8, 1859, in his *Journal*, vol. XII, p. 121

The smokes from a dozen clearings far and wide, from a portion of the earth thirty miles or more in diameter, reveal the employment of many husbandmen at this season. Thus I see the woods burned up from year to year. The telltale smokes reveal it. The smokes will become rarer and thinner year by year, till I shall detect only a mere feathery film and there is no more brush to be burned.

Written October 10, 1857, in his *Journal*, vol. X, p. 83

The Anglo American can indeed cut down and grub up all this waving forest and make a stump speech and vote for Buchanan on its ruins, but he cannot converse with the spirit of the tree he fells—he cannot read the poetry and mythology which retire as he advances. He ignorantly erases mythological tablets in order to print his handbills and town meeting warrants on them.

The Maine Woods, p. 229

I seek acquaintance with Nature,—to know her moods and manners. Primitive Nature is the most interesting to me. I take infinite pains to know all the phenomena of the spring, for instance, thinking that I have here the entire poem, and then, to my chagrin, I learn that it is but an imperfect copy that I possess and have read, that my ancestors have torn out many of the first leaves and grandest passages, and mutilated it in many places. I should not like to think that some demigod had come before me and picked out some of the best of the stars. I wish to know an entire heaven and an entire earth.

Written March 23, 1856, in his *Journal*, vol. VIII, p. 221; emended from manuscript Journal (MA 1302, The Morgan Library & Museum, New York)

CONVERSATION AND TALK

I am thinking by what long discipline and at what cost a man learns to speak simply at last.

Written December 12, 1851, in his *Journal*, vol. 4, p. 202

It is vain to talk.

> Written February 20, 1842, in his *Journal*, vol. 1, p. 369

Say what you have to say, not what you ought.

> *Walden*, p. 327

The most constant phenomenon when men or women come together is talking.

> Written between 1842 and 1844, in his *Journal*, vol. 2, p. 67

All words are gossip.

> Written between 1847 and 1848, in his *Journal*, vol. 2, p. 380

Men cannot stay long together without talking, according to the rules of polite society.

> Written between 1842 and 1844, in his *Journal*, vol. 2, p. 67

We had nothing to say to one another, and therefore we said a great deal!

> To Ralph Waldo Emerson, January 24, 1843, after meeting John L. O'Sullivan, founder and editor of the *United States Magazine and Democratic Review*, in *The Correspondence of Henry David Thoreau*, p. 77

Surface meets surface. When our life ceases to be inward and private, conversation degenerates into mere gossip.

> "Life without Principle" in *Reform Papers*, p. 169

I have sometimes heard a conversation beginning again when it should have ceased for want of fuel.

Passage omitted from *A Week on the Concord and Merrimack Rivers* as published in Linck C. Johnson, *Thoreau's Complex Weave*, p. 468

The gregariousness of men is their most contemptible and discouraging aspect.

Written April 3, 1858, in his *Journal*, vol. X, p. 350

We are in great haste to construct a magnetic telegraph from Maine to Texas; but Maine and Texas, it may be, have nothing important to communicate. Either is in such a predicament as the man who was earnest to be introduced to a distinguished deaf woman, but when he was presented, and one end of her ear trumpet was put into his hand, had nothing to say.

Walden, p. 52

Do not speak for other men—Speak for yourself.

Written December 25, 1851, in his *Journal*, vol. 4, p. 223

DAY AND NIGHT

In the morning we do not believe in expediency—we will start afresh, and have no patching—no temporary fixtures. The after-noon man has an interest in the past;

his eye is divided and he sees indifferently well either way.

Written April 4, 1839, in his *Journal*, vol. 1, p. 69

For my panacea . . . let me have a draught of undiluted morning air. Morning air! If men will not drink of this at the fountain-head of the day, why, then, we must even bottle up some and sell it in the shops, for the benefit of those who have lost their subscription ticket to morning time in this world.

Walden, p. 138

Have you knowledge of the morning? Do you sympathise with that season of nature? Are you abroad early, brushing the dews aside? If the sun rises on you slumbering, if you do not hear the morning cockcrow, if you do not witness the blushes of Aurora, if you are not acquainted with Venus as the morning star, what relation have you to wisdom & purity? You have then forgotten your creator in the days of your youth.

Written July 18, 1851, in his *Journal*, vol. 3, p. 312

Morning brings back the heroic ages.

Walden p. 88

Morning is when I am awake and there is a dawn in me.

Walden, p. 90

The day is an epitome of the year. The night is the winter, the morning and evening are the spring and fall, and the noon is the summer.

Walden, p. 301

Many men walk by day, few walk by night. It is a very different season.

Written after July 1, 1850, in his *Journal*, vol. 3, p. 92

Is not the midnight like central Africa to most?

Written February 1, 1852, in his *Journal*, vol. 4, p. 315

To see the sun rise or go down every day would preserve us sane forever—so to relate ourselves for our mind's & body's health to a universal fact.

Written January 20, 1852, in his *Journal*, vol. 4, p. 270

It is day & we have more of that same light that the moon sent us but not reflected now but shining directly. The sun is a fuller moon. Who knows how much brighter day there may be?

Written June 11, 1852, in his *Journal*, vol. 5, p. 92

The voice of the crickets heard at noon from deep in the grass allies day to night. It is unaffected by sun & moon. It is a mid-night sound heard at noon—a mid-day sound heard at midnight.

Written June 29, 1851, in his *Journal*, vol. 3, p. 280

The morning hope is soon lost in what becomes the routine of the day & we do not recover ourselves again until we land on the pensive shores of evening.

Written January 8, 1854, in his *Journal*, vol. 7, p. 227

How swiftly the earth appears to revolve at sunset which at midday appears to rest on its axle.

Written December 21, 1851, in his *Journal*, vol. 4, p. 215

We never tire of the drama of sunset. . . . Can Washington Street or Broad-Way show anything as good? Every day a new picture is painted and framed, held up for half an hour in such lights as the great artist chooses & then withdrawn & the curtain falls.

Written January 7, 1852, in his *Journal*, vol. 4, p. 242

The man is blessed who every day is permitted to behold anything so pure & serene as the western sky at sunset while revolutions vex the world.

Written December 27, 1851, in his *Journal*, vol. 4, p. 225

If I were to choose a time for a friend to make a passing visit to this world for the first time in the full possession of all his faculties perchance it would be at a moment when the sun was setting with splendor in the west—his light reflected far & wide through the clarified air after a rain—and a brilliant rain-bow as now oerarching the eastern sky.

Written August 7, 1852, in his *Journal*, vol. 5, p. 287

Every sunset which I witness inspires me with the desire to go to a west as distant and as fair as that into which the Sun goes down.

"Walking" in *Excursions*, p. 197

So is not shade as good as sunshine—night as day? Why be eagles and thrushes always, and owls and whippoor-wills never?

Written June 16, 1840, in his *Journal*, vol. 1, p. 129

As the twilight deepens and the moonlight is more & more bright I begin to distinguish myself, who I am & where. As my walls contract I become more collected & composed & sensible of my own existence—as when a lamp is brought into a dark apartment & I see who the company are.

Written August 5, 1851, in his *Journal*, vol. 3, pp. 353–354

By moonlight all is simple. We are enabled to erect ourselves, our minds, on account of the fewness of objects. We are no longer distracted. It is simple as bread and water. It is simple as the rudiments of an art.

Written September 22, 1854, in his *Journal*, vol. VII, p. 51

Nature seems not have designed that man should be much abroad by night and in the moon proportioned the light fitly. By the faintness & rareness of the light compared with that of the sun she expresses her intention with regard to him.

Written June 14, 1851, in his *Journal*, vol. 3, p. 269

When man is asleep & day fairly forgotten, then is the beauty of moon light seen over lonely pastures where cattle are silently feeding.

Written June 14, 1851, in his *Journal*, vol. 3, p. 268

The night is oracular.

Written October 27, 1851, in his *Journal*, vol. 4, p. 156

There is a certain glory attends on water by night. By it the heavens are related to the earth—Undistinguishable from a sky beneath you.

Written June 13, 1851, in his *Journal*, vol. 3, p. 260

When I am outside on the outskirts of the town enjoying the still majesty of the moon I am wont to think that all men are aware of this miracle—that they too are silently worshipping this manifestation of divinity elsewhere—but when I go into the house I am undeceived, they are absorbed in checquers or chess or novel, though they may have been advertised of the brightness through the shutters.

Written May 16, 1851, in his *Journal*, vol. 3, p. 219

DRESS AND FASHION

We know but few men, a great many coats and breeches.

Walden, p. 22

Fig. 3. Edward Emerson's copy of Daniel Ricketson's pencil sketch of Thoreau originally drawn on December 12, 1854. The Raymond Adams Collection (The Thoreau Society® Collections at the Thoreau Institute). Courtesy of the Thoreau Society.

No man ever stood the lower in my estimation for having a patch in his clothes.

Walden, p. 22

It is highly important to invent a dress which will enable us to be abroad with impunity in the severest storms. We cannot be said to have fully invented clothing yet.

Written April 22, 1856, in his *Journal*, vol. VIII, pp. 299–300

I say, beware of all enterprises that require new clothes, and not rather a new wearer of clothes.

Walden, p. 23

We worship not the Graces, nor the Parcae, but Fashion. She spins and weaves and cuts with full authority. The head monkey at Paris puts on a traveller's cap, and all the monkeys in America do the same.

Walden, p. 25

When I see a fine lady or gentleman dressed to the top of the fashion, I wonder what they would do if an earthquake should happen, or a fire suddenly break out, for they seem to have counted only on fair weather, and that things will go on smoothly and without jostling.

Written July 12, 1840, in his *Journal*, vol. 1, p. 157

The walker and naturalist does not wear a hat, or a shoe, or a coat, to be looked at, but for other uses. When a citizen comes to take a walk with me I commonly find that he is lame,—disabled by his shoeing. He is sure to wet his feet, tear his coat, and jam his hat, and the superior qualities of my boots, coat, and hat appear. I once went into the woods with a party for a fortnight. I wore my old and common clothes, which were of Vermont gray. They wore, no doubt, the best they had for such an occasion,—of a fashionable color and quality. I thought that they were a little ashamed of me while we were in the towns. They all tore their clothes badly but myself, and I, who, it chanced, was the only one provided with needles and thread, enabled them to mend them. When we came out of the woods I was the best dressed of any of them.

Written March 26, 1860, in his *Journal*, vol. XIII, pp. 231–232

How different are men and women, *e.g.* in respect to the adornment of their heads! Do you ever see an old or jammed bonnet on the head of a woman at a public meeting? But look at any assembly of men with their hats on; how large a proportion of the hats will be old, weather-beaten, and indented, but I think so much the more picturesque and interesting!

Written December 25, 1859, in his *Journal*, vol. XIII, p. 51

The chief recommendation of the Kossuth hat is that it looks old to start with, and almost as good as new to end with.

Written December 25, 1859, in his *Journal*, vol. XIII, p. 52

It is generally conceded that a man does not look the worse for a somewhat dilapidated hat.

Written December 25, 1859, in his *Journal*, vol. XIII, p. 52

Men wear their hats for use; women theirs for ornament.

Written December 25, 1859, in his *Journal*, vol. XIII, p. 52

Ladies are in haste to dress *as if* it were cold or *as if* it were warm,—though it may not yet be so,—merely to display a new dress.

Written December 25, 1859, in his *Journal*, vol. XIII, p. 52

It is astonishing how far a merely well-dressed and good-looking man may go without being challenged by any sentinel.

Written January 3, 1856, in his *Journal*, vol. VIII, p. 82

Every day our garments become more assimilated to ourselves, receiving the impress of the wearer's character, until we hesitate to lay them aside, without such delay and medical appliances and some such solemnity even as our bodies.

Walden, pp. 21–22

I have had made a pair of corduroy pants, which cost when done $1.60. They are of that peculiar clay-color, reflecting the light from portions of their surface. They have this advantage, that, beside being very strong, they will look about as well three months hence as now,—or as ill, some would say.

Written May 8, 1857, in his *Journal*, vol. IX, p. 359

When I go a-visiting I find that I go off the fashionable street—not being inclined to change my dress—to where man meets man and not polished shoe meets shoe.

Written June 11, 1855, in his *Journal*, vol. VII, p. 416

I have just got a letter from Ricketson, urging me to come to New Bedford, which possibly I may do. He says I can wear my old clothes there.

To H.G.O. Blake, September 26, 1855, in *The Correspondence of Henry David Thoreau*, p. 385

I just had a coat come home from the tailors—ah me—who am I that I should wear this coat? It was fitted upon one of the Devil's angels about my size. Of what use that measuring of me if he did not measure my character? This is not the figure that I cut—this is the figure the tailor cuts.

Written January 14, 1854, in his *Journal*, vol. 7, p. 241

I was pleased the other day to see a son of Concord return after an absence of eight years, not in a shining suit of black, with polished boots and a beaver or silk hat, as if on a furlough from human duties generally,—a mere clothes-horse,— but clad in an honest clay-colored suit and a snug every-day cap. It showed unusual manhood.

Written May 8, 1857, in his *Journal*, vol. IX, pp. 359–360

EDUCATION AND LEARNING

I would make education a pleasant thing both to the teacher and the scholar. This discipline, which we allow to be the end of life, should not be one thing in the schoolroom, and another in the street. We should seek to be fellow students with the pupil, and we should learn of, as well as with him, if we would be most helpful to him.

To Orestes Brownson, December 30, 1837, in *The Correspondence of Henry David Thoreau*, p. 20

Which would have advanced the most at the end of a month,—the boy who had made his own jackknife from the ore which he had dug and smelted, reading as much as would be necessary for this,—or the boy who had attended the lectures on metallurgy at the Institute in the mean while, and had received a Rodgers' pen-knife from his father?

Walden, p. 51

I served my apprenticeship and have since done considerable journeywork in the huckleberry field. Though I never paid for my schooling and clothing in that way, it was some of the best schooling that I got and paid for itself.

"Huckleberries," p. 26

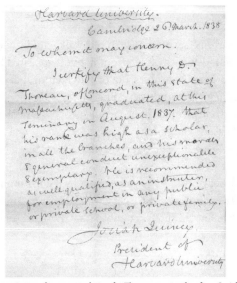

FIG. 4. Letter of recommendation for Thoreau as a teacher from Josiah Quincy, president of Harvard University, March 26, 1838. The Raymond Adams Collection (The Thoreau Society* Collections at the Thoreau Institute). Courtesy of the Thoreau Society

Knowledge does not come to us by details but by lief-erungs from the gods.

Written July 7, 1851, in his *Journal*, vol. 3, p. 291

Knowledge does not come to us by details, but in flashes of light from heaven.

"Life without Principle" in *Reform Papers*, p. 173

What we do best or most perfectly is what we have most thoroughly learned by the longest practice, and at length it falls from us without our notice, as a leaf from a tree.

Written March 11, 1859, in his *Journal*, vol. XII, p. 39

We saw one school-house in our walk, and listened to the sounds which issued from it; but it appeared like a place where the process, not of enlightening, but of ob-fuscating the mind was going on, and the pupils received only so much light as could penetrate the shadow of the Catholic church.

"A Yankee in Canada" in *Excursions*, p. 116

Knowledge is to be acquired only by a corresponding experience. How can we *know* what we are *told* merely? Each man can interpret another's experience only by his own.

A Week on the Concord and Merrimack Rivers, p. 365

I have noticed that whatever is thought to be covered by the word *education*—whether reading, writing or 'rithmetick—is a great thing, but almost all that constitutes education is a little thing in the estimation of such speakers as I refer to.

"Huckleberries," p. 3

Those things for which the most money is demanded are never the things which the student most wants. Tuition, for instance, is an important item in the term bill, while for the far more valuable education which he gets by associating with the most cultivated of his contemporaries no charge is made.

Walden, p. 50

The audience are never tired of hearing how far the wind carried some man woman or child—or family bible—but they are immediately tired if you undertake to give them a scientific account of it.

Written February 4, 1852, in his *Journal*, vol. 4, p. 328

All the branches and none of the roots.

On hearing Emerson remark that most of the branches of knowledge were taught at Harvard, as reported by John Albee in *Remembrances of Emerson*, p. 30

We spend more on almost any article of bodily aliment or ailment than on our mental aliment.

Walden, p. 108

It is time that we had uncommon schools, that we did not leave off our education when we begin to be men and women. It is time that villages were universities, and their elder inhabitants the fellows of universities, with leisure—if they are indeed so well off—to pursue liberal studies the rest of their lives.

Walden, pp. 108–109

I have never declined paying the highway tax, because I am as desirous of being a good neighbor as I am of being a bad subject; and, as for supporting schools, I am doing my part to educate my fellow-countrymen now.

On spending a night in jail for nonpayment of taxes in "Resistance to Civil Government" in *Reform Papers*, p. 84

Men have a respect for scholarship and learning greatly out of proportion to the use they commonly serve.

A Week on the Concord and Merrimack Rivers, p. 105

What does education often do! It makes a straight-cut ditch of a free meandering brook.

Written after October 31, 1850, in his *Journal*, vol. 3, p. 130

Many College text books which were a weariness & a stumbling block when *studied* I have since read a little in with pleasure & profit.

Written February 19, 1854, in his *Journal*, vol. 8, p. 10

During the berry season the Schools have a vacation and many little fingers are busy picking these small fruits. . . . I remember how glad I was when I was kept from school a half a day to pick huckleberries on a neighboring hill all by myself to make a pudding for the family dinner. Ah, they got nothing but the pudding—but I got invaluable experience beside.

Written July 16, 1851, in his *Journal*, vol. 3, p. 307

I well remember with what a sense of freedom and spirit of adventure I used to take my way across the fields with my pail . . . toward some distant hill or swamp, when dismissed for all day, and I would not now exchange such an expansion of all my being for all the learning in the world. Liberation and enlargement—such is the fruit which all culture aims to secure. I suddenly knew more about my books than if I had never ceased studying them. I found myself in a schoolroom where I could not fail to see and hear things worth seeing and hearing—where I could not help getting my lesson—for my lesson came to me. Such experience often repeated, was the chief encouragement to go to the Academy and study a book at last.

"Huckleberries," pp. 27–28

Do not think that the fruits of New England are mean and insignificant, while those of some foreign land are noble and memorable. Our own, whatever they may be, are far more important to us than any others can be. They educate us, and fit us to live in New England. Better for us is the wild strawberry than the pineapple, the wild apple than the orange, the hazelnut or pignut than the cocoanut or almond, and not on account of their flavor merely, but the part they play in our education.

Written November 26, 1860, in his *Journal*, vol. XIV, p. 274

It is strange that men are in such haste to get fame as teachers rather than knowledge as learners.

Written March 11, 1856, in his *Journal*, vol. VIII, p. 205

Who knows whence his education is to come!

To Isaac Hecker, after August 15, 1844, in *The Correspondence of Henry David Thoreau*, p. 158

I am still a learner, not a teacher, feeding somewhat omnivorously, browsing both stalk & leaves.

To H.G.O. Blake, May 21, 1856, in *The Correspondence of Henry David Thoreau*, pp. 423–424

We of Massachusetts boast a good deal of what we do for the education of our people—of our district-school system—& yet our district schools are as it were but infant schools & we have no system for the education of the great mass who are grown up.

Written September 27, 1851, in his *Journal*, vol. 4, p. 101

We boast that we belong to the 19th century and are making the most rapid strides of any nation. But consider how little this village does for its own culture—perchance a comparatively decent system of common schools—schools for infants only, as it were, but excepting the half starved lyceum in the winter, no school for ourselves.

Written August 29, 1852, in his *Journal*, vol. 5, p. 318

With a little more deliberation in the choice of their pursuits, all men would perhaps become essentially students and observers, for certainly their nature and destiny are interesting to all alike.

Walden, p. 99

The poet says the proper study of mankind is man. I say study to forget all that—take wider views of the universe.

Written April 2, 1852, in his *Journal*, vol. 4, p. 418

The universe is wider than our views of it.

Walden, p. 320

It is only when we forget all our learning that we begin to know.

Written October 4, 1859, in his *Journal*, vol. XII, p. 371

EXPECTATION

What is hope, what is expectation, but a seed-time whose harvest cannot fail, an irresistible expedition of the mind, at length to be victorious?

Written February 20, 1857, in his *Journal*, vol. IX, p. 275

Fishermen, hunters, woodchoppers, and others, spending their lives in the fields and woods, in a peculiar sense a part of Nature themselves, are often in a more favorable mood for observing her, in the intervals of their pursuits, than philosophers or poets even, who approach her with expectation.

Walden, p. 210

What is this heaven which they expect, if it is no better than they expect? Are they prepared for a better than they can now imagine?

A Week on the Concord and Merrimack Rivers, p. 379

Consider the infinite promise of a man, so that the sight of his roof at a distance suggests an idyll or pastoral, or of his grave an Elegy in a Country Churchyard.

Written October 3, 1859, in his *Journal*, vol. XII, p. 369

Most men can keep a horse or keep up a certain fashionable style of living, but few indeed can keep up great expectations.

Written May 6, 1858, in his *Journal*, vol. X, p. 405

Can I not by expectation affect the revolutions of nature—make a day to bring forth something new?

Written April 18, 1852, in his *Journal*, vol. 4, p. 468

We soon get through with Nature. She excites an expectation which she cannot satisfy. The merest child which has rambled into a copse wood dreams of a wilderness so wild and strange & inexhaustible as Nature can never show him.

Written May 23, 1854, in his *Journal*, vol. 8, p. 146

Give me the old familiar walk, post-office and all, with this ever new self, with this infinite expectation and faith, which does not know when it is beaten. We'll go nutting once more. We'll pluck the nut of the world, and crack it in the winter evenings. Theatres and all other sightseeing are puppet-shows in comparison.

Written November 1, 1858, in his *Journal*, vol. XI, p. 274

The truest account of heaven is the fairest & I will accept none which disappoints expectation. It is more glorious to expect a better, than to enjoy a worse.

Written January 26, 1852, in his *Journal*, vol. 4, p. 290

We must learn to reawaken and keep ourselves awake, not by mechanical aids, but by an infinite expectation of the dawn, which does not forsake us in our soundest sleep.

Walden, p. 90

We may well be ashamed to tell what things we have read or heard in our day. I do not know why my news should be so trivial,—considering what one's dreams and expectations are, why the developments should be so paltry.

"Life without Principle," in *Reform Papers*, p. 170

With what infinite & unwearied expectation and proclamations the cocks usher in every dawn as if there had never been one before.

Written March 16, 1852, in his *Journal*, vol. 4, p. 391

Show men unlimited faith as the coin with which you will deal with them, and they will invariably exhibit the best wares they have.

Written January 28, 1841, in his *Journal*, vol. 1, p. 233

May I go to my slumbers as expecting to arise to a new & more perfect day.

Written July 16, 1851, in his *Journal*, vol. 3, p. 311

Expectation may amount to prophecy.

Written April 2, 1852, in his *Journal*, vol. 4, p. 415

Our circumstances answer to our expectations and the demand of our natures.

A Week on the Concord and Merrimack Rivers, p. 292

Is not the attitude of expectation somewhat divine?—a sort of home-made divineness?

To H.G.O. Blake, May 28, 1850, in *The Correspondence of Henry David Thoreau*, p. 259

They who are ready to go are already invited.

Written July 2, 1840, in his *Journal*, vol. 1, p. 147

EXPERIENCE

Who is old enough to have learned from experience?

Written March 21, 1842, in his *Journal*, vol. 1, p. 385

My only integral experience is in my vision.

> To H.G.O. Blake, May 2, 1848, in *The Correspondence of Henry David Thoreau*, p. 222

All we have experienced is so much gone within us and there lies. It is the company we keep.

> Written February 8, 1841, in his *Journal*, vol. 1, p. 258

In the summer we lay up a stock of experiences for the winter, as the squirrel of nuts. Something for conversation in winter evenings.

> Written September 4, 1851, in his *Journal*, vol. 4, p. 40

Surely one may as profitably be soaked in the juices of a swamp for one day as pick his way dry-shod over sand. Cold and damp,—are they not as rich experience as warmth and dryness?

> *A Week on the Concord and Merrimack Rivers*, p. 300

Going a-berrying implies more things than eating the berries.

> "Huckleberries," pp. 26–27

The poet deals with his privatest experience.

> Written April 8, 1854, in his *Journal*, vol. 8, p. 57

It is a grand fact that you cannot make the fairer fruits or parts of fruits matter of commerce; that is, you cannot buy the highest use and enjoyment of them. You cannot buy that pleasure which it yields to him who truly plucks it.

> *Wild Fruits*, p. 5

The chief want is ever a life of deep experiences.

Written June 8, 1854, in his *Journal*, vol. 8, p. 181

Our mother's faith has not grown with her experience. Her experience has been too much for her. The lesson of life was too hard for her to learn.

A Week on the Concord and Merrimack Rivers, p. 77

Methinks my present experience is nothing, my past experience is all in all. I think that no experience which I have today comes up to or is comparable with the experiences of my boyhood.

Written July 16, 1851, in his *Journal*, vol. 3, p. 305

Our life is not altogether a forgetting but also alas to a great extent a remembering of that which perchance we should never have been conscious of—the consciousness of what should not be permitted to disturb a man's waking hours.

Written November 10, 1851, in his *Journal*, vol. 4, p. 174

The value of any experience is measured, of course, not by the amount of money, but the amount of development we get out of it.

Written November 26, 1860, in his *Journal*, vol. XIV, p. 274

Do not tread on the heels of your experience. Be impressed without making a minute of it.

Written July 23, 1851, in his *Journal*, vol. 3, p. 331

There is no such thing as pure *objective* observation. Your observation to be interesting i.e. to be significant must be *subjective*.

Written May 6, 1854, in his *Journal*, vol. 8, p. 98

Early for several mornings I have heard the sound of a flail. It leads me to ask if I have spent as industrious a spring & summer as the farmer & gathered as rich a crop of experience. Let the sound of my flail be heard, by those who have ears to hear, separating the kernel from the chaff all the fall & winter & a sound no less cheering it will be.

Written August 29, 1854, in his *Journal*, vol. 8, p. 307

FARMERS AND FARMING

I must not lose any of my freedom by being a farmer and land holder. Most who enter on any profession are doomed men. The world might as well sing a dirge over them forthwith. The farmer's muscles are rigid— he can do one thing long not many well. His pace seems determined henceforth—he never quickens it. A very rigid Nemesis is his fate. When the right wind blows or a star calls, I can leave this arable and grass ground, without making a will or settling my estate. I would buy a farm as freely as a silken streamer. Let me not think my front windows must face east henceforth because a particular hill slopes that way. My life must undulate still. I will not feel that my wings are clipt when once I have settled on ground which the law calls my own but find new pinions grown to the old and talaria to my feet beside.

Written after March 27, 1841, in his *Journal*, vol. 1, p. 291

I talked of buying Conantum once but for want of money we did not come to terms—but I have farmed it in my own fashion every year since.

Written August 31, 1851, in his *Journal*, vol. 4, p. 25

Buy a farm! What have I to pay for a farm which a farmer will take?

A Week on the Concord and Merrimack Rivers, p. 350

As for farming, I am convinced it is too tame for me and my genius dates from an older era than the agricultural. I would strike my spade into the earth with such careless freedom, but accuracy, as the woodpecker his bill into a tree.

Written between 1842 and 1844, in his *Journal*, vol. 2, p. 22

I see young men, my townsmen, whose misfortune it is to have inherited farms, houses, barns, cattle, and farming tools; for these are more easily acquired than got rid of. Better if they had been born in the open pasture and suckled by a wolf, that they might have seen with clearer eyes what field they were called to labor in. Who made them serfs of the soil?

Walden, p. 5

I respect not his labors, his farm where every thing has its price; who would carry the landscape, who would carry his God, to market, if he could get any thing for him; who goes to market *for* his god as it is; on whose farm nothing grows free, whose fields bear no crops, whose meadows no flowers, whose trees no fruits, but dollars; who loves not the beauty of his fruits, whose fruits are not ripe for him till they are turned to dollars.

Walden, p. 196

Farms are for sale all around here—and so I suppose men are for purchase.

To his parents, June 8, 1843, in *The Correspondence of Henry David Thoreau*, p. 114

When I witness the first plowing and planting, I acquire a long-lost confidence in the earth,—that it will nourish the seed that is committed to its bosom.

Written March 28, 1857, in his *Journal*, vol. IX, p. 310

The scholar's & the farmer's work are strictly analogous. . . . He is doing like myself. My barn-yard is my journal.

Written January 20, 1852, in his *Journal*, vol. 4, p. 269

The farmer has always come to the field after some material thing; that is not what a philosopher goes there for.

Written October 14, 1857, in his *Journal*, vol. X, p. 94

Successful farming admits of no idling.

Written July 23, 1852, in his *Journal*, vol. 5, p. 240

I have faith that the man who redeemed some acres of land the past summer redeemed also some parts of his character.

Written March 1, 1852, in his *Journal*, vol. 4, p. 369

The farmer increases the extent of habitable earth. He makes soil. That is an honorable occupation.

Written March 2, 1852, in his *Journal*, vol. 4, p. 371

It is a novel sight, that of the farmer distributing manure with a shovel in the field and planting again. The earth looks warm and genial again. . . . I could almost lie down in the furrow and be warmed into her life and growth.

Written March 26, 1857, in his *Journal*, vol. IX, p. 303

What noble work is plowing, with the broad and solid earth for material, the ox for fellow-laborer, and the simple but efficient plow for tool! . . . It comes pretty near to making a world.

Written March 28, 1857, in his *Journal*, vol. IX, pp. 310–311

It is agreeable once more to put a spade into the warm mould. The victory is ours at last, for we remain and take possession of the field.

Written March 31, 1857, in his *Journal*, vol. IX, p. 312

FOOD AND DIET

He who distinguishes the true savor of his food can never be a glutton; he who does not cannot be otherwise.

Walden, p. 218

We live too fast & coarsely just as we eat too fast & do not know the true savor of our food.

Written December 28, 1852, in his *Journal*, vol. 5, p. 412

The indecent haste and grossness with which our food is swallowed, have cast a disgrace on the very act of eating itself.

Written after July 16, 1845, in his *Journal*, vol. 2, p. 165

A man may use as simple a diet as the animals, and yet retain health and strength.

Walden, p. 61

It is a common saying among country people that if you eat much fried hasty pudding it will make your hair curl. My experience which was considerable did not confirm this assertion.

Written November 20, 1850, in his *Journal*, vol. 3, p. 146

Some men are excited by the smell of burning powder but I thought in my dream last night how much saner to be excited by the smell of new bread.

Written September 25, 1851, in his *Journal*, vol. 4, p. 97

Is it not a reproach that man is a carnivorous animal? True, he can and does live, in a great measure, by preying on other animals; but this is a miserable way,—as any one who will go to snaring rabbits, or slaughtering lambs, may learn,—and he will be regarded as a benefactor of his race who shall teach man to confine himself to a more innocent and wholesome diet.

Walden, pp. 215–216

Like many of my contemporaries I had rarely for many years used animal food or tea or coffee, &c &c not so much because of any ill effects which I had traced to them in my own case, though I could theorize extensively in that direction as because it was not agreeable to my imagination. It appeared more beautiful to live low & fare hard in many respects, and though I never did so I went just far enough to please my imagination. But now I find myself somewhat less particular in these respects. I carry less religion to the table, ask no blessing—not because I am wiser than I was—but I am obliged to confess, because, however much it is to be regretted, with years I have grown more coarse and indifferent.

Written November 28, 1852, in his *Journal*, vol. 5, p. 399

Whatever my own practice may be, I have no doubt that it is a part of the destiny of the human race, in its gradual improvement, to leave off eating animals, as surely as the savage tribes have left off eating each other when they came in contact with the more civilized.

Walden, p. 216

One farmer says to me, "You cannot live on vegetable food solely, for it furnishes nothing to make bones with;" and so he religiously devotes a part of his day to supplying his system with the raw material of bones; walking all the while he talks behind his oxen, which, with vegetable-made bones, jerk him and his lumbering plow along in spite of every obstacle.

Walden, p. 9

A man may esteem himself happy when that which is his food is also his medicine.

A Week on the Concord and Merrimack Rivers, p. 256

Man for once stands in such relation to Nature as the animals—they pluck & eat as they go. The fields & hills are a table constantly spread. Wines of all kinds & qualities of noblest vintages are bottled up in the skins of countless berries for the taste of men & animals. To men they seem offered not so much for food as for sociality that they may picnic with nature—Diet drinks—cordials—wines—We pluck & eat in remembrance of Her. It is a sacrament—a communion.

Written July 24, 1853, in his *Journal*, vol. 6, pp. 266–267

We have not had such a year for berries this long time—the earth is actually blue with them. High blueberries, three kinds of low—thimble and rasp-berries, constitute my diet at present. (Take notice—I only diet between meals.)

To his brother, John, July 8, 1838, in *The Correspondence of Henry David Thoreau*, p. 27

I have carried an apple in my pocket tonight. . . . I realize the existence of a goddess Pomona and that the gods have really intended that men should feed divinely, like themselves, on their own nectar & ambrosia. They have so painted this fruit and freighted it with such a fragrance that it satisfies much more than an animal appetite.

Written after July 16, 1845, in his *Journal*, vol. 2, p. 165

The bitter-sweet of a white oak acorn which you nibble in a bleak November walk over the tawny earth is more to me than a slice of imported pineapple. We do not think much of table-fruits. They are especially for aldermen and epicures. They do not feed the imagination. That would starve on them. These wild fruits, whether eaten or not, are a dessert for the imagination.

Written November 24, 1860, in his *Journal*, vol. XIV, p. 265

I cannot but believe that acorns were intended to be the food of man. They are agreeable to the palate as the mother's milk to the babe.

Written October 8, 1851, in his *Journal*, vol. 4, p. 133

Drink the wines not of your bottling but nature's bottling—not kept in goat skins or pig skins but the skins of a myriad fair berries.

Written August 23, 1853, in his *Journal*, vol. 7, p. 16

I have drank tea & coffee & made myself cheap and vulgar. My days have been all noon tide without sacred mornings & evenings.

Written August 13, 1854, in his *Journal*, vol. 8, p. 265

Wine is not a noble liquor, except when it is confined to the pores of the grape.

Written after September 19, 1850, in his *Journal*, vol. 3, p. 119

I am glad to have drunk water so long, as I prefer the natural sky to an opium eater's heaven—would keep sober always, and lead a sane life, not indebted to stimulants. Whatever my practice may be, I believe that it is the only drink for a wise man, and only the foolish habitually use any other.

Written after September 19, 1850, in his *Journal*, vol. 3, p. 119

The common perch. . . . is the firmest and toughest of our fishes and by those who are not epicures most preferred for food.

Written after August 1, 1844, in his *Journal*, vol. 2, p. 108

It is hard to provide and cook so simple and clean a diet as will not offend the imagination.

Walden, p. 215

The fruits eaten temperately need not make us ashamed of our appetites, nor interrupt the worthiest pursuits. But put an extra condiment into your dish, and it will poison you.

Walden, p. 215

It is not worth the while to live by rich cookery.

Walden, p. 215

Most men would feel shame if caught preparing with their own hands precisely such a dinner, whether of animal or vegetable food, as is every day prepared for them by others.

Walden, p. 215

The greater or less abundance of food determines migrations.

Written April 23, 1852, in his *Journal*, vol. 4, p. 486

FREEDOM AND SLAVERY

FIG. 5. Detail from "Protest of 400 inhabitants of Concord against the execution of Washington Goode," 1849. The Thoreau Society Archives (The Thoreau Society® Collections at the Thoreau Institute). Courtesy of the Thoreau Society.

Perhaps I am more than usually jealous with respect to my freedom.

"Life without Principle" in *Reform Papers*, p. 160

I am freer than any planet.

Written March 21, 1840, in his *Journal*, vol. 1, p. 118

I never met a man who cast a free and healthy glance over life.

Written August 1, 1841, in his *Journal*, vol. 1, p. 315

What other liberty is there worth having, if we have not freedom & peace in our minds, if our inmost & most private man is but a sour & turbid pool.

Written October 26, 1853, in his *Journal*, vol. 7, p.115

When on my way this after noon shall I go down this long hill in the rain to fish in the pond "I ask myself" and I say to my-self yes roam far—grasp life & conquer it—learn much—& live—Your fetters are knocked off—you are really free.

Written August 23, 1845, in his *Journal*, vol. 2, p. 177

Do we call this the land of the free? What is it to be free from King George the IV. and continue the slaves of prejudice? What is it be born free & equal & not to live. What is the value of any political freedom, but as a means to moral freedom. Is it a freedom to be slaves or a freedom to be free, of which we boast.

Written February 16, 1851, in his *Journal*, vol. 3, p. 194

We would fain express our appreciation of the freedom and steady wisdom, so rare in the reformer, with which

he declared that he was not born to abolish slavery, but
to do right.

"Wendell Phillips Before Concord Lyceum" in *Reform Papers*,
p. 61

I cannot for an instant recognize that political organization as *my* government which is the *slave's* government also.

"Resistance to Civil Government" in *Reform Papers*, p. 67

Wait not till slaves pronounce the word
    To set the captive free,
Be free yourselves, be not deferred,
    And farewell slavery.

Untitled poem in *Collected Poems of Henry Thoreau*, p. 198

Let the State dissolve her union with the slaveholder.
She may wriggle and hesitate, and ask leave to read the
Constitution once more; but she can find no respectable law or precedent which sanctions the continuance
of such a Union for an instant.

"Slavery in Massachusetts" in *Reform Papers*, p. 104

What is the character of that calm which follows *the
success* when the law and the slave-holder prevail?

Written October 19, 1859, in his *Journal*, vol. XII, p. 404;
emended from manuscript Journal (MA 1302, The Morgan
Library & Museum, New York)

A government that pretends to be Christian and cruci-
fies a million Christs every day!

Written October 19, 1859, in his *Journal*, vol. XII, p. 404

Talk about slavery! It is not the peculiar institution of the South. It exists wherever men are bought and sold, wherever a man allows himself to be made a mere thing or a tool, and surrenders his inalienable rights of reason and conscience. Indeed, this slavery is more complete than that which enslaves the body alone.

Written December 4, 1860, in his *Journal*, vol. XIV, p. 292

There are thousands who are *in opinion* opposed to slavery and to the war, who yet in effect do nothing to put an end to them; who, esteeming themselves children of Washington and Franklin, sit down with their hands in their pockets, and say that they know not what to do, and do nothing; who even postpone the question of freedom to the question of free-trade, and quietly read the prices-current along with the latest advices from Mexico, after dinner, and, it may be, fall asleep over them both. What is the price-current of an honest man and patriot to-day?

"Resistance to Civil Government" in *Reform Papers*, p. 69

As long as you *know of* it, you are *particeps criminis*.

To Parker Pillsbury, April 10, 1861, in *The Correspondence of Henry David Thoreau*, p. 611

I do not wish, it happens, to be associated with Massachusetts, either in holding slaves or in conquering Mexico. I am a little better than herself in these respects.

A Week on the Concord and Merrimack Rivers, p. 130

I know this well, that if one thousand, if one hundred, if ten men whom I could name,—if ten *honest* men only,—aye, if *one* HONEST man, in this State of Massachusetts, *ceasing to hold slaves*, were actually to withdraw from this copartnership, and be locked up in the county jail therefor, it would be the abolition of slavery in America. For it matters not how small the beginning may seem to be: what is once well done is done for ever. But we love better to talk about it: that we say is our mission. Reform keeps many scores of newspapers in its service, but not one man.

"Resistance to Civil Government" in *Reform Papers*, p. 75

There has not been anything which you could call union between the North and South in this country for many years, and there cannot be so long as slavery is in the way. I only wish that Northern—that any men— were better material, or that I for one had more skill to deal with them; that the north had more spirit and would settle the question at once, and here instead of struggling feebly and protractedly away off on the plains of Kansas.

To Thomas Cholmondeley, October 20, 1856, in *The Correspondence of Henry David Thoreau*, p. 436

Men talk of freedom! How many are free to think? free from fear, from perturbation, from prejudice?

Written May 6, 1858, in his *Journal*, vol. X, p. 404

I wonder men can be so frivolous almost as to attend to the gross form of negro slavery—there are so many keen and subtle masters, who subject us both. Self-emancipation in the West Indies of a man's thinking and imagining provinces, which should be more than his island territory. One emancipated heart & intellect—It would knock off the fetters from a million slaves.

Written July 6, 1845, in his *Journal*, vol. 2, p. 156

It hath not entered into the heart of man to conceive the full import of that word—Freedom—not a paltry Republican freedom, with a *posse comitatus* at his heels to administer it in doses as to a sick child—but a freedom proportionate to the dignity of his nature—a freedom that shall make him feel that he is a man among men, and responsible only to that Reason of which he is a particle, for his thoughts and his actions.

To Orestes Brownson, December 30, 1837, in *The Correspondence of Henry David Thoreau*, p. 20

You know we have hardly done our own deeds, thought our own thoughts, or lived our own lives, hitherto. For a man to act himself, he must be perfectly free; otherwise, he is in danger of losing all sense of responsibility or of self-respect.

To his sister, Helen, October 27, 1837, in *The Correspondence of Henry David Thoreau*, p. 15

Thank God, no Hindoo tyranny prevailed at the framing of the world, but we are freemen of the universe, and not sentenced to any cast.

A Week on the Concord and Merrimack Rivers, p. 148

It is hard to have a southern over-seer it is worse to have a northern one but worst of all when you are yourself the slave driver.

Written winter 1845–1846, in his *Journal*, vol. 2, pp. 219–220

The stern command is—move or ye shall be moved—be the master of your own action or you shall unawares become the tool of the meanest slave. Any can command him who doth not command himself.

Written after July 24, 1846, in his *Journal*, vol. 2, p. 263

It is our children's children who may perchance be essentially free.

Written February 16, 1851, in his *Journal*, vol. 3, p. 194

I would say to my fellows, once for all, As long as possible live free and uncommitted. It makes but little difference whether you are committed to a farm or the county jail.

Walden, p. 84

The question is whether you can bear freedom. At present the vast majority of men whether black or white require the discipline of labor which enslaves them for their good.

Written September 1, 1853, in his *Journal*, vol. 7, p. 29

Freedom of speech! It hath not entered into your hearts to conceive what those words mean. It is not leave given me by your sect to say this or that; it is when leave is given to your sect to withdraw. The church, the state, the school, the magazine, think they are liberal and free! It is the freedom of a prison-yard. I ask only that one fourth part of my honest thoughts be spoken aloud.

Written November 16, 1858, in his *Journal*, vol. XI, p. 324

If you are prepared to leave father and mother, and brother and sister, and wife and child and friends, and never see them again; if you have paid your debts, and made your will, and settled all your affairs, and are a free man; then you are ready for a walk.

"Walking" in *Excursions*, p. 186

We have felt that we almost alone hereabouts practiced this noble art; though, to tell the truth, at least, if their own assertions are to be received, most of my towns-men would fain walk sometimes, as I do, but they cannot. No wealth can buy the requisite leisure, free-dom, and independence, which are the capital in this profession. It comes only by the grace of God.

"Walking" in *Excursions*, p. 186

Eastward I go only by force; but westward I go free. Thither no business leads me. It is hard for me to be-lieve that I shall find fair landscapes, or sufficient Wild-ness and Freedom behind the eastern horizon.

"Walking" in *Excursions*, p. 196

I rarely walk by moonlight without hearing the sound of a flute or a horn or a human voice. It is a performer I never see by day—should not recognise him if pointed out—but you may hear his performance in every horizon. He plays but one strain and goes to bed early but I know by the character of that single strain that he is deeply dissatisfied with the manner in which he spends his day. He is a slave who is purchasing his freedom. He is Apollo watching the flocks of Admetus on every hill & this strain he plays every evening to remind him of his heavenly descent, it is all that saves him—his one redeeming trait.

Written August 5, 1851, in his *Journal*, vol. 3, p. 355

My life more civil is and free
Than any civil polity.

"Independence" in *Collected Poems of Henry Thoreau*, p. 132

Have we resigned the protection of our hearths and civil liberties to that feathered race of wading birds & marching men who drill but once a month & I mean no reproach to our Concord train bands—who make a handsome appearance—and dance well. Do we enjoy the sweets of domestic life undisturbed because the naughty boys are all shut up in that white-washed "stone-yard" as it is called and see the Concord meadows only through a grating?

No. Let us live amid the free play of the elements. Let the dogs bark. Let the cocks crow & the sun shine and the winds blow.

Written after August 1, 1844, in his *Journal*, vol. 2, p. 118

When I converse with the freest of my neighbors, I perceive that, whatever they may say about the magnitude and seriousness of the question, and their regard for the public tranquility, the long and the short of the matter is, that they cannot spare the protection of the existing government, and they dread the consequences of disobedience to it to their property and families.

"Resistance to Civil Government" in *Reform Papers*, p. 78

I have paid no poll-tax for six years. I was put into a jail once on this account, for one night; and, as I stood considering the walls of solid stone, two or three feet thick, the door of wood and iron, a foot thick, and the iron grating which strained the light, I could not help being struck with the foolishness of that institution which treated me as if I were mere flesh and blood and bones, to be locked up. I wondered that it should have concluded at length that this was the best use it could put me to, and had never thought to avail itself of my services in some way. I saw that, if there was a wall of stone between me and my townsmen, there was a still more difficult one to climb or break through, before they could get to be as free as I was. I did not for a moment feel confined, and the walls seemed a great waste of stone and mortar.

"Resistance to Civil Government" in *Reform Papers*, pp. 79–80

The information which the gods vouchsafe to give us is never concerning anything which we wished to know. We are not wise enough to put a question to them. Tell me some truth about society and you will annihilate it. What though we are its ailing members and prisoners. We cannot always be detained by your measures for

reform. All that is called hindrance without is but occasion within. The prisoner who is free in spirit, on
whose innocent life some rays of light and hope still
fall, will not delay to be a reformer of prisons, an in-
ventor of superior prison disciplines, but walks forth
free on the path by which those rays penetrated to his
cell. Has the Green Mountain boy made no better nor
more thrilling discovery than that the church is rotten
and the state corrupt? Thank heaven, we have not to
choose our calling out of those enterprises which society has to offer. Is he then indeed called, who chooses
to what he is called? Obey your calling rather, and it
will not be whither your neighbors and kind friends
and patrons expect or desire, but be true nevertheless,
and choose not, nor go whither they will call you.

"Reform and the Reformers" in *Reform Papers*, p. 188

We would have some pure product of man's hands,
some pure labor, some life got in this old trade of getting a living—some work done which shall not be a
mending, a cobbling, a reforming. Show me the mountain boy, the city boy, who never heard of an abuse,
who has not *chosen* his calling. It is the delight of the
ages, the free labor of man, even the creative and beautiful arts.

"Reform and the Reformers" in *Reform Papers*, p. 188

Yet we think that if rail-fences are pulled down, and
stone-walls piled up on our farms, bounds are henceforth set to our lives and our fates decided. If you are
chosen town-clerk, forsooth, you cannot go to Tierra

del Fuego this summer: but you may go to the land of infernal fire nevertheless.

Walden, p. 320

Most men, even in this comparatively free country, through mere ignorance and mistake, are so occupied with the factitious cares and superfluously coarse labors of life that its finer fruits cannot be plucked by them.

Walden, p. 6

The necessaries of life for man in this climate may, accurately enough, be distributed under the several heads of Food, Shelter, Clothing, and Fuel; for not till we have secured these are we prepared to entertain the true problems of life with freedom and a prospect of success.

Walden, p. 12

I also have in my mind that seemingly wealthy, but most terribly impoverished class of all, who have accumulated dross, but know not how to use it, or get rid of it, and thus have forged their own golden or silver fetters.

Walden, p. 16

In those days when how to get my living honestly with freedom left for my proper pursuits, was a question which vexed me even more than it does now, I used to see a large box by the railroad, 6 feet long by 3 wide, in which the workmen locked up their tools at night— And it suggested to me that every man who was hard pushed might get such a one for a dollar, and having bored a few auger holes in it to admit the air at least— get into it when it rained and at night, & so have freedom in his mind and in his soul be free. This did not seem the worst alternative nor by any means a despicable resource. You could sit up as late as you pleased & you would not have any creditor dogging you for rent. I should not be in a bad box. Many a man is harassed to death to pay the rent of a larger and more luxurious box who would not have frozen to death in such a box as this. I should not be in so bad a box as many a man is in now.

Written January 28, 1852, in his *Journal*, vol. 4, pp. 297–298

I would rather ride on earth in an ox cart with a free circulation, than go to heaven in the fancy car of an excursion train and breathe a *malaria* all the way.

Walden, p. 37

If I seem to boast more than is becoming, my excuse is that I brag for humanity rather than for myself; and my shortcomings and inconsistencies do not affect the truth of my statement. Notwithstanding much cant and hypocrisy,—chaff which I find it difficult to separate from my wheat, but for which I am as sorry as any man,—I will breathe freely and stretch myself in this respect, it is such a relief to both the moral and physical system; and I am resolved that I will not through humility become the devil's attorney. I will endeavor to speak a good word for the truth.

Walden, pp. 49–50

I am wont to think that men are not so much the keepers of herds as herds are the keepers of men, the former are so much the freer.

Walden, p. 56

As I preferred some things to others, and especially valued my freedom, as I could fare hard and yet succeed well, I did not wish to spend my time in earning rich carpets or other fine furniture, or delicate cookery, or a house in the Grecian or the Gothic style just yet. If there are any to whom it is no interruption to acquire these things, and who know how to use them when acquired, I relinquish to them the pursuit.

Walden, p. 70

Those who would not know what to do with more leisure than they now enjoy, I might advise to work twice as hard as they do.

Walden, p. 70

I found that the occupation of a day-laborer was the most independent of any, especially as it required only thirty or forty days in a year to support one. The laborer's day ends with the going down of the sun, and he is then free to devote himself to his chosen pursuit, independent of his labor; but his employer, who speculates from month to month, has no respite from one end of the year to the other.

Walden, p. 70

Just before sundown we reached some more falls in the town of Bedford, where some stone-masons were employed repairing the locks in a solitary part of the river. They were interested in our adventures, especially one young man of our own age ... and when he had heard our story, and examined our outfit, asked us other questions, but temperately still, and always turning to his work again, though as if it were become his duty. It was plain that he would like to go with us, and as he looked up the river, many a distant cape and wooded shore were reflected in his eye, as well as in his thoughts.

A Week on the Concord and Merrimack Rivers, p. 234

What is produced by a free stroke charms us, like the forms of lichens and leaves. There is a certain perfection in accident which we never consciously attain.

A Week on the Concord and Merrimack Rivers, p. 329

Now I yearn for one of those old meandering dry uninhabited roads which lead away from towns—which lead us away from temptation, which conduct to the outside of earth—over its uppermost crust—where you may forget in what country you are travelling— where no farmer can complain that you are treading down his grass—no gentleman who has recently constructed a seat in the country that you are trespassing—on which you can go off at half cock—and wave adieu to the village—along which you may travel like a pilgrim—going nowhither. Where travellers are not too often to be met. Where my spirit is free—

... There I have freedom in my thought & in my soul am free.

Written July 21, 1851, in his *Journal*, vol. 3, pp. 317–320

In short, all good things are wild and free.

"Walking" in *Excursions*, p. 210

FRIENDSHIP

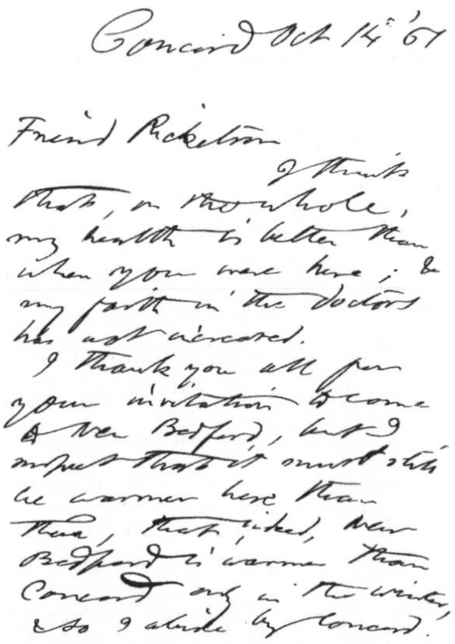

Concord Oct 14th '61

Friend Ricketson

I think that, on the whole, my health is better than when you were here; & my faith in the doctors has not increased.

I thank you all for your invitation to come to New Bedford, but I suspect that it must still be warmer here than there, that, indeed, New Bedford is warmer than Concord only in the winter, & so I abide by Concord.

FIG. 6. Thoreau to Daniel Ricketson, October 14, 1861. Reproduced from *Daniel Ricketson and His Friends: Letters, Poems, Sketches, etc.* The Walden Woods Project Collection at the Thoreau Institute at Walden Woods. Courtesy of the Walden Woods Project.

Two sturdy oaks I mean, which side by side,
Withstand the winter's storm,
And spite of wind and tide,

Grow up the meadow's pride,
   For both are strong

Above they barely touch, but undermined
   Down to their deepest source,
   Admiring you shall find
   Their roots are intertwined
      Insep'rably.

"Friendship" in *Collected Poems of Henry Thoreau*, pp. 90–91

What a difference, whether, in all your walks, you meet only strangers, or in one house is one who knows you, and whom you know. To have a brother or a sister! To have a gold mine on your farm! To find diamonds in the gravel heaps before your door! How rare these things are! To share the day with you,—to people the earth. Whether to have a god or a goddess for companion in your walks, or to walk alone with hinds and villains and carles. Would not a friend enhance the beauty of the landscape as much as a deer or hare? Everything would acknowledge and serve such a relation; the corn in the field, and the cranberries in the meadow. The flowers would bloom, and the birds sing, with a new impulse. There would be more fair days in the year.

"Love" in *Early Essays and Miscellanies*, p. 273

Treat your friends for what you know them to be—regard no surfaces. Consider not what they did, but what they intended.

Written December 31, 1851, in his *Journal*, vol. 4, p. 232

The language of friendship is not words but meanings. It is an intelligence above language.

A Week on the Concord and Merrimack Rivers, p. 273

All that has been said of friendship is like botany to flowers.

Written between 1842 and 1844, in his *Journal*, vol. 2, p. 87

A Friend is one who incessantly pays us the compliment of expecting from us all the virtues, and who can appreciate them in us.

A Week on the Concord and Merrimack Rivers, p. 267

It would give me such joy to know that a friend had come to see me and yet that pleasure I seldom if ever experience.

Written December 23, 1851, in his *Journal*, vol. 4, p. 217

How is it that we are impelled to treat our old friends so ill when we obtain new ones?

A Week on the Concord and Merrimack Rivers, p. 260

I would that I were worthy to be any man's Friend.

A Week on the Concord and Merrimack Rivers, p. 265

I hate that my motive for visiting a friend should be that I want society. That it should lie in my poverty & weakness & not in his and my riches & strength.

Written February 14, 1852, in his *Journal*, vol. 4, p. 350

Fatal is the discovery that our friend is fallible—that he has prejudices. He is then only prejudiced in our favor.

Written February 15, 1851, in his *Journal*, vol. 3, p. 193

Some men may be my acquaintances merely but one whom I have been accustomed to regard to idealize to have dreams about as a friend & mix up intimately with myself can never degenerate into an acquaintance. I must know him on that higher ground or not know him at all.

Written November 24, 1850, in his *Journal*, vol. 3, p. 150

The Friend asks no return but that his Friend will religiously accept and wear and not disgrace his apotheosis of him. They cherish each other's hopes. They are kind to each other's dreams.

A Week on the Concord and Merrimack Rivers, p. 270

The Friend is some fair floating isle of palms eluding the mariner in Pacific seas. Many are the dangers to be encountered, equinoctial gales and coral reefs, ere he may sail before the constant trades. But who would not sail through mutiny and storm even over Atlantic waves, to reach the fabulous retreating shores of some continent man?

A Week on the Concord and Merrimack Rivers, p. 262

To say that a man is your Friend, means commonly no more than this, that he is not your enemy.

A Week on the Concord and Merrimack Rivers, p. 266

How I love the simple, reserved countrymen, my neighbors, who mind their own business and let me alone, who never waylaid nor shot at me, to my knowledge, when I crossed their fields, though each one has a gun at his house! For nearly twoscore years I have known, at a distance, these long-suffering men, whom I never spoke to, who never spoke to me, and now I feel a certain tenderness for them, as if this long probation were but the prelude to an eternal friendship.

Written December 3, 1856, in his *Journal*, vol. IX, p. 151; emended from manuscript Journal (MA 1302, The Morgan Library & Museum, New York)

I have never met with a friend who furnished me sea-room. I have only tacked a few times & come to anchor—not sailed—made no voyage—carried no venture.

Written August 24, 1852, in his *Journal*, vol. 5, p. 310

There are times when we have had enough even of our Friends.

A Week on the Concord and Merrimack Rivers, p. 272

My friend is one whom I meet, who takes me for what I am. A stranger takes me for something else than what I am.

Written October 23, 1852, in his *Journal*, vol. 5, p. 382

How can they keep together who are going different ways!

Written July 12, 1851, in his *Journal*, vol. 3, p. 302

I see two great fish hawks (*possibly* blue herons) slowly beating northeast against the storm, by what a curious tie circling ever near each other and in the same direction. . . . Where is my mate, beating against the storm with me?

> Written October 26, 1857, in his *Journal*, vol. X, pp. 126–127

You may buy a servant or slave, in short, but you cannot buy a friend.

> Written November 28, 1860, in his *Journal*, vol. XIV, p. 277

A man cannot be said to succeed in this life who does not satisfy one friend.

> Written February 19, 1857, in his *Journal*, vol. IX, p. 272

If I had never thought of you as a friend, I could make much use of you as an acquaintance.

> Written January 31, 1852, in his *Journal*, vol. 4, p. 313

What if we feel a yearning to which no breast answers? I walk alone. My heart is full. Feelings impede the current of my thoughts. I knock on the earth for my friend. I expect to meet him at every turn; but no friend appears, and perhaps none is dreaming of me. I am tired of frivolous society, in which silence is forever the most natural and the best manners. I would fain walk on the deep waters, but my companions will only walk on shallows and puddles.

> Written June 11, 1855, in his *Journal*, vol. VII, pp. 416–417

One complains that I do not take his jokes. I took them before he had done uttering them, and went my way.

One talks to me of his apples and pears, and I depart with my secret untold. His are not the apples that tempt me.

Written June 11, 1855, in his *Journal*, vol. VII, p. 417

I have some good friends from whom I am wont to part with disappointment for they neither care what I think nor mind what I say.

Written January 27, 1854, in his *Journal*, vol. 7, p. 251

In what concerns you much do not think that you have companions—know that you are alone in the world.

To H.G.O. Blake, March 27, 1848, in *The Correspondence of Henry David Thoreau*, pp. 216–217

Often, I would rather undertake to shoulder a barrel of pork and carry it a mile than take into my company a man. It would not be so heavy a weight upon my mind. I could put it down and only feel my *back* ache for it.

Written August 31, 1856, in his *Journal*, vol. IX, p. 48

Nothing makes the earth seem so spacious as to have friends at a distance; they make the latitudes and longitudes.

Written on Staten Island to Lidian Emerson, May 22, 1843, in *The Correspondence of Henry David Thoreau*, p. 103

The price of friendship is the total surrender of yourself; no lesser kindness, no ordinary attentions and offerings will buy it.

Written July 13, 1857, in his *Journal*, vol. IX, p. 479

I sometimes awake in the night and think of friendship and its possibilities, a new life and revelation to me, which perhaps I had not experienced for many months. Such transient thoughts have been my nearest approach and realization of it, thoughts which I know of no one to communicate to. . . . I wake up in the night to these higher levels of life, as to a day that begins to dawn, as if my intervening life had been a long night. I catch an echo of the great strain of Friendship played somewhere, and feel compensated for months and years of commonplace.

Written July 13, 1857, in his *Journal*, vol. IX, p. 480; emended from manuscript Journal (MA 1302, The Morgan Library & Museum, New York)

Woe to him who wants a companion for he is unfit to be the companion even of himself.

Written June 9, 1850, in his *Journal*, vol. 3, p. 84

Who are the estranged? Two friends explaining.

Written December 21, 1851, in his *Journal*, vol. 4, p. 213

There are enough who will flatter me with sweet words, and anon use bitter ones to balance them, but they are not my friends. Simple sincerity and truth are rare indeed.

Written September 9, 1852, in his *Journal*, vol. 5, p. 341

We love to talk with those who can make a good guess at us—not with those who talk to us as if we were somebody else all the while.

Written September 9, 1852, in his *Journal*, vol. 5, p. 341

Suspicion creates the stranger & substitutes him for the friend.

Written October 23, 1852, in his *Journal*, vol. 5, p. 383

If my friend would take a quarter part the pains to show me himself that he does to show me a piece of roast beef, I should feel myself irresistibly invited.

Written May 19, 1856, in his *Journal*, vol. VIII, p. 348

I never realized so distinctly as this moment that I am peacefully parting company with the best friend I ever had, by each pursuing his proper path. I perceive that it is possible that we may have a better *understanding* now than when we were more at one. Not expecting such essential agreement as before. Simply our paths diverge.

Written January 21, 1852, in his *Journal*, vol. 4, p. 274

I know but one with whom I can walk. I might as well be sitting in a bar room with them as walk and talk with most. We are never side by side in our thoughts & we cannot bear each other's silence. Indeed we cannot be silent. We are forever breaking silence, that is all, and mending nothing.

Written July 12, 1851, in his *Journal*, vol. 3, p. 302

I love my friends very much but I find that it is of no use to go to see them. I hate them commonly when I am near them. They belie themselves & deny me continually.

Written November 16, 1850, in his *Journal*, vol. 3, p. 141

To obtain to a true relation to one human creature is enough to make a year memorable.

Written March 30, 1851, in his *Journal*, vol. 3, p. 202

My Friend is not of some other race or family of men, but flesh of my flesh, bone of my bone. He is my real brother.

A Week on the Concord and Merrimack Rivers, p. 284

The only danger in Friendship is that it will end.

A Week on the Concord and Merrimack Rivers, p. 277

GENIUS

What is called genius is the abundance of life or health so that whatever addresses the senses—as the flavor of these berries—or the lowing of that cow—which sounds as if it echoed along a cool mountain side just before night—where odoriferous dews perfume the air and there is everlasting vigor serenity & expectation of perpetual untarnished morning—each sight & sound & scent & flavor intoxicates with a healthy intoxication. The shrunken stream of life overflows its banks, makes & fertilizes broad intervals from which generations derive their sustenances. This is the true overflowing of the Nile. So exquisitely sensitive are we it makes us embrace our fates & instead of suffering or indifference, we enjoy & bless.

Written July 11, 1852, in his *Journal*, vol. 5, p. 215

Genius is a light which makes the darkness visible, like the lightning's flash, which perchance shatters the temple of knowledge itself—and not a taper lighted at the hearthstone of the race which pales before the light of common day.

"Walking" in *Excursions*, p. 208

I was not anchored to a house or farm, but could follow the bent of my genius, which is a very crooked one, every moment.

Walden, p. 56

Nature is full of genius, full of the divinity.

Written January 5, 1856, in his *Journal*, vol. VIII, p. 88

I would not stand between any man and his genius.

Walden, p. 73

Go not so far out of your way for a truer life—keep strictly onward in that path alone which your genius points out. Do the things which lie nearest to you but which are difficult to do.

Written January 12, 1852, in his *Journal*, vol. 4, p. 249

Follow your genius closely enough, and it will not fail to show you a fresh prospect every hour.

Walden, p. 112

A man cannot wheedle nor overawe his Genius. It requires to be conciliated by nobler conduct than the world demands or can appreciate. These winged thoughts are like birds, and will not be handled.

A Week on the Concord and Merrimack Rivers, p. 339

Genius is the worst of lumber, if the poet would float upon the breeze of popularity.

A Week on the Concord and Merrimack Rivers, p. 340

My genius makes distinctions which my understanding can not and which my senses do not report.

Written July 23, 1851, in his *Journal*, vol. 3, p. 329

Be faithful to your genius.

Written December 20, 1851, in his *Journal*, vol. 4, p. 211

The Man of Genius, referred to mankind, is an originator, an inspired or demonic man, who produces a perfect work in obedience to laws yet unexplored.

A Week on the Concord and Merrimack Rivers, p. 328

There has been no man of pure Genius; as there has been none wholly destitute of Genius.

A Week on the Concord and Merrimack Rivers, p. 328

No doubt it is an important difference between men of genius or poets, and men not of genius, that the latter are unable to grasp and confront the thought which visits them.

A Week on the Concord and Merrimack Rivers, p. 341

Genius is inspired by its own works; it is hermaphroditic.

Written October 10, 1858, in his *Journal*, vol. XI, p. 204

In all important crises one can only consult his genius.

Written December 27, 1858, in his *Journal*, vol. XI, p. 379

For a companion, I require one who will make an equal demand on me with my own genius.

A Week on the Concord and Merrimack Rivers, p. 279

No man ever followed his genius till it misled him.

Walden, p. 216

The Good Genius is sure to prevail.

A Week on the Concord and Merrimack Rivers, p. 116

GOOD AND EVIL

The greater part of what my neighbors call good I believe in my soul to be bad, and if I repent of any thing it is very likely to be my good behavior.

Walden, p. 10

All genuine goodness is original and as free from cant and tradition as the air.

Written June 16, 1857, in his *Journal*, vol. IX, p. 425

Men have a singular desire to be good without being good for any thing, because, perchance, they think vaguely that so it will be good for them in the end.

A Week on the Concord and Merrimack Rivers, p. 74

Our whole life is startlingly moral. There is never an instant's truce between virtue and vice. Goodness is the only investment that never fails.

Walden, p. 218

It is not so important that many should be as good as you, as that there be some absolute goodness somewhere; for that will leaven the whole lump.

"Resistance to Civil Government" in *Reform Papers*, p. 69

All good things are cheap—all bad are very dear.

Written March 3, 1841, in his *Journal*, vol. 1, p. 277

There is no ill which may not be dissipated like the dark, if you let in a stronger light upon it. Overcome evil with good.

"The Service" in *Reform Papers*, p. 7

If I ever *did* a man any good, in their sense, of course it was something exceptional, and insignificant compared with the good or evil which I am constantly doing by being what I am.

To H.G.O. Blake, February 27, 1853, in *The Correspondence of Henry David Thoreau*, p. 297

Men invite the devil in at every angle and then prate about the garden of Eden and the fall of man.

Written November 5, 1855, in his *Journal*, vol. VIII, p. 8

Every one has a devil in him that is capable of any crime in the long run.

A Week on the Concord and Merrimack Rivers, p. 284

Where an angel travels it will be paradise all the way, but where Satan travels it will be burning marl and cinders.

"Paradise (to be) Regained" in *Reform Papers*, p. 46

Be not *simply* good—be good for something.

To H.G.O. Blake, March 27, 1848, in *The Correspondence of Henry David Thoreau*, p. 216

GOVERNMENT AND POLITICS

That certainly is the best government where the inhabitants are least often reminded of the government.

Written August 21, 1851, in his *Journal*, vol. 4, p. 3

I please myself with imagining a State at last which can afford to be just to all men, and to treat the individual with respect as a neighbor; which even would not think it inconsistent with its own repose, if a few were to live aloof from it, not meddling with it, nor embraced by it, who fulfilled all the duties of neighbors and fellow-men. A State which bore this kind of fruit, and suffered it to drop off as fast as it ripened, would prepare the way for a still more perfect and glorious State, which I have also imagined, but not yet anywhere seen.

"Resistance to Civil Government" in *Reform Papers*, pp. 89–90

Is it not possible that an individual may be right and a government wrong?

"A Plea for Captain John Brown" in *Reform Papers*, p. 136

It is not to be forgotten, that while the law holds fast the thief and murderer, it lets itself go loose.

A Week on the Concord and Merrimack Rivers, p. 130

I went to the store the other day to buy a bolt for our front door, for, as I told the storekeeper, the Governor was coming here. "Aye," said he, "and the Legislature too." "Then I will take two bolts," said I.

Written September 8, 1859, in his *Journal*, vol. XII, pp. 317–318

What makes the United States government, on the whole, more tolerable,—I mean for us lucky *white* men,—is the fact that there is so much less government with us.

"A Yankee in Canada" in *Excursions*, p. 148

If we were left solely to the wordy wit of legislators in Congress for our guidance, uncorrected by the seasonable experience and the effectual complaints of the people, America would not long retain her rank among the nations.

"Resistance to Civil Government" in *Reform Papers*, p. 89

A government which deliberately enacts injustice, and persists in it, will at length ever become the laughing-stock of the world.

"Slavery in Massachusetts" in *Reform Papers*, p. 96

Let every man make known what kind of government would command his respect, and that will be one step toward obtaining it.

"Resistance to Civil Government" in *Reform Papers*, p. 64

If you aspire to anything better than politics, expect no coöperation from men.

Written April 3, 1858, in his *Journal*, vol. X, p. 351

Under a government which imprisons any unjustly, the true place for a just man is also in prison.

"Resistance to Civil Government" in *Reform Papers*, p. 76

The ring-leader of the mob will soonest be admitted into the councils of state.

Written February 12, 1840, in his *Journal*, vol. 1, p. 108

I heartily accept the motto,—"That government is best which governs least;" and I should like to see it acted up to more rapidly and systematically. Carried out, it finally amounts to this, which also I believe,—"That government is best which governs not at all;" and when men are prepared for it, that will be the kind of government which they will have.

"Resistance to Civil Government" in *Reform Papers*, p. 63

Unjust laws exist: shall we be content to obey them, or shall we endeavor to amend them, and obey them until we have succeeded, or shall we transgress them at once?

"Resistance to Civil Government" in *Reform Papers*, pp. 72–73

The poor President, what with preserving his popularity and doing his duty, is completely bewildered.

"Life without Principle" in *Reform Papers*, p. 178

Nobody legislates for me for the way would be not to legislate at all.

Written March 23, 1853, in his *Journal*, vol. 6, p. 31

Law never made men a whit more just.

"Resistance to Civil Government" in *Reform Papers*, p. 65

Politics is, as it were, the gizzard of society—full of grit & gravel and the two political parties are its two opposite halves which grind on each other.

Written November 10, 1851, in his *Journal*, vol. 4, p. 174

The fate of the country does not depend on how you vote at the polls—the worst man is as strong as the best at that game; it does not depend on what kind of paper you drop into the ballot-box once a year, but on what kind of man you drop from your chamber into the street every morning.

"Slavery in Massachusetts" in *Reform Papers*, p. 104

To one who habitually endeavors to contemplate the true state of things, the political state can hardly be said to have any existence whatever. It is unreal, incredible, and insignificant to him, and for him to endeavor to extract the truth from such lean material is like making sugar from linen rags, when sugar cane may be had.

A Week on the Concord and Merrimack Rivers, p. 129

The law will never make men free; it is men who have got to make the law free. They are the lovers of law and order, who observe the law when the government breaks it.

"Resistance to Civil Government" in *Reform Papers*, p. 98

The authority of government, even such as I am willing to submit to,—for I will cheerfully obey those who know and can do better than I, and in many things even those who neither know nor can do so well,—is still an impure one: to be strictly just, it must have the sanction and consent of the governed. It can have no pure right over my person and property but what I concede to it.

"Resistance to Civil Government" in *Reform Papers*, p. 89

It is for no particular item in the tax-bill that I refuse to pay it. I simply wish to refuse allegiance to the State, to withdraw and stand aloof from it effectually. I do not care to trace the course of my dollar, if I could, till it buys a man, or a musket to shoot one with,—the dollar is innocent,—but I am concerned to trace the effects of my allegiance.

"Resistance to Civil Government" in *Reform Papers*, p. 84

Trade and commerce, if they were not made of India rubber, would never manage to bounce over the obstacles which legislators are continually putting in their way; and, if one were to judge these men wholly by the effects of their actions, and not partly by their intentions, they would deserve to be classed and punished with those mischievous persons who put obstructions on the railroads.

"Resistance to Civil Government" in *Reform Papers*, p. 64

The progress from an absolute to a limited monarchy, from a limited monarchy to a democracy, is a progress toward a true respect for the individual.

"Resistance to Civil Government" in *Reform Papers*, p. 89

Why will men be such fools as to trust to lawyers for a *moral* reform?

Written June 16, 1854, in his *Journal*, vol. 8, p. 200

But as for politics, what I most admire now-a-days, is not the regular governments but the irregular primitive ones, like the Vigilance committee in California and even the free state men in Kansas. They are the most divine.

To Thomas Cholmondeley, October 20, 1856, in *The Correspondence of Henry David Thoreau*, p. 436

The effect of a good government is to make life more valuable—of a bad government to make it less valuable. We can afford that railroad and all merely material stock should depreciate—for that only compels us to live more simply & economically—but suppose the value of life itself should be depreciated.

Written June 16, 1854, in his *Journal*, vol. 8, p. 198

HEALTH AND ILLNESS

In society you will not find health, but in nature.

"Natural History of Massachusetts" in *Excursions*, p. 4

To the healthy man the winter of his discontent never comes.

Written October 13, 1851, in his *Journal*, vol. 4, p. 145

It is the faith with which we take medicine that cures us.

Written June 27, 1852, in his *Journal*, vol. 5, p. 159

Nature, the earth herself, is the only panacea.

Written September 24, 1859, in his *Journal*, vol. XII, p. 350

A healthy man, indeed, is the complement of the seasons, and in winter, summer is in his heart.

"A Winter Walk" in *Excursions*, p. 60

'Tis healthy to be sick sometimes.

Written after January 10, 1851, in his *Journal*, vol. 3, p. 178

All nature is doing her best each moment to make us well—she exists for no other end. Do not resist her. With the least inclination to be well we should not be sick.

Written August 23, 1853, in his *Journal*, vol. 7, p. 16

Sickness should not be allowed to extend further than the body. We need only to retreat further within us, to preserve uninterrupted the continuity of serene hours to the end of our lives.

Written February 14, 1841, in his *Journal*, vol. 1, pp. 265–266

Cultivate the habit of early-rising. It is unwise to keep the head long on a level with the feet.

Written June 8, 1850, in his *Journal*, vol. 3, p. 82

The unwise are accustomed to speak as if some were not sick; but methinks the difference between men in respect to health is not great enough to lay much stress upon.

A Week on the Concord and Merrimack Rivers, p. 36

It is a very remarkable and significant fact that though no man is quite well or healthy yet every one believes practically that health is the rule & disease the exception—And each invalid is wont to think of himself in a minority.

Written September 3, 1851, in his *Journal*, vol. 4, p. 34

Disease is not the accident of the individual nor even of the generation but of life itself. In some form & to some degree or other it is one of the permanent conditions of life.

Written September 3, 1851, in his *Journal*, vol. 4, p. 35

In sickness all is deranged. I had yesterday a kink in my back and a general cold, and as usual it amounted to a cessation of life. I lost for the time my *rapport* or relation to nature. Sympathy with nature is an evidence of perfect health.

Written November 18, 1857, in his *Journal*, vol. X, p. 188

I have noticed that notional nervous invalids, who report to the community the exact condition of their heads and stomachs every morning, as if they alone were blessed or cursed with these parts; who are old betties and quiddles, if men; who can't eat their breakfasts when they are ready, but play with their spoons, and hanker after an ice-cream at irregular hours; who go more than half-way to meet any invalidity, and go to bed to be sick on the slightest occasion, in the middle of the brightest forenoon,—improve the least opportunity to be sick;—I observe that such are self-indulgent persons, without any regular and absorbing employment.

Written May 26, 1857, in his *Journal*, vol. IX, p. 379

If you look over a list of medicinal recipes in vogue in the last century, how foolish and useless they are seen to be! And yet we use equally absurd ones with faith to-day.

Written February 18, 1860, in his *Journal*, vol. XIII, p. 155

I have been sick so long that I have almost forgotten what it is to be well, yet I feel that it all respects only my envelope.

To Daniel Ricketson, August 15, 1861, in *The Correspondence of Henry David Thoreau*, p. 625

Measure your health by your sympathy with morning and spring. If there is no response in you to the awakening of nature,—if the prospect of an early morning walk does not banish sleep, if the warble of the first bluebird does not thrill you,—know that the morning and spring of your life are past. Thus may you feel your pulse.

Written February 25, 1859, in his *Journal*, vol. XI, p. 455

Men have discovered or think they have discovered the salutariness of a few wild things only and not of all nature. Why nature is but another name for health & the seasons are but different states of health. Some men think that they are not well in Spring or Summer or Autumn or Winter—it is only because they are not *well* in them.

Written August 23, 1853, in his *Journal*, vol. 7, p. 16

No doubt the healthiest man in the world is prevented from doing what he would like by sickness.

Written December 21, 1855, in his *Journal*, vol. VIII, p. 56

I am inclined to think of late that as much depends on the state of the bowels as of the stars.

Written December 12, 1859, in his *Journal*, vol. XIII, p. 22

The invalid brought to the brink of the grave by an unnatural life instead of imbibing only the great influence that nature is—drinks only the tea made of a particular herb—while he still continues his unnatural life—saves at the spile & wastes at the bung. He does not love nature or his life & so sickens & dies & no doctor can cure him.

Written August 23, 1853, in his *Journal*, vol. 7, pp. 15–16

THE HEARD AND THE UNHEARD

Fig. 7. Thoreau's flute. Photographer: Alfred W. Hosmer. Thoreau Society Archives (The Thoreau Society® Collections at the Thoreau Institute). Courtesy of the Thoreau Society.

Sound

In the midst of a gentle rain . . . I was suddenly sensible of such sweet and beneficent society in Nature, in the very pattering of the drops, and in every sound and sight around my house, an infinite and unaccountable friendliness all at once like an atmosphere sustaining me, as made the fancied advantages of human neighborhood insignificant, and I have never thought of them since.

Walden, pp. 131–132

Far in the night, as we were falling asleep on the bank of the Merrimack, we heard some tyro beating a drum incessantly, in preparation for a country muster. . . . This stray sound from a far-off sphere came to our ears from time to time, far, sweet, and significant, and we listened with such an unprejudiced sense as if for the first time we heard at all.

A Week on the Concord and Merrimack Rivers, p. 173

I used to strike with a paddle on the side of my boat on Walden Pond filling the surrounding woods with circling & dilating sound. . . . We wake the echo of the place we are in—its slumbering music.

Written after October 31, 1850, in his *Journal*, vol. 3, p. 129

I should think that savages would have made a god of echo.

Written after October 31, 1850, in his *Journal*, vol. 3, p. 129

The ringing of the church bell is a much more melodious sound than any that is heard within the church.

Written Sunday, January 2, 1842, in his *Journal*, vol. 1, p. 355

The whistle of the locomotive penetrates my woods summer and winter, sounding like the scream of a hawk sailing over some farmer's yard, informing me that many restless city merchants are arriving within the circle of the town, or adventurous country traders from the other side. As they come under one horizon, they shout their warning to get off the track to the other, heard sometimes through the circles of two towns.

Walden, p. 115

Each summer sound
Is a summer round.

Written February 19, 1838, in his *Journal*, vol. 1, p. 30

Debauched and worn-out senses require the violent vibrations of an instrument to excite them, but *sound* and still youthful senses, not enervated by luxury, hear music in the wind and rain and running water. One would think from reading the critics that music was intermittent as a spring in the desert, depending on some Paganini or Mozart, or heard only when the Pierians or Euterpeans drive through the villages; but music is perpetual, and only hearing is intermittent.

Written February 8, 1857, in his *Journal*, vol. IX, pp. 244–245

Only in their saner moments do men hear the crickets. It is balm to the philosopher. It tempers his thoughts.

Written May 22, 1854, in his *Journal*, vol. 8, p. 144

The earth song of the cricket! Before Christianity was, it is. Health, health, health, is the burden of its song.

Written June 17, 1852, in his *Journal*, vol. 5, p. 105

The ring of the first toad leaks into the general stream of sound, unnoticed by most, as the mill-brook empties into the river and the voyager cannot tell if he is above or below its mouth. The bell was ringing for town meeting, and every one heard it, but none heard this older and more universal bell, rung by more native Americans all the land over.

Written May 1, 1857, in his *Journal*, vol. IX, p. 349

What a contrast to sink your head so as to cover your ears with water, and hear only the confused noise of the rushing river, and then to raise your ears above water and hear the steady creaking of crickets in the aerial universe!

Written September 7, 1858, in his *Journal*, vol. XI, p. 150

I hear faintly the cawing of a crow far, far away, echoing from some unseen wood-side, as if deadened by the spring-like vapor which the sun is drawing from the ground. It mingles with the slight murmur of the village, the sound of children at play, as one stream empties gently into another, and the wild and tame are one. What a delicious sound. It is not merely crow calling to crow, for it speaks to me too. I am part of one great creature with him; if he has voice, I have ears.

Written January 12, 1855, in his *Journal*, vol. VII, pp 112–113; emended from manuscript *Journal* (MA 1302, The Morgan Library & Museum, New York)

The other evening I was determined I would silence this shallow din; that I would walk in various directions and see if there was not to be found any depth of silence around. As Bonaparte sent out his horsemen in the Red Sea on all sides to find shallow water, so I sent forth my mounted thoughts to find deep water. I left the village and paddled up the river to Fair Haven Pond. As the sun went down, I saw a solitary boatman disporting on the smooth lake. The falling dews seemed to strain and purify the air, and I was soothed with an infinite stillness. I got the world, as it were, by the nape of the neck, and held it under in the tide of its own events, till it was drowned, and then I let it go downstream like a dead dog. Vast hollow chambers of silence stretched away on every side, and my being expanded in proportion and filled them. Then first could I appreciate sound, and find it musical.

> To H.G.O. Blake, August 8, 1854, in *The Correspondence of Henry David Thoreau*, p. 331

SILENCE

Silence is the communing of a conscious soul with itself.

> From an essay on "Sound and Silence" written in the latter half of December 1838 in his *Journal*, vol. 1, p. 60

I have been breaking silence these twenty three years and have hardly made a rent in it.

> Written February 9, 1841, in his *Journal*, vol. 1, p. 262

As I walk the railroad causeway I am disturbed by the sound of my steps on the frozen ground. I wish to hear the silence of the night. I cannot walk with my ears covered. The silence is something positive & to be heard. I must stand still & listen with open ear far from the noises of the village that the night may make its impression on me—a fertile & eloquent silence. Sometimes the silence is merely negative, an arid & barren waste in which I shudder—where no ambrosia grows. I must hear the whispering of a myriad voices. Silence alone is worthy to be heard.

Written January 21, 1853, in his *Journal*, vol. 5, p. 448

The silence rings—it is musical & thrills me. A night in which the silence was audible—I hear the unspeakable.

Written January 21, 1853, in his *Journal*, vol. 5, p. 448

The man I meet with is not often so instructive as the silence he breaks.

Written January 7, 1857, in his *Journal*, vol. IX, p. 209

I mean always to spend only words enough to purchase silence with; and I have found that this, which is so valuable, though many writers do not prize it, does not cost much, after all.

To James Elliot Cabot, March 8, 1848, in *The Correspondence of Henry David Thoreau*, p. 210

The longest silence is the most pertinent question most pertinently put. Emphatically silent. The most

important questions whose answers concern us more
than any are never put in any other way.

Written January 4, 1851, in his *Journal*, vol. 3, p. 173

MUSIC

Listen to music religiously as if it were the last strain
you might hear.

Written June 12, 1851, in his *Journal*, vol. 3, p. 259

All music is only a sweet striving to express character.

Written November 12, 1841, in his *Journal*, vol. 1, p. 341

So few habitually intoxicate themselves with music, so
many with alcohol. I think, perchance, I may risk it, it
will whet my senses so.

Written October 16, 1857, in his *Journal*, vol. X, p. 103

The music of all creatures has to do with their loves,
even of toads & frogs. Is it not the same with man?

Written May 6, 1852, in his *Journal*, vol. 5, p. 34

Each more melodious note I hear
Brings this reproach to me,
That I alone afford the ear,
Who would the music be.

"The Service" in *Reform Papers*, p. 9

I awoke into a music which no one about me heard.
Whom shall I thank for it?

Written June 22, 1851, in his *Journal*, vol. 3, p. 275

Music is the sound of the circulation in nature's veins.

Written April 24, 1841, in his *Journal*, vol. 1, p. 303

I sailed on the north river last night with my flute and my music was a tinkling stream which meandered with the river and fell from note to note as a brook from rock to rock.

Written August 18, 1841, in his *Journal*, vol. 1, p. 320

Unpremeditated music is the true gage which measures the current of our thoughts—the very undertow of our life's stream.

Written August 18, 1841, in his *Journal*, vol. 1, p. 321

Even music is wont to be intoxicating.

Written after September 19, 1850, in his *Journal*, vol. 3, p. 119

The music of all creatures has to do with their loves, even of toads & frogs. Is it not the same with man?

Written May 6, 1852, in his *Journal*, vol. 5, p. 34

When I *hear* music I fear no danger, I am invulnerable, I see no foe. I am related to the earliest times and to the latest.

Written January 13, 1857, in his *Journal*, vol. IX, p. 218

What is there in music that it should so stir our deeps? We are all ordinarily in a state of desperation; such is our life; ofttimes it drives us to suicide. To how many, perhaps to most, life is barely tolerable, and if it were not for the fear of death or of dying, what a multitude would immediately commit suicide! But let us hear a strain of music, we are at once advertised of a life which no man had told us of, which no preacher preaches. Suppose I try to describe faithfully the prospect which a strain of music exhibits to me. The field of my life becomes a boundless plain, glorious to tread, with no death nor disappointment at the end of it. All meanness and trivialness disappear. I become adequate to any deed. No particulars survive this expansion; persons do not survive it. In the light of this strain there is no thou nor I. We are actually lifted above ourselves.

Written January 15, 1857, in his *Journal*, vol. IX, p. 222

I hear one thrumming a guitar below stairs. It reminds me of moments that I have lived. What a comment on our life is the least strain of music! It lifts me up above all the dust and mire of the universe. I soar or hover with clean skirts over the field of my life. It is ever life within life, in concentric spheres. The field wherein I toil or rust at any time is at the same time the field for such different kinds of life! The farmer's boy or hired man has an instinct which tells him as much indistinctly, and hence his dreams and his restlessness; hence, even, it is that he wants money to realize his dreams with. The identical field where I am leading my humdrum life, let but a strain of music be heard there, is seen to be the field of some unrecorded crusade or tournament the thought of which excites in us an ecstasy of joy. The way in which I am affected by this faint thrumming advertises me that there is still some health and immortality in the springs of me. What an elixir is this sound! I, who but lately came and went and lived under *a dish cover*, live now under the heavens. It releases me; it bursts my bonds.

Written January 13, 1857, in his *Journal*, vol. IX, p. 217

A man's life should be a stately march to a sweet but unheard music, and when to his fellows it shall seem irregular and inharmonious, he will only be stepping to a livelier measure; or his nicer ear hurry him into a thousand symphonies and concordant variations. There will be no halt ever but at most a marching on his post, or such a pause as is richer than any sound, when the melody runs into such depth and wildness as to be no longer heard, but implicitly consented to with the whole life and being. He will take a false step never, even in the most arduous times; for then the music will not fail to swell into greater sweetness and volume, and itself rule the movement it inspired.

Written June 30, 1840, in his *Journal*, vol. 1, p. 146

You cannot hear music and noise at the same time.

Written April 27, 1854, in his *Journal*, vol. 8, p. 89

Was awakened in the night to a strain of music dying away,—passing travellers singing. My being was so expanded and infinitely and divinely related for a brief season that I saw how unexhausted, how almost wholly unimproved, was man's capacity for a divine life. When I remembered what a narrow and finite life I should anon awake to!

Written April 19, 1856, in his *Journal*, vol. VIII, p. 294

A thrumming of piano strings beyond the gardens & through the elms—at length the melody steals into my being. I know not when it began to occupy me. By some fortunate coincidence of thought or circumstance I am attuned to the universe—I am fitted to hear—my being moves in a sphere of melody—my fancy and imagination are excited to an inconceivable degree. This is no longer the dull earth on which I stood.

Written August 3, 1852, in his *Journal*, vol. 5, p. 272

THE HEAVENS: SUN, MOON, AND STARS

We begin to have an interest in sun, moon, and stars.

Written August 31, 1839, and copied on June 21, 1840 into his *Journal*, vol. 1, p. 135

If there is nothing new on earth, still there is something new in the heavens. We have always a resource in the skies. They are constantly turning a new page to view. The wind sets the types in this blue ground, and the inquiring may always read a new truth.

Written November 17, 1837, in his *Journal*, vol. 1, p. 13

Truly the stars were given for a consolation to man.

"A Walk to Wachusett" in *Excursions*, p. 40

The heavens are as deep as our aspirations are high.

To H.G.O. Blake, May 2, 1848, in *The Correspondence of Henry David Thoreau*, p. 220

When I consider how, after sunset, the stars come out gradually in troops from behind the hills and woods, I confess that I could not have contrived a more curious and inspiring night.

Written July 26, 1840, in his *Journal*, vol. 1, p. 158

The World run to see the panorama when there is a panorama in the sky which few go out to see.

Written January 17, 1852, in his *Journal*, vol. 4, p. 264

I cannot see the bottom of the sky, because I cannot see to the bottom of myself. It is the symbol of my own infinity.

Written June 23, 1840, in his *Journal*, vol. 1, p. 140

Only the Hunter's & Harvest moons are famous but I think that each full moon deserves to be & has its own character well marked. One might be called the midsummer night moon.

Written June 11, 1851, in his *Journal*, vol. 3, p. 252

A sky without clouds is a meadow without flowers.

Written June 24, 1852, in his *Journal*, vol. 5, p. 142

The most beautiful thing in Nature is the sun reflected from a tear-ful cloud.

Written September 7, 1851, in his *Journal*, vol. 4, p. 56

What form of beauty could be imagined more striking & conspicuous—An arch of the most brilliant &

glorious colors completely spanning heavens before the eyes of men.

On rainbows, written August 6, 1852, in his *Journal*, vol. 5, p. 284

The sky is always ready to answer to our moods.

Written December 28, 1851, in his *Journal*, vol. 4, p. 225

HEROES AND THE HEROIC: COURAGE AND FEAR, RIGHT AND WRONG

The hero is commonly the simplest and obscurest of men.

"Walking" in *Excursions*, p. 202

When a noble deed is done, who is likely to appreciate it? They who are noble themselves.

"A Plea for Captain John Brown" in *Reform Papers*, p. 148

To march sturdily through life patiently and resolutely looking defiance at one's foes, that is one way, but we cannot help being more attracted by that kind of heroism which relaxes its brows in the presence of danger, and does not need to maintain itself strictly, but by a kind of sympathy with the universe, generously adorns the scene and the occasion, and loves valor so well that itself would be the defeated party only to behold it.

"Sir Walter Raleigh" in Early *Essays and Miscellanies*, p. 217

Any landscape would be glorious to me, if I were assured that its sky was arched over a single hero.

Written September 26, 1851, in his *Journal*, vol. 4, p. 101

A man sits as many risks as he runs.

Walden, p. 153

The monster is never just there where we think he is. What is truly monstrous is our cowardice and sloth.

To H.G.O. Blake, December 19, 1854, in *The Correspondence of Henry David Thoreau*, p. 355

What is heroism? That which we are not.

"Sir Walter Raleigh" second draft manuscript (Walden Woods Project Collection at the Thoreau Institute at Walden Woods)

It was not the hero I admired but the reflection from his epaulet or helmet.

To H.G.O. Blake, February 27, 1853, in *The Correspondence of Henry David Thoreau*, p. 299

If a man were to place himself in an attitude to bear manfully the greatest evil that can be inflicted on him, he would find suddenly that there was no such evil to bear.

To H.G.O. Blake, December 19, 1854, in *The Correspondence of Henry David Thoreau*, p. 354

Greatness is in the ascent.

Written February 7, 1841, in his *Journal*, vol. 1, p. 256

Cowards suffer, heroes enjoy.

To H.G.O. Blake, May 20, 1860, in *The Correspondence of Henry David Thoreau*, p. 579

Whatever your sex or position life is a battle in which you are to show your pluck & woe be to the coward.... Despair & postponement are Cowardice & defeat.

Written March 21, 1853, in his *Journal*, vol. 6, p. 23

He who receives an injury is an accomplice of the wrong doer.

Written July 9, 1840, in his *Journal*, vol. 1, p. 154

The hero obeys his own law.

Written February 1, 1852, in his *Journal*, vol. 4, p. 314

The great person never wants an opportunity to be great but makes occasion for all about him.

Written June 1, 1841, in his *Journal*, vol. 1, p. 312

Most things are strong in one direction; a straw longitudinally; a board in the direction of its edge; a knee transversely to its grain; but the brave man is a perfect sphere, which cannot fall on its flat side, and is equally strong every way.

"The Service" in *Reform Papers*, pp. 5–6

Not to grieve long for any action but to go immediately and do freshly and otherwise subtracts so much from the wrong.

Written January 9, 1842, in his *Journal*, vol. 1, p. 363

Marching is when the pulse of the hero beats in unison with the pulse of Nature, and he steps to the measure of the universe; then there is true courage and invincible strength.

A Week on the Concord and Merrimack Rivers, p. 175

You are expected to do your duty, not in spite of every thing but *one*, but in spite of *everything*.

Written September 24, 1859, in his *Journal*, vol. XII, p. 344

We should impart our courage, and not our despair, our health and ease, and not our disease, and take care that this does not spread by contagion.

Walden, p. 77

What the prophets even have said is forgotten, and the oracles are decayed, but what heroes and saints have done is still remembered, and posterity will tell it again and again.

"Reform and the Reformers," in *Reform Papers*, p. 185

Be of good courage! That is the main thing.

To H.G.O. Blake, December 19, 1854, in *The Correspondence of Henry David Thoreau*, p. 354

HIGHER LAW

What is wanted is men of principle who recognize a higher law than the decision of the majority.

Written June 9, 1854, in his *Journal*, vol. 8, p. 185

The Christians now & always are they who obey the higher law.

> Written June 17, 1854, in his *Journal*, vol. 8, p. 204

He who lives according to the highest law is in one sense lawless.

> Written February 27, 1851, in his *Journal*, vol. 3, p. 201

No man loses ever on a lower level by magnanimity on a higher.

> *Walden*, p. 329

The unwritten laws are the most stringent.

> Written September 6, 1851, in his *Journal*, vol. 4, p. 49

There will never be a really free and enlightened State, until the State comes to recognize the individual as a higher and independent power, from which all its own power and authority are derived, and treats him accordingly.

> "Resistance to Civil Government" in *Reform Papers*, p. 89

What force has a multitude? They only can force me who obey a higher law than I.

> "Resistance to Civil Government" in *Reform Papers*, p. 81

Whoever has discerned truth, has received his commission from a higher source than the chiefest justice in the world, who can discern only law.

> "Slavery in Massachusetts" in *Reform Papers*, p. 98

It is by obeying the suggestions of a higher light within you that you escape from yourself.

Written August 30, 1856, in his *Journal*, vol. IX, p. 38

What is wanted is men, not of policy, but of probity—who recognize a higher law than the Constitution, or the decision of the majority.

"Slavery in Massachusetts" in *Reform Papers*, p. 104

HUMAN NATURE

The Mass of Men

The deep places in the river are not so obvious as the shallow ones and can only be found by carefully probing it. So perhaps it is with human nature.

Written July 5, 1859, in his *Journal*, vol. XII, p. 222

The mass of men lead lives of quiet desperation. What is called resignation is confirmed desperation.

Walden, p. 8

As boys are sometimes required to show an excuse for being absent from school, so it seems to me that men should have to show some excuse for being here.

Written January 3, 1861, in his *Journal*, vol. XIV, p. 307

When I meet gentlemen and ladies, I am reminded of the extent of the inhabitable and uninhabitable globe;

I exclaim to myself, Surfaces! surfaces! If the outside of a man is so variegated and extensive, what must the inside be?

Written March 10, 1859, in his *Journal*, vol. XII, p. 31

How sweet it would be to treat men and things, for an hour, for just what they are!

To H.G.O. Blake, April 3, 1850, in *The Correspondence of Henry David Thoreau*, p. 256

Only make something to take the place of something, and men will behave as if it was the very thing they wanted.

A Week on the Concord and Merrimack Rivers, p. 128

The mass of men serve the State thus, not as men mainly, but as machines, with their bodies. They are the standing army, and the militia, jailers, constables, *posse comitatus*, &c. In most cases there is no free exercise whatever of the judgment or of the moral sense; but they put themselves on a level with wood and earth and stones, and wooden men can perhaps be manufactured that will serve the purpose as well.

"Resistance to Civil Government" in *Reform Papers*, p. 66

Men have become the tools of their tools.

Written July 16, 1845, in his *Journal*, vol. 2, p. 162

The mass of men are very easily imposed on. They have their runways in which they always travel, and are sure to fall into any pit or box trap set therein. Whatever a great many grown-up boys are seriously engaged in is considered great and good, and, as such, is sure of the recognition of the churchman and statesman.

Written November 28, 1860, in his *Journal*, vol. XIV, p. 278

We must not confound man and man. We cannot conceive of a greater difference than between the life of one man and that of another. I am constrained to believe that the mass of men are never so lifted above themselves that their destiny is seen to be transcendently beautiful and grand.

Written January 13, 1857, in his *Journal*, vol. IX, p. 218

The mass of men do not know how to cultivate the fields they traverse. The mass glean only a scanty pittance where the thinker reaps an abundant harvest.

Written May 6, 1858, in his *Journal*, vol. X, pp. 404–405

Men will pay something to look into a travelling showman's box but not to look upon the fairest prospects on the earth.

Written May 25, 1851, in his *Journal*, vol. 3, p. 235

It would be sweet to deal with men more, I can imagine, but where dwell they? Not in the fields which I traverse.

Written January 4, 1857, in his *Journal*, vol. IX, p. 205

The way to compare men is to compare their respective ideals—The actual man is too complex to deal with.

Written winter 1845–1846, in his *Journal*, vol. 2, p. 222

What troubles men lay up for want of a little energy and precision!

Written September 16, 1859, in his *Journal*, vol. XII, p. 329

We slander the hyena; man is the fiercest and cruelest animal.

"Paradise (to be) Regained" in *Reform Papers*, p. 22

Men think that it is essential that the *Nation* have commerce, and export ice, and talk through a telegraph, and ride thirty miles an hour, without a doubt, whether *they* do or not; but whether we should live like baboons or like men, is a little uncertain.

Walden, p. 92

When we want culture more than potatoes, and illumination more than sugar-plums, then the great resources of a world are taxed and drawn out, and the result, or staple production, is, not slaves, nor operatives, but men,—those rare fruits called heroes, saints, poets, philosophers, and redeemers.

"Life without Principle" in *Reform Papers*, p. 177

There are nine hundred and ninety-nine patrons of virtue to one virtuous man.

"Resistance to Civil Government" in *Reform Papers*, p. 69

But why should not the New Englander try new adventures, and not lay so much stress on his grain, his potato and grass crop, and his orchards?—raise other crops than these? Why concern ourselves so much about our beans for seed, and not be concerned at all about a new generation of men?

Walden, p. 164

Instead of noblemen, let us have noble villages of men. If it is necessary, omit one bridge over the river, go round a little there, and throw one arch at least over the darker gulf of ignorance which surrounds us.

Walden, p. 110

Every man should stand for a force which is perfectly irresistible. How can any man be weak who dares *to be* at all? Even the tenderest plants force their way up through the hardest earth, and the crevices of rocks; but a man no material power can resist. What a wedge, what a beetle, what a catapult, is an *earnest* man! What can resist him?

To H.G.O. Blake, May 2, 1848, in *The Correspondence of Henry David Thoreau*, pp. 220–221

An ordinary man will work every day for a year at shovelling dirt to support his body, or a family of bodies, but he is an extraordinary man who will work a whole day in a year for the support of his soul.

To H.G.O Blake, February 27, 1853, in *The Correspondence of Henry David Thoreau*, p. 298

The wood-sawyer, through his effort to do his work well, becomes not merely a better wood-sawyer, but measurably a better *man*.

To H.G.O. Blake, December 19, 1853, in *The Correspondence of Henry David Thoreau*, p. 311

Only think, for a moment, of a man about his affairs! How we should respect him! How glorious he would appear! Not working for any corporation, its agent, or president, but fulfilling the end of his being! A man about *his business* would be the cynosure of all eyes.

To H.G.O. Blake, August 8, 1854, in *The Correspondence of Henry David Thoreau*, p. 331

A man cannot be too circumspect in order to keep in the straight road, and be sure that he sees all that he may at any time see, that so he may distinguish his true path.

To H.G.O. Blake, May 2, 1848, in *The Correspondence of Henry David Thoreau*, p. 221

How prompt we are to satisfy the hunger & thirst of our bodies; how slow to satisfy the hunger & thirst of our *souls*!

To H.G.O. Blake, February 27, 1853, in *The Correspondence of Henry David Thoreau*, p. 298

If a man believes and expects great things of himself, it makes no odds where you put him, or what you show him, (of course, you cannot put him anywhere nor show him anything), he will be surrounded by grandeur.

To H.G.O. Blake, May 20, 1860, in *The Correspondence of Henry David Thoreau*, p. 579

I cannot conceive of persons more strange to me than they *actually* are; not thinking, not believing, not doing as I do; interrupted by me. My only distinction must be that I am the greatest bore they ever had. Not in a single thought agreed; regularly balking one another. But when I get far away, my thoughts return to them. That is the way I can visit them.

Written November 3, 1858, in his *Journal*, vol. XI, p. 282; emended from manuscript Journal (MA 1302, The Morgan Library & Museum, New York)

Shall not a man have his spring as well as the plants?

Written June 9, 1850, in his *Journal*, vol. 3, p. 84

The more we know about the ancients the more we find that they were like the moderns.

Written September 2, 1851, in his *Journal*, vol. 4, p. 30

Many seem to be so constituted that they can respect only somebody who is dead or something which is distant.

Written November 28, 1860, in his *Journal*, vol. XIV, p. 277

Everyman proposes fairly and does not willfully take the devil for his guide, as our shadows never fall between us and the sun. Go towards the sun and your shadow will fall behind you.

Written February 8, 1841, in his *Journal*, vol. 1, p. 261

I think that the existence of man in nature is the divinest and most startling of all facts. It is a fact which few have realized.

Written May 21, 1851, in his *Journal*, vol. 3, p. 229

Why is it that in the lives of men we hear more of the dark wood than of the sunny pasture?

Written October 29, 1857, in his *Journal*, vol. X, p. 143

In order to avoid delusions I would fain let man go by & behold a universe in which man is but as a grain of sand.

Written April 2, 1852, in his *Journal*, vol. 4, p. 419

With all this opportunity, this comedy and tragedy, how near all men come to doing nothing! It is strange that they did not make us more intense and emphatic, that they do not goad us into some action. Generally, with all our desires and restlessness, we are no more likely to embark in any enterprise than a tree is to walk to a more favorable locality.

Written May 29, 1857, in his *Journal*, vol. IX, p. 390

The New Englander is a pagan suckled in a creed outworn.

Superstition has always reigned.

It is absurd to think that these farmers dressed in their Sunday clothes proceeding to church differ essentially in this respect from the Roman peasantry. They have merely changed the names & numbers of their gods.

Written June 5, 1853, in his *Journal*, vol. 6, p. 179

One sensible act will be more memorable than a monument as high as the moon.

Written June 26, 1852, in his *Journal*, vol. 5, p. 154

Man has a million eyes & the race knows infinitely more than the individual. Consent to be wise through your race.

> Written September 15, 1850, in his *Journal*, vol. 3, p. 115

It is for want of a man that there are so many men.

> "Life without Principle" in *Reform Papers*, p. 171

INDIVIDUALITY

Do what nobody else can do for you. Omit to do anything else.

> To H.G.O. Blake, August 9, 1850, in *The Correspondence of Henry David Thoreau*, p. 265

Let him see that he does only what belongs to himself and to the hour.

> "Resistance to Civil Government" in *Reform Papers*, p. 84

A man does best when he is most himself.

> Written January 21, 1852, in his *Journal*, vol. 4, p. 274

If a man does not keep pace with his companions, perhaps it is because he hears a different drummer. Let him step to the music which he hears, however measured or far away.

> *Walden*, p. 326

How many men have you seen that did not belong to any sect, or party, or clique?

> Written August 9, 1858, in his *Journal*, vol. XI, p. 88

At each step man measures himself against the system.

Written January 31, 1841, in his *Journal*, vol. 1, p. 242

We are constantly invited to be what we are.

Written February 3, 1841, in his *Journal*, vol. 1, p. 245

Do a little more of that work which you have sometime confessed to be good—which you feel that society & your justest judge rightly demands of you. Do what you reprove yourself for not doing. Know that you are neither satisfied nor dissatisfied with yourself without reason. Let me say to you & to myself in one breath— Cultivate the tree which you have found to bear fruit in your soil.

Written after July 29, 1850, in his *Journal*, vol. 3, p. 95

The universe seems bankrupt as soon as we begin to discuss the character of individuals.

A Week on the Concord and Merrimack Rivers, p. 260

To be sure there is no telling what an individual may do, but it is easy to tell what half a dozen men may *not* do unless they are to a certain extent united as one.

To Ralph Waldo Emerson, May 21, 1848, in *The Correspondence of Henry David Thoreau*, p. 227

If you would learn to speak all tongues and conform to the customs of all nations, if you would travel farther than all travellers, be naturalized in all climes, and cause the Sphinx to dash her head against a stone, even obey the precept of the old philosopher, and Explore thyself. . . . Start now on that farthest western way, which does not pause at the Mississippi or the Pacific, nor conduct toward a worn-out China or Japan, but leads on direct a tangent to this sphere, summer and winter, day and night, sun down, moon down, and at last earth down too.

Walden, p. 322

HUNTING AND FISHING

Fig. 8. The slug with which Thoreau's cousin, George Thatcher, killed a moose, as described in "Chesuncook" in *The Maine Woods*. Thoreau wrote, "My companion keeps it to show to his grandchildren." Photographer: Jim Cunningham. Courtesy of Nathaniel T. Wheelwright and Jim Cunningham.

These modern ingenious sciences and arts do not affect me as those more venerable arts of hunting and fishing, and even of husbandry in its primitive and simple form; as ancient and honorable trades as the sun and moon and winds pursue, coeval with the faculties of man, and invented when these were invented.

A Week on the Concord and Merrimack Rivers, p. 57

As I ran down the hill toward the reddening west, with the rainbow over my shoulder, and some faint tinkling sounds borne to my ear through the cleansed air, from I know not what quarter, my Good Genius seemed to say,—Go fish and hunt far and wide day by day,— farther and wider,—and rest thee by many brooks and hearth-sides without misgiving.

Walden, p. 207

Perhaps the hunter is the greatest friend of the animals hunted, not excepting the Humane Society.

Walden, p. 211

It is remarkable that many men will go with eagerness to Walden Pond in the winter to fish for pickerel & yet not seem to care for the landscape. Of course it cannot be *merely* for the pickerel they may catch. There is some adventure in it but any love of nature which they may feel is certainly very slight & indefinite. They call it going a-fishing & so indeed it is, though perchance their natures know better. Now I go a-fishing & a-hunting every day but omit the fish & the game—which are the least important part. I have learned to do without them. They were indispensable only as long as I was a boy.

Written January 26, 1853, in his *Journal*, vol. 5, pp. 455–456

Such is oftenest the young man's introduction to the forest, and the most original part of himself. He goes thither at first as a hunter and fisher, until at last, if he has the seeds of a better life in him, he distinguishes his proper objects, as a poet or naturalist it may be, and leaves the gun and fish-pole behind. The mass of men are still and always young in this respect.

Walden, pp. 212–213

As for fowling, during the last years that I carried a gun my excuse was that I was studying ornithology, and sought only new or rare birds. But I confess that I am now inclined to think that there is a finer way of studying ornithology than this. It requires so much closer attention to the habits of the birds, that, if for that reason only, I have been willing to omit the gun.

Walden, pp. 211–212

I like sometimes to take rank hold on life and spend my day more as the animals do.

Perhaps I have owed to this employment and to hunting, when quite young, my closest acquaintance with Nature.

Walden, p. 210

Yet notwithstanding the objection on the score of humanity, I am compelled to doubt if equally valuable sports are ever substituted for these; and when some of my friends have asked me anxiously about their boys, whether they should let them hunt, I have answered, yes,—remembering that it was one of the best parts of my education,—*make* them hunters, though sports-men only at first, if possible, mighty hunters at last, so that they shall not find game large enough for them in this or any vegetable wilderness,—hunters as well as fishers of men.

Walden, p. 212

In California and Oregon, if not nearer home, it is common to treat men exactly like deer which are hunted, and I read from time to time in Christian newspapers how many "bucks," that is, Indian men, their sportsmen have killed.

Written October 21, 1859, in his *Journal*, vol. XII, pp. 416–417

But this hunting of the moose merely for the satisfac-tion of killing him—not even for the sake of his hide, without making any extraordinary exertion or run-ning any risk yourself, is too much like going out by night to some woodside pasture and shooting your neighbor's horses.

The Maine Woods, p. 119

We cannot but pity the boy who has never fired a gun; he is no more humane, while his education has been sadly neglected. This was my answer with respect to those youths who were bent on this pursuit, trusting that they would soon outgrow it. No humane being, past the thoughtless age of boyhood, will wantonly murder any creature, which holds its life by the same tenure that he does. The hare in its extremity cries like a child.

Walden, p. 212

I hunt with a glass; for a gun gives you but the body while a glass gives you the bird.

Reported by Frederick L. H. Willis in *Alcott Memoirs*, p. 92

Do you think that I should shoot you if I wanted to study you?

In reply to George Bartlett on being asked if he ever shoots a bird to study it, as recorded in Hector Waylen's "A Visit to Walden Pond" (*Natural Food*, July 1895)

Can he who has discovered only some of the values of whalebone and whale oil be said to have discovered the true use of the whale? Can he who slays the elephant for his ivory be said to have "seen the elephant"? These are petty and accidental uses; just as if a stronger race were to kill us in order to make buttons and flageolets of our bones; for everything may serve a lower as well as a higher use. Every creature is better alive than dead, men and moose and pine-trees, and he who understands it aright will rather preserve its life than destroy it.

The Maine Woods, p. 121

There is unquestionably this instinct in me which belongs to the lower orders of creation; yet with every year I am less a fisherman, though without more humanity or even wisdom; at present I am no fisherman at all. But I see that if I were to live in a wilderness I should again be tempted to become a fisher and hunter in earnest.

Walden, p. 214

IMAGINATION

When one man has reduced a fact of the imagination to be a fact to his understanding, I foresee that all men will at length establish their lives on that basis.

Walden, p. 11

I find that actual events, notwithstanding the singular prominence which we all allow them, are far less real than the creations of my imagination.

To H.G.O. Blake, August 9, 1850, in *The Correspondence of Henry David Thoreau*, p. 265

This world is but canvass to our imaginations. I see men with infinite pains endeavoring to realize to their bodies, what I, with at least equal pains, would realize to my imagination,—its capacities; for certainly there is a life of the mind above the wants of the body and independent of it. Often the body is warmed, but the imagination is torpid; the body is fat, but the imagination is lean and shrunk. But what avails all other wealth if this is wanting?

A Week on the Concord and Merrimack Rivers, p. 292

Sometimes in our prosaic moods, life appears to us but a certain number more of days like those which we have lived, to be cheered not by more friends and friendship, but probably fewer and less. As, perchance, we anticipate the end of this day before it is done, close the shutters, and with a cheerless resignation commence the barren evening whose fruitless end we clearly see, we despondingly think that all of life that is left is only this experience reflected a certain number of times. And so it would be, if it were not for the faculty of imagination.

Written February 13, 1859, in his *Journal*, vol. XI, p. 445; emended from manuscript Journal (MA 1302, The Morgan Library & Museum, New York)

Often an inquisitive eye may detect the shores of a primitive lake in the low horizon hills, and no subsequent elevation of the plain has been necessary to conceal their history. But it is easiest, as they who work on the highways know, to find the hollows by the puddles after a shower. The amount of it is, the imagination, give it the least license, dives deeper and soars higher than Nature goes.

Walden, p. 288

Generally speaking, a howling wilderness does not howl: it is the imagination of the traveller that does the howling.

The Maine Woods, p. 219

They are of sick and diseased imaginations who would toll the world's knell so soon.

"Natural History of Massachusetts," in *Excursions*, p. 5

What a faculty must that be which can paint the most barren landscape and humblest life in glorious colors. It is pure & invigorated senses reacting on a sound & strong imagination.

> Written August 21, 1851, in his *Journal*, vol. 4, p. 3

It is the imagination of poets which puts those brave speeches into the mouths of their heroes.

> *A Week on the Concord and Merrimack Rivers*, p. 379

We should endeavor practically in our lives to correct all the defects which our imagination detects.

> To H.G.O. Blake, May 2, 1848, in *The Correspondence of Henry David Thoreau*, p. 220

The excursions of the imagination are so boundless.

> Written September 20, 1851, in his *Journal*, vol. 4, p. 85

There is this moment proposed to me every kind of life that men lead anywhere or at any time—or that imagination can paint. By another spring I may be a mail carrier in Peru, or a South African planter, or a Siberian exile, or a Greenland whaler, or a settler on the Columbia River—or a Canton merchant, or a soldier in Mexico, or a mackerel fisher off Cape Sable, or a Robinson Crusoe in the Pacific, or a silent navigator of any sea.

> "Reform and the Reformers" in *Reform Papers*, p. 196

INDIANS

I have much to learn of the Indian, nothing of the missionary.

The Maine Woods, p. 181

Myriads of arrow-points lie sleeping in the skin of the revolving earth, while meteors revolve in space. The footprint, the mind-print of the oldest men.

Written March 28, 1859, in his *Journal*, vol. XII, p. 92

Time will soon destroy the works of famous painters and sculptors, but the Indian arrowhead will balk his efforts and Eternity will have to come to his aid. They are not fossil bones, but, as it were, fossil thoughts, forever reminding me of the mind that shaped them. I would fain know that I am treading in the tracks of human game,—that I am on the trail of mind,—and those little reminders never fail to set me right.

Written March 28, 1859, in his *Journal*, vol. XII, p. 91

We survive in one sense in our posterity and in the continuance of our race—but when a race of men, of Indians for instance, becomes extinct, is not this the end of the world for them? Is not the world forever beginning & coming to an end both to men and races?

Written December 29, 1853, in his *Journal*, vol. 7, p. 209

The ferry here took us past the Indian island. As we left the shore, I observed a short shabby washerwoman-looking Indian; they commonly have the woe-begone look of the girl that cried for spilt milk— just from "up river,"—land on the Oldtown side near a grocery, and drawing up his canoe, take out a bundle of skins in one hand, and an empty keg or half-barrel in the other, and scramble up the bank with them. This picture will do to put before the Indian's history, that is, the history of his extinction.

The Maine Woods, p. 6

I think that the farmer displaces the Indian even because he redeems the meadow, and so makes himself stronger and in some respects more natural.

"Walking" in *Excursions*, p. 206

Here and there still you will find a man with Indian blood in his veins. An eccentric farmer descended from an Indian Chief—Or you will see a solitary pure blooded Indian looking as wild as ever among the pines—one of the last of the Massachusetts tribes stepping into a railroad car with his gun & pappoose.

Still here and there an Indian squaw with her dog— her only companion—lives in some lone house—insulted by school children—making baskets & picking berries her employment.... A lone Indian woman without children—accompanied by her dog—weaving the shroud of her race—performing the last services for her departed race.

Written after July 16, 1850, in his *Journal*, vol. 3, p. 93

A squaw came to our door today, with two pappooses, and said—"Me want a pie." Theirs is not common begging. You are merely the rich Indian who shares his goods with the poor. They merely offer you an opportunity to be generous and hospitable.

Written after October 31, 1850, in his *Journal*, vol. 3, p. 130

There is, in fact, a remarkable and unexpected resemblance between the degraded savage and the lowest classes in a great city. The one is no more a child of nature than the other. In the progress of degradation, the distinction of races is soon lost.

The Maine Woods, p. 78

Our Indian said that he was a doctor, and could tell me some medicinal use for every plant I could show him. . . . According to his account, he had acquired such knowledge in his youth from a wise old Indian with whom he associated, and he lamented that the present generation of Indians "had lost a great deal."

The Maine Woods, p. 235

The muskrat and the fresh water muscle are very native to our river. The Indian, their human compere, has departed.

Written October 7, 1851, in his *Journal*, vol. 4, p. 12

The arrow shot by the Indian is still found occasionally sticking in the trees of our forest.

Written after July 1, 1850, in his *Journal*, vol. 3, p. 91

But the Indian is absolutely forgotten but by some persevering poets. By an evident fate the white man has commenced a new era. What do our anniversaries commemorate but white men's exploits? For Indian deeds there must be an Indian memory—the white man will remember his own only.

Written between 1842 and 1844, in his *Journal*, vol. 2, pp. 38–39

The French respected the Indians as a separate & independent people and speak of them & contrast themselves with them as the English have never done. They not only went to war with them but they lived at home with them.

Written February 8, 1852, in his *Journal*, vol. 4, p. 337

The constitution of the Indian mind appears to be the very opposite of that of the white man. He is acquainted with a different side of nature. He measures his life by winters not summers. His year is not measured by the sun but consists of a certain number of moons, & his moons are measured not by days but by nights. He has taken hold of the dark side of nature—the white man the bright side.

Written October 25, 1852, in his *Journal*, vol. 5, p. 385

Indians generally, with whom I have talked, are not able to describe dimensions or distances in our measures with any accuracy. He could tell, perhaps, at what time we should arrive, but not how far it was.

The Maine Woods, p. 131

The charm of the Indian to me is that he stands free and unconstrained in nature—is her inhabitant and not her guest—and wears her easily and gracefully. But the civilized man has the habits of the house. His house is a prison in which he finds himself oppressed and confined, not sheltered and protected. He walks as if he sustained the roof. He carries his arms as if the walls would fall in and crush him and his feet remember the cellar beneath. His muscles are never relaxed.

Written April 26, 1841, in his *Journal*, vol. 1, p. 304

There can be no more startling evidence of their being a distinct and comparatively aboriginal race, than to hear this unaltered Indian language, which the white man cannot speak nor understand. We may suspect change and deterioration in almost every other particular, but the language which is so wholly unintelligible to us. It took me by surprise, though I had found so many arrow-heads, and convinced me that the Indian was not the invention of historians and poets. It was a purely wild and primitive American sound.

The Maine Woods, p. 136

When a new country like North America is discovered, a few feeble efforts are made to Christianize the natives before they are all exterminated, but they are not found to pay, in any sense. But then energetic traders of the discovering country organize themselves, or rather inevitably crystallize, with a vast rat-catching society, tempt the natives to become mere vermin-hunters and rum-drinkers, reserving half a continent for the field of *their* labors. Savage meets savage, and the white man's only distinction is that he is the chief.

Written April 8, 1859, in his *Journal*, vol. XII, p. 124; emended from manuscript Journal (MA 1302, The Morgan Library & Museum, New York)

Our orators might learn much from the Indians. They are remarkable for their precision—nothing is left at loose ends. They address more senses than one so as to preclude misunderstanding.

Written January 1, 1854, in his *Journal*, vol. 7, p. 221

The Jesuits were quite balked by those Indians who, being burned at the stake, suggested new modes of torture to their tormentors. Being superior to physical suffering, it sometimes chanced that they were superior to any consolation which the missionaries could offer; and the law to do as you would be done by fell with less persuasiveness on the ears of those, who, for their part, did not care how they were done by, who loved their enemies after a new fashion, and came very near freely forgiving them all they did.

Walden, p. 75

My companion and I having a minute's discussion on some point of ancient history, were amused by the attitude which the Indian, who could not tell what we were talking about, assumed. He constituted himself umpire, and, judging by our air and gesture, he very seriously remarked from time to time, "you beat," or "he beat."

The Maine Woods, p. 242

Indians like to get along with the least possible communication and ado.

The Maine Woods, p. 272

I had observed that he did not wish to answer the same
question more than once, and was often silent when it
was put again for the sake of certainty, as if he were
moody. Not that he was incommunicative, for he frequently commenced a long-winded narrative of his
own accord,—repeated at length the tradition of some
old battle, or some passage in the recent history of his
tribe in which he had acted a prominent part, from
time to time drawing a long breath, and resuming the
thread of his tale, with the true story-teller's leisureli-
ness, perhaps after shooting a rapid,—prefacing with
"we-ll-by-by," &c., as he paddled along.

The Maine Woods, p. 289

I have made a short excursion into the new world
which the Indian dwells in, or is. He begins where we
leave off. It is worth the while to detect new faculties in
man,—he is so much the more divine; and anything
that fairly excites our admiration expands us. The Indian, who can find his way so wonderfully in the
woods, possesses so much intelligence which the white
man does not,—and it increases my own capacity, as
well as faith, to observe it. I rejoice to find that intelligence flows in other channels than I knew.

To H.G.O. Blake, August 18, 1857, in *The Correspondence of
Henry David Thoreau*, p. 491

If we could listen but for an instant to the chaunt of the Indian muse, we should understand why he will not exchange his savageness for civilization.

A Week on the Concord and Merrimack Rivers, p. 56

The Indian does well to continue Indian.

A Week on the Concord and Merrimack Rivers, p. 56

INSTITUTIONS

To the thinker, all the institutions of men, as all imperfection, viewed from the point of equanimity, are legitimate subjects of humor.

"Thomas Carlyle and His Works" in *Early Essays and Miscellanies*, pp. 235–236

In short, as a snow-drift is formed where there is a lull in the wind, so, one would say, where there is a lull of truth, an institution springs up.

"Life without Principle" in *Reform Papers*, p. 177

One generation abandons the enterprises of another. Many an institution which was thought to be an essential part of the order of society, has, in the true order of events, been left like a stranded vessel on the sand.

"Reform and the Reformers" in *Reform Papers*, p. 189

The way in which men cling to old institutions after the life has departed out of them & out of themselves reminds me of those monkies which cling by their tails— aye whose tails contract about the limbs—even the dead limbs of the forest and they hang suspended beyond the hunters reach long after they are dead. It is of no use to argue with such men. They have not the apprehensive intellect but merely as it were a prehensile tail.

Written August 19, 1851, in his *Journal*, vol. 3, p. 376

In my short experience of human life I have found that the outward obstacles which stood in my way were not living men but dead institutions.

Written after June 20, 1846, in his *Journal*, vol. 2, p. 262

I love mankind. I hate the institutions of their forefathers.

Written after June 20, 1846, in his *Journal*, vol. 2, p. 262

The rich man . . . is always sold to the institution which makes him rich.

"Resistance to Civil Government" in *Reform Papers*, p. 77

Most with whom you endeavor to talk soon come to a stand against some institution in which they appear to hold stock,—that is, some particular, not universal, way of viewing things. They will continually thrust their own low roof, with its narrow skylight, between you and the sky, when it is the unobstructed heavens you wish to view.

"Life without Principle" in *Reform Papers*, pp. 167–168

I do not value any view of the universe into which man & the institutions of man enter very largely & absorb much of the attention. Man is but the place where I stand & the prospect (thence) hence is infinite.

Written April 2, 1852, in his *Journal*, vol. 4, pp. 419–420

The Reformer who comes recommending any institution or system to the adoption of men, must not rely solely on logic and argument, or on eloquence and oratory for his success, but see that he represents one pretty perfect institution in himself, the centre and circumference of all others, an erect man.

"Reform and the Reformers" in *Reform Papers*, p. 184

What institutions of man can survive a morning experience?

Written May 24, 1851, in his *Journal*, vol. 3, p. 234

Some institutions—most institutions, indeed, have had a divine origin. But of most that we see prevailing in society nothing but the form, the shell, is left—the life is extinct—and there is nothing divine in them.

Written August 19, 1851, in his *Journal*, vol. 3, pp. 377–378

It is surprising to what extent the world is ruled by cliques. They who constitute, or at least lead, New England or New York society, in the eyes of the world, are but a clique, a few "men of the age" and of the town, who work best in the harness provided for them. The institutions of almost all kinds are thus of a sectarian or party character. Newspapers, magazines, colleges, and all forms of government and religion express superficial activity of a few, the mass either conforming or not attending.

Written August 9, 1858, in his *Journal*, vol. XI, p. 86

How much of the life of certain men *goes* to sustain— to make respected—the institutions of society.

Written September 6, 1851, in his *Journal*, vol. 4, p. 48

The startings and arrivals of the cars are now the epochs in the village day. They go and come with such regularity and precision, and their whistle can be heard so far, that the farmers set their clocks by them, and thus one well conducted institution regulates a whole country.

Walden, pp. 117–118

Some years ago, the State met me in behalf of the church, and commanded me to pay a certain sum toward the support of a clergyman whose preaching my father attended, but never I myself.... I did not see why the schoolmaster should be taxed to support the priest, and not the priest the schoolmaster.... However, at the request of the selectmen, I condescended to make some such statement as this in writing:—"Know all men by these presents, that I, Henry Thoreau, do not wish to be regarded as a member of any incorporated society which I have not joined."

"Resistance to Civil Government" in *Reform Papers*, p. 79

LAND: MOUNTAINS, BOGS, AND
MEADOWS

How little appreciation of the beauty of the landscape there is among us!

"Walking" in *Excursions*, p. 217

A man can never say of any landscape that he has exhausted it.

Written April 19, 1850, in his *Journal*, vol. 3, p. 54

When the far mountains are invisible the near ones look the higher.

Written after May 12, 1850, in his *Journal*, vol. 3, p. 72

Summer and winter our eyes had rested on the dim outline of the mountains in our horizon, to which distance and indistinctness lent a grandeur not their own, so that they served equally to interpret all the allusions of poets and travellers.

"A Walk to Wachusett" in *Excursions*, p. 29

Many a man when I tell him that I have been on to a mountain asks if I took a glass with me. No doubt, I could have seen further with a glass and particular objects more distinctly—could have counted more meeting-houses; but this has nothing to do with the peculiar beauty and grandeur of the view which an elevated position affords. It was not to see a few particular objects as if they were near at hand as I had been accustomed to see them, that I ascended the mountain, but to see an infinite variety far & near in their relation to each other thus reduced to a single picture.

Written October 20, 1852, in his *Journal*, vol. 5, p. 378

We could, at length, realize the place mountains occupy on the land, and how they come into the general scheme of the universe. When first we climb their summits, and observe their lesser irregularities, we do not give credit to the comprehensive intelligence which shaped them; but when afterward we behold their outlines in the horizon, we confess that the hand which moulded their opposite slopes, making one to balance the other, worked round a deep centre, and was privy to the plan of the universe.

"A Walk to Wachusett" in *Excursions*, p. 42

If I wished to see a mountain or other scenery under the most favorable auspices, I would go to it in foul weather, so as to be there when it cleared up; we are then in the most suitable mood, and nature is most fresh and inspiring. There is no serenity so fair as that which is just established in a tearful eye.

The Maine Woods, p. 175

When once I have learned my place in the sphere I will fill it once for all.

Written February 4, 1841, in his *Journal*, vol. 1, p. 246

I doubt if in the landscape there can be anything finer than a distant mountain-range. They are a constant elevating influence.

Written May 17, 1858, in his *Journal*, vol. X, p. 430

An island always pleases my imagination, even the smallest, as a small continent and integral portion of the globe.

A Week on the Concord and Merrimack Rivers, p. 243

The land seemed to grow fairer as we withdrew from it.

A Week on the Concord and Merrimack Rivers, p. 22

When, formerly, I have analyzed my partiality for some farm which I had contemplated purchasing, I have frequently found that I was attracted solely by a few square rods of impermeable and unfathomable bog—a natural sink in one corner of it. That was the jewel which dazzled me. I derive more of my subsistence from the swamps which surround my native town than from the cultivated gardens in the village.

"Walking" in *Excursions*, p. 204

Beck Stow's swamp! What an incredible spot to think of in town or city! When life looks sandy & barren—is reduced to its lowest terms—we have no appetite & it has no flavor—then let me visit such a swamp as this deep & impenetrable where the earth quakes for a rod around you at every step,—with its open water where the swallows skim & twitter—its meadow & cotton grass—its dense patches of dwarf andromeda now brownish green—with clumps of blue-berry bushes—its spruces & its verdurous border of woods imbowering it on every side.

Written July 17, 1852, in his *Journal*, vol. 5, p. 226

I enter a swamp as a sacred place—a sanctum sanctorum. There is the strength—the marrow of Nature.

"Walking" in *Excursions*, p. 205

LIFE AND DEATH

Let me not live as if time was short. Catch the pace of the seasons. Have leisure to attend to every phenomenon of nature and to entertain every thought that comes to you. Let your life be a leisurely progress through the realms of nature.

Written January 11, 1852, in his *Journal*, vol. 4, p. 244

However mean your life is, meet it and live it; do not shun it and call it hard names.

Walden, p. 328

Even the death of Friends will inspire us as much as their lives. They will leave consolation to the mourners, as the rich leave money to defray the expenses of their funerals, and their memories will be incrusted over with sublime and pleasing thoughts, as monuments of other men are overgrown with moss; for our Friends have no place in the graveyard.

A Week on the Concord and Merrimack Rivers, p. 286

To the eyes of men there is something tragic in death. We hear of the death of any member of the human family with something more than regret,—not without a slight shudder and feeling of commiseration. The churchyard is a *grave* place.

Written August 8, 1856, in his *Journal*, vol. VIII, p. 457

On the death of a friend, we should consider that the fates through confidence have devolved on us the task of a double living—that we have henceforth to fulfill the promise of our friend's life also, in our own, to the world.

Written February 28, 1840, in his *Journal*, vol. 1, p. 114

This life is not for complaint, but for satisfaction.

To Daniel Ricketson, November 4, 1860, in *The Correspondence of Henry David Thoreau*, p. 600

As the afternoon grows shorter, and the early evening drives us home to complete our chores, we are reminded of the shortness of life, and become more pensive, at least in this twilight of the year. We are prompted to make haste to finish our work before the night comes.

Written November 1, 1858, in his *Journal*, vol. XI, p. 273

I am not afraid that I shall exaggerate the value and significance of life, but that I shall not be up to the occasion which it is. I shall be sorry to remember that I was there, but noticed nothing remarkable,—not so much as a prince in disguise; lived in the golden age a hired man; visited Olympus even, but fell asleep after dinner, and did not hear the conversation of the gods.

> To H.G.O. Blake, April 3, 1850, in *The Correspondence of Henry David Thoreau*, pp. 257–258

We do not commonly live our life out & full—we do not fill all our pores with our blood—we do not inspire & expire fully & entirely enough.

> Written June 13, 1851, in his *Journal*, vol. 3, p. 261

It is life near the bone where it is sweetest.

> *Walden*, p. 329

Love your life, poor as it is.

> *Walden*, p. 328

My life will wait for nobody but is being matured still irresistibly while I go about the streets, and chaffer with this man and that to secure it a living. It will cut its own channel like the mountain stream which by the longest ridges and by level prairies is not kept from the sea finally. So flows a man's life—and will reach the sea water, if not by an earthy channel—yet in dew and rain overleaping all barriers—with rainbows to announce its victory. It can wind as cunningly and unerringly as water that seeks its level, and shall I complain if the gods make it meander.

> Written April 7, 1841, in his *Journal*, vol. 1, p. 297

I am astonished at the singular pertinacity and endurance of our lives. The miracle is, that what is *is*, when it is so difficult, if not impossible, for any thing else to be; that we walk on in our particular paths so far, before we fall on death and fate, merely because we must walk in some path; that every man can get a living, and so few can do any more. So much only can I accomplish ere health and strength are gone, and yet this suffices.

A Week on the Concord and Merrimack Rivers, p. 293

The world is a cow that is hard to milk,—life does not come so easy,—and ah, how thinly it is watered ere we get it! But the young bunting calf, he will get at it. There is no way so direct.

To Ralph Waldo Emerson, November 14, 1847, in *The Correspondence of Henry David Thoreau*, pp. 188–189; emended from manuscript letter (Robert H. Taylor Collection, Manuscripts Division, Department of Rare Books and Special Collections, Manuscripts Division, Princeton University Library)

I have heard of some who were 15 years a dying—a shiftless business for which neither gods nor mortals have any sympathy to spare.

Passage omitted from *A Week on the Concord and Merrimack Rivers* as published in Linck C. Johnson, *Thoreau's Complex Weave*, p. 465

How meanly and miserably we live for the most part! We escape fate continually by the skin of our teeth, as the saying is. We are practically desperate. But as every man, in respect to material wealth, aims to become independent or wealthy, so, in respect to our spirits and imagination, we should have some spare capital and superfluous vigor, have some margin and leeway in which to move. What kind of gift is life unless we have spirits to enjoy it and taste its true flavor?

Written August 10, 1857, in his *Journal*, vol. X, p. 6

I had this advantage, at least, in my mode of life, over those who were obliged to look abroad for amusement, to society and the theatre, that my life itself was become my amusement and never ceased to be novel. It was a drama of many scenes and without an end.

Walden, p. 112

The simplest and most lumpish fungus has a peculiar interest to us, compared with a mere mass of earth, because it is so obviously organic and related to ourselves, however mute. It is the expression of an idea; growth according to a law; matter not dormant, not raw, but inspired, appropriated by spirit. If I take up a handful of earth, however separately interesting the particles may be, their relation to one another appears to be that of mere juxtaposition generally. I might have thrown them together thus. But the humblest fungus betrays a life akin to my own. It is a successful poem in its kind. There is suggested something superior to any particle of matter, in the idea or mind which uses and arranges the particles.

Written October 10, 1858, in his *Journal*, vol. XI, p. 204

There are infinite degrees of life, from that which is next to sleep and death, to that which is forever awake and immortal.

Written January 13, 1857, in his *Journal*, vol. IX, p. 218

When we are unhurried and wise, we perceive that only great and worthy things have any permanent and absolute existence,—that petty fears and petty pleasures are but the shadow of the reality. This is always exhilarating and sublime. By closing the eyes and slumbering, and consenting to be deceived by shows, men establish and confirm their daily life of routine and habit every where, which still is built on purely illusory foundations. Children, who play life, discern its true law and relations more clearly than men, who fail to live it worthily, but who think that they are wiser by experience, that is, by failure.

Walden, pp. 95–96

We who walk the streets and hold time together, are but the refuse of ourselves, and that life is for the shells of us—of our body & our mind—for our scurf—a thoroughly *scurvy* life. It is coffee made of coffee-grounds the twentieth time, which was only coffee the first time—while the living water leaps and sparkles by our doors.

To H.G.O. Blake, May 28, 1850, in *The Correspondence of Henry David Thoreau*, p. 259

He is the true artist whose life is his material—every stroke of the chisel must enter his own flesh and bone, and not grate dully on marble.

Written June 23, 1840, in his *Journal*, vol. 1, p. 139

This, our respectable daily life, in which the man of common sense, the Englishman of the world, stands so squarely, and on which our institutions are founded, is in fact the veriest illusion, and will vanish like the baseless fabric of a vision; but that faint glimmer of reality which sometimes illuminates the darkness of daylight for all men, reveals something more solid and enduring than adamant, which is in fact the corner-stone of the world.

To H.G.O. Blake, March 27, 1848, in *The Correspondence of Henry David Thoreau*, p. 215

Pursue, keep up with, circle round and round your life, as a dog does his master's chaise. Do what you love. Know your own bone; gnaw at it, bury it, unearth it, and gnaw it still.

To H.G.O. Blake, March 27, 1848, in *Familiar Letters*, pp. 163–164

The life which men praise and regard as successful is but one kind. Why should we exaggerate any one kind at the expense of the others?

Walden, p. 19

It is essential that a man confine himself to pursuits—a scholar for instance to studies, which lie next to & conduce to his life—which do not go against the grain either of his will or his imagination. The scholar finds in his experience some studies to be moist fertile & radiant with light—others, dry, barren & dark. If he is wise he will not persevere in the last as a plant in a cellar will strive toward the light. He will confine the observations of his mind as closely as possible to the experience or life of his senses.

Written March 12, 1853, in his *Journal*, vol. 6, pp. 6–7

As a man grows older his ability to sit still and follow in-door occupations increases.

"Walking" in *Excursions*, p. 188

I think that the ancient practice of burning the dead is far more tasteful and beautiful, for so the body is most speedily and cleanly returned to dust again, and its elements dispersed throughout nature.

Passage omitted from *A Week on the Concord and Merrimack Rivers* as published in Linck C. Johnson, *Thoreau's Complex Weave*, p. 458

There is not one of my readers who has yet lived a whole human life.

Walden, p. 331

The life in us is like the water in the river. It may rise this year higher than man has ever known it, and flood the parched uplands; even this may be the eventful year, which will drown out all our muskrats.

Walden, p. 333

This life we live is a strange dream, and I don't believe at all any account men give of it.

To his mother, August 6, 1843, in *The Correspondence of Henry David Thoreau*, p. 131

That which properly constitutes the life of every man is
a profound secret. Yet this is what every one would give
most to know but is himself most backward to impart.

Written March 14, 1838, in his *Journal*, vol. 1, p. 36

It is a record of the mellow & ripe moments that I
would keep.

Written December 23, 1851, in his *Journal*, vol. 4, p. 217

I would not preserve the husk of life, but the kernel.

Written December 23, 1851, in his *Journal*, vol. 4, p. 217

The art of life, of a poet's life is, not having any thing to
do, to do something.

Written April 29, 1852, in his *Journal*, vol. 5, p. 8

In proportion as our inward life fails, we go more constantly and desperately to the post-office. You may depend upon it, that the poor fellow who walks away
with the greatest number of letters, proud of his extensive correspondence, has not heard from himself this
long while.

"Life without Principle" in *Reform Papers*, p. 169

Some men endeavor to live a constrained life—to subject their whole lives to their will as he who said he
would give a sign if he were conscious after his head
was cut off but he gave no sign. Dwell as near as possible to the channel in which your life flows.

Written March 12, 1853, in his *Journal*, vol. 6, p. 7

Above all, we cannot afford not to live in the present.

"Walking" in *Excursions*, p. 220

All our life, *i.e.* the living part of it, is a persistent dreaming awake. The boy does not camp in his father's yard. That would not be adventurous enough, there are too many sights and sounds to disturb the illusion; so he marches off twenty or thirty miles and *there* pitches his tent, where stranger inhabitants are tamely sleeping in their beds just like his father at home, and camps in their yard, perchance. But then he dreams uninterruptedly that he is any where but where he is.

Written August 27, 1859, in his *Journal*, vol. XII, pp. 296–297; emended from manuscript Journal (MA 1302, The Morgan Library & Museum, New York)

I will not plant beans and corn with so much industry another summer, but such seeds, if the seed is not lost, as sincerity, truth, simplicity, faith, innocence, and the like, and see if they will not grow in this soil, even with less toil and manurance, and sustain me, for surely it has not been exhausted for these crops. Alas! I said this to myself; but now another summer is gone, and another, and another, and I am obliged to say to you, Reader, that the seeds which I planted, if indeed they *were* the seeds of those virtues, were wormeaten or had lost their vitality, and so did not come up.

Walden, pp. 183–184

I left the woods for as good a reason as I went there. Perhaps it seemed to me that I had several more lives to live, and could not spare any more time for that one.

Walden, p. 323

Soon after John's death I listened to a music-box, and if, at any time, that event had seemed inconsistent with the beauty and harmony of the universe, it was then gently constrained into the placid course of nature by those steady notes, in mild and unoffended tone echoing far and wide under the heavens. But I find these things more strange than sad to me. What right have I to grieve, who have not ceased to wonder? ... Only Nature has a right to grieve perpetually, for she only is innocent. Soon the ice will melt, and the blackbirds sing along the river which he frequented, as pleasantly as ever. The same everlasting serenity will appear in this face of God, and we will not be sorrowful if he is not.

To Mrs. Lucy Brown, March 2, 1842, in *Familiar Letters*, p. 41

We begin to die not in our senses or extremities but in our divine faculties. Our members may be sound, our sight & hearing perfect, but our genius and imagination betray signs of decay.

Written January 27, 1854, in his *Journal*, vol. 7, p. 252

As one year passes into another through the medium of winter so does this our life pass into another through the medium of death.

Written September 8, 1851, in his *Journal*, vol. 4, p. 63

This event advertises me that there is such a fact as death—the possibility of a man's dying. It seems as if no man had ever died in America before, for in order to die you must first have lived.

On the hanging of John Brown in "A Plea for Captain John Brown" in *Reform Papers*, p. 134

Let the dead bury their dead.

"A Plea for Captain John Brown" in *Reform Papers*, p. 134

I hear a good many pretend that they are going to die;—or that they have died for aught that I know. Nonsense! I'll defy them to do it. They haven't got life enough in them. They'll deliquesce like fungi, and keep a hundred eulogists mopping the spot where they left off. Only half a dozen or so have died since the world began.

"A Plea for Captain John Brown" in *Reform Papers*, p. 134

The sad memory of departed friends is soon incrusted over with sublime & pleasing thoughts as their monuments are overgrown with moss. Nature doth thus kindly heal every wound.

Written March 14, 1842, in his *Journal*, vol. 1, p. 372

One moment of serene and confident life is more glorious than a whole campaign of daring. We should be ready for all issues; not daring to die, but daring to live.

Written December, 1839, in his *Journal*, vol. 1, p. 91

The death scenes of great men are agreeable to consider only when they make another and harmonious chapter of their lives.

"Sir Walter Raleigh" in *Early Essays and Miscellanies*, p. 195

FROM HIS DEATH-BED

I *suppose* that I have not many months to live; but, of course, I know nothing about it. I may add that I am enjoying existence as much as ever, and regret nothing.

To Myron B. Benton, March 21, 1862, in *The Correspondence of Henry David Thoreau*, p. 641

One world at a time.

In answer to Parker Pillsbury's statement to Thoreau that he was "so near the brink of the dark river, that I almost wonder how the opposite shore may appear to you," as recorded in Franklin B. Sanborn's *The Personality of Thoreau*, p. 69

I did not know we had ever quarreled.

On having been asked if he had made his peace with God, as recorded in Edward Emerson's *Henry Thoreau as Remembered by a Young Friend*, p. 117

This is a beautiful world, but soon I shall see one that is fairer.

Told to Edmund Hosmer, as recorded in Emil R. Lyman's *Thoreau*, p. 5

FIG. 9. Thoreau family plot, Sleepy Hollow Cemetery, Concord. Photographer: Herbert W. Gleason. Reproduced from *The Writings of Henry D. Thoreau*. The Walden Woods Project Collection at the Thoreau Institute at Walden Woods. Courtesy of the Walden Woods Project.

LITERARY MATTERS

FIG. 10. Thoreau's signature. Reproduced from *The Writings of Henry D. Thoreau*. The Walden Woods Project Collection at the Thoreau Institute at Walden Woods. Courtesy of the Walden Woods Project.

WRITING AND WRITERS

My work is writing.

Written October 18, 1856, in his *Journal*, vol. IX, p. 121

We commonly do not remember that it is, after all, always the first person that is speaking.

Walden, p. 3

The writer needs the suggestion and correction that a correspondent or companion is.

Written August 23, 1858, in his *Journal*, vol. XI, p. 120

It is enough if I have pleased myself with writing—I am then sure of an audience.

Written March 24, 1842, in his *Journal*, vol. 1, p. 388

Write in the strain that interests you most. Consult not the popular taste.

Written December 20, 1851, in his *Journal*, vol. 4, p. 211

A Journal.—a book that shall contain a record of all your joy—your extacy.

Written July 13, 1852, in his *Journal*, vol. 5, p. 219

All that interests the reader is the depth and intensity of the life excited.

Written October 18, 1856, in his *Journal*, vol. IX, p. 121

It is the uncivilized free and wild thinking in Hamlet and the Iliad, in all the scriptures and mythologies, not learned in the Schools, that delights us.

"Walking" in *Excursions*, pp. 207–208

Give me simple, cheap, and homely themes.

Written October 18, 1856, in his *Journal*, vol. IX, p. 121

There are two kinds of writing, both great and rare; one that of genius, or the inspired, the other of intellect and taste, in the intervals of inspiration.

A Week on the Concord and Merrimack Rivers, p. 375

It is the height of art that on the first perusal plain common sense should appear—on the second serene truth—and on a third beauty—and having these warrants for its depth and reality, we may then enjoy the beauty forever more.

To Emerson, July 8, 1843, in *The Correspondence of Henry David Thoreau*, p. 125

How vain it is to sit down to write when you have not stood up to live! Methinks that the moment my legs begin to move my thoughts begin to flow.

Written August 19, 1851, in his *Journal*, vol. 3, p. 378

A perfectly healthy sentence is extremely rare. Sometimes we read one which was written while the world went round, while grass grew and water ran. But for the most part we miss the hue and fragrance of the thought.

"Sir Walter Raleigh" in *Early Essays and Miscellanies*, p. 214

In Literature, it is only the wild that attracts us. Dullness is but another name for tameness.

"Walking" in *Excursions*, p. 207

Whatever book or sentence will bear to be read twice, we may be sure was thought twice.

Written March 18, 1842, in his *Journal*, vol. 1, p. 379

It is fatal to the writer to be too much possessed by his thought. Things must lie a little remote to be described.

Written November 11, 1851, in his *Journal*, vol. 4, p. 177

If you would get money as a writer or lecturer, you must be popular, which is to go down perpendicularly.

"Life without Principle" in *Reform Papers*, p. 158

We sometimes experience a mere fullness of life, which does not find any channels to flow into. We are stimulated but to no obvious purpose. I feel myself uncommonly prepared for *some* literary work, but I can select no work. I am prepared not so much for contemplation, as for force-ful expression. I am braced both physically and intellectually. It is not so much the music as the marching to the music that I feel.

Written September 7, 1851, in his *Journal*, vol. 4, pp. 50–51

A genuine thought or feeling can find expression for itself, if it have to invent hieroglyphics.

Written September 8, 1851, in his *Journal*, vol. 4, p. 61

Nothing goes by luck in composition—it allows of no trick. The best you can write will be the best you are. Every sentence is the result of a long probation. The author's character is read from title-page to end—of this he never corrects the proofs.

Written February 28, 1841, in his *Journal*, vol. 1, p. 276

I find that I use many words for the sake of emphasis which really add nothing to the force of my sentences and they look relieved the moment I have cancelled these. Words by which I express my mood, my conviction, rather than the simple truth.

Written January 26, 1852, in his *Journal*, vol. 4, pp. 291–292

No man's thoughts are new, but the style of their expression is the never failing novelty which cheers and refreshes men.

"Thomas Carlyle and His Works" in *Early Essays and Miscellanies*, p. 233

It is vain to try to write unless you feel strong in the knees.

Written August 9, 1841, in his *Journal*, vol. 1, p. 317

Though I write every day yet when I say a good thing, it seems as if I wrote but rarely.

Written February 28, 1841, in his *Journal*, vol. 1, p. 273

There are two classes of authors—the one write the history of their times; the other their biography.

Written April 20, 1841, in his *Journal*, vol. 1, p. 302

I do not always state the facts exactly in the order in which they were observed, but select out of my numerous observations extended over a series of years the most important ones, and describe them in a natural order.

"The Dispersion of Seeds" in *Faith in a Seed*, p. 104

As for style of writing—if one has any thing to say, it drops from him simply & directly, as a stone falls to the ground.

To Daniel Ricketson, August 18, 1857, in *The Correspondence of Henry David Thoreau*, p. 489

Let me suggest a theme for you: to state to yourself precisely and completely what that walk over the mountains amounted to for you,—returning to this essay again and again, until you are satisfied that all that was important in your experience is in it. Give this good reason to yourself for having gone over the mountains, for mankind is ever going over a mountain. Don't suppose that you can tell it precisely the first dozen times you try, but at 'em again, especially when, after a sufficient pause, you suspect that you are touching the heart or summit of the matter, reiterate your blows there, and account for the mountain to yourself. Not that the story need be long, but it will take a long while to make it short. It did not take very long to get over the mountain, you thought; but have you got over it indeed? If you have been to the top of Mount Washington, let me ask, what did you find there? That is the way they prove witnesses, you know. Going up there and being blown on is nothing. We never do much climbing while we are there, but we eat our luncheon, etc., very much as at home. It is after we get home that we really go over the mountain, if ever. What did the mountain say? What did the mountain do?

To H.G.O. Blake, November 16, 1857, in *The Correspondence of Henry David Thoreau*, p. 498

I know very well what Goethe meant when he said that he never had a chagrin but he made a poem out of it.

To H.G.O. Blake, May 2, 1848, in *The Correspondence of Henry David Thoreau*, p. 222

The writer must to some extent inspire himself. Most of his sentences may at first lie dead in his essay, but when all are arranged, some life and color will be reflected on them from the mature and successful lines; they will appear to pulsate with fresh life, and he will be enabled to eke out their slumbering sense, and make them worthy of their neighborhood. . . . The writer has much to do even to create a theme for himself. Most that is first written on any subject is a mere groping after it, mere rubble-stone and foundation. It is only when many observations of different periods have been brought together that he begins to grasp his subject and can make one pertinent and just observation.

Written February 3, 1859, in his *Journal*, vol. XI, pp. 438–439

Time never passes so quickly and unaccountably as when I am engaged in composition, *i.e.* in writing down my thoughts. Clocks seem to have been put forward.

Written January 27, 1858, in his *Journal*, vol. X, p. 263

The forcible writer does not go far for his themes—his ideas are not far-fetched.

Written January 29, 1852, in his *Journal*, vol. 4, p. 301

The forcible writer stands bodily behind his words with his experience. He does not make books out of books, but he has been *there* in person.

Written February 3, 1852, in his *Journal*, vol. 4, p. 326

For a year or 2 past my *publisher* falsely so called, has been writing from time to time to ask what disposition should be made of the copies of "A Week on the Concord and Merrimack Rivers" still on hand, and at last suggesting that he had use for the room they occupied in his cellar. So I had them all sent to me here & they have arrived today by express, filling the man's wagon, 706 copies out of an edition of 1000 which I bought of Munroe 4 years ago & have been ever since paying for & have not quite paid for yet. The wares are sent to me at last, and I have an opportunity to examine my purchase. They are something more substantial than fame—as my back knows which has borne them up two flights of stairs to a place similar to that to which they trace their origin. . . . I have now a library of nearly 900 volumes over 700 of which I wrote myself.

Written October 28 1853, in his *Journal*, vol. 7, pp. 122–123

It is not easy to write in a journal what interests us at any time, because to write it is not what interests us.

A Week on the Concord and Merrimack Rivers, p. 332

It is of no use to plow deeper than the soil is, unless you mean to follow up that mode of cultivation persistently, manuring highly and carting on muck at each plowing,—making a soil, in short. Yet many a man likes to tackle mightily themes like immortality, but in his discourse he turns up nothing but yellow sand, under which what little fertile and available surface soil he may have is quite buried and lost. He should teach frugality rather,—how to postpone the fatal hour,—should plant a crop of beans. He might have raised enough of these to make a deacon of him, though never a preacher. Many a man runs his plow so deep in heavy or stony soil that it sticks fast in the furrow. It is a great art in the writer to improve from day to day just that soil and fertility which he has, to harvest that crop which his life yields, whatever it may be, not be straining as if to reach apples or oranges when he yields only ground-nuts. He should be digging, not soaring. Just as earnest as your life is, so deep is your soil. If strong and deep, you will sow wheat and raise bread of life in it.

Written November 9, 1858, in his *Journal*, vol. XI, p. 304; emended from manuscript Journal (MA 1302, The Morgan Library & Museum, New York)

It is wise to write on many subjects to try many themes that so you may find the right & inspiring one. Be greedy of occasions to express your thought. Improve the opportunity to draw analogies.

Written September 4, 1851, in his *Journal*, vol. 4, p. 41

It is not in vain that the mind turns aside this way or that. Follow its leading—apply it whither it inclines to go. Probe the universe in a myriad points. Be avaricious of these impulses. You must try a thousand themes before you find the right one—as nature makes a thousand acorns to get one oak.

Written September 4, 1851, in his *Journal*, vol. 4, p. 41

What if there were a tariff on words, on language, for the encouragement of home manufactures? Have we not the genius to coin our own?

Written October 16, 1859, in his *Journal*, vol. XII, p. 390

How many there are who advise you to print! How few who advise you to lead a more interior life! In the one case there is all the world to advise you, in the other there is none to advise you but yourself.

Written April 16, 1852, in his *Journal*, vol. 4, p. 453

I wish I could buy at the shops some kind of India rubber that would rub out at once all that in my writing which it now costs me so many perusals—so many months if not years & so much reluctance to erase.

Written December 27, 1853, in his *Journal*, vol. 7, p. 208

I find incessant labor with the hands which engrosses the attention also, the best method to remove palaver out of one's style.

Written January 5, 1842, in his *Journal*, vol. 1, p. 358

The scholar may be sure that he writes the tougher truth for the calluses on his palms. They give firmness to the sentence. Indeed, the mind never makes a great and successful effort without a corresponding energy of the body. We are often struck by the force and precision of style to which hard-working men, unpracticed in writing, easily attain, when required to make the effort. As if plainness, and vigor, and sincerity, the ornaments of style, were better learned on the farm and in the workshop than in the schools. The sentences written by such rude hands are nervous and tough, like hardened thongs, the sinews of the deer, or the roots of the pine.

A Week on the Concord and Merrimack Rivers, p. 106

Language is the most perfect work of art in the world. The chisel of a thousand years retouches it.

Written July 27, 1840, in his *Journal*, vol. 1, p. 160

In this part of the world it is considered a ground for complaint if a man's writings admit of more than one interpretation.

Walden, p. 325

Who cares what a man's style is, so it is intelligible—as intelligible as his thought. Literally and really, the style is no more than the *stylus*, the pen he writes with—and it is not worth scraping and polishing, and gilding, unless it will write his thoughts the better for it. It is something for use, and not to look at. The question for us is not whether Pope had a fine style, wrote with a peacock's feather, but whether he uttered useful thoughts. Translate a book a dozen times from one language to another, and what becomes of its style? Most books would be worn out and disappear in this ordeal.

The pen which wrote it is soon destroyed, but the poem survives.

"Thomas Carlyle and His Works" in *Early Essays and Miscellanies*, p. 232

A well built sentence in the rapidity and force with which it works may be compared to a modern corn planter which furrows out, drops the seed and covers it up at one movement.

Written January 5, 1842, in his *Journal*, vol. 1, p. 359

The writer must direct his sentences as carefully & leisurely as the marks-man his rifle—who shoots sitting & with a rest—with patent sights & conical balls beside. He must not merely seem to speak the truth. He must really speak it. If you foresee that a part of your essay will topple down after the lapse of time, throw it down now yourself.

Written January 26, 1852, in his *Journal*, vol. 4, p. 289

Write while the heat is in you. When the farmer burns a hole in his yoke, he carries the hot iron quickly from the fire to the wood, for every moment it is less effectual to penetrate (pierce) it. It must be used instantly or it is useless. The writer who postpones the recording of his thoughts uses an iron which has cooled to burn a hole with. He cannot inflame the minds of his audience.

Written February 10, 1852, in his *Journal*, vol. 4, pp. 340–341

The words of some men are thrown forcibly against you and adhere like burs.

Written June 4, 1839, in his *Journal*, vol. 1, p. 74

We like to read a good description of no thing so well as that which we already know the best, as our friend, or ourselves even.

Written October 13, 1860, in his *Journal*, vol. XIV, p. 119

From the weak and flimsy periods of the politician and literary man, we are glad to turn even to the description of work, the simple record of the month's labor in the farmer's almanac, to restore our tone and spirits. A sentence should read as if its author, had he held a plow instead of a pen, could have drawn a furrow deep and straight to the end.

A Week on the Concord and Merrimack Rivers, p. 107

Improve every opportunity to express yourself in writing as if it were your last.

Written December 17, 1851, in his *Journal*, vol. 4, p. 207

Thinkers & writers are in foolish haste to come before the world with crude works. Young men are persuaded by their friends or by their own restless ambition, to write a course of lectures in a summer against the ensuing winter—And what it took the lecturer a summer to write it will take his audience but an hour to forget.

Written November 16, 1851, in his *Journal*, vol. 4, p. 191

One more merit in Carlyle let the subject be what it may, is the freedom of prospect he allows, the entire absence of cant and dogma. He removes many cartloads of rubbish, and leaves open a broad highway. His writings are all unfenced on the side of the future and the possible. He does not place himself across the passage out of his books, so that none may go freely out, but rather by the entrance, inviting all to come in and go through. No gins, no net-work, no pickets here, to restrain the free thinking reader.

"Thomas Carlyle and His Works" in *Early Essays and Miscellanies*, p. 252

He speaks as an unconcerned spectator, whose object is faithfully to describe what he sees, and that, for the most part, in the order in which he sees it. Even his reflections do not interfere with his descriptions.

On Goethe in *A Week on the Concord and Merrimack Rivers*, p. 326

POETS AND POETRY

How differently the poet and the naturalist look at objects!

"Autumnal Tints" in *Excursions*, p. 257

The poet is more in the air than the naturalist though they may walk side by side. Granted that you are out of door—but what if the outer door *is* open, if the inner door is shut.

Written August 21, 1851, in his *Journal*, vol. 4, p. 6

If we respected only what is inevitable and has a right to be, music and poetry would resound along the streets.

Walden, p. 95

The poet cherishes his chagrins & sets his sighs to music.

> Written June 1, 1853, in his *Journal*, vol. 6, p. 168

There are two classes of men called poets. The one cultivates life, the other art,—one seeks food for nutriment, the other for flavor; one satisfies hunger, the other gratifies the palate.

> *A Week on the Concord and Merrimack Rivers*, p. 375

As naturally as the oak bears an acorn, and the vine a gourd, man bears a poem, either spoken or done.

> *A Week on the Concord and Merrimack Rivers*, p. 91

Poetry *implies* the whole truth. Philosophy *expresses* a particle of it.

> Written January 26, 1852, in his *Journal*, vol. 4, p. 291

I omit the unusual, the hurricanes & earthquakes, & describe the common. This has the greatest charm and is the true theme of poetry.

> Written August 28, 1851, in his *Journal*, vol. 4, p. 17

One sentence of perennial poetry would make me forget—would atone for volumes of mere science.

> Written August 5, 1851, in his *Journal*, vol. 3, p. 354

The science of Humboldt is one thing, poetry is another thing. The poet today, notwithstanding all the discoveries of science, and the accumulated learning of mankind, enjoys no advantage over Homer.

> "Walking" in *Excursions*, p. 208

Poetry is the only life got, the only work done, the only pure product and free labor of man, performed only when he has put all the world under his feet, and conquered the last of his foes.

"Thomas Carlyle and His Works" in *Early Essays and Miscellanies*, p. 249

The poet leaves not a single chord untouched if the reader will but yield himself up to his influence.

"L' Allegro & Il Penseroso" in *Early Essays and Miscellanies*, p. 75

The poet will write for his peers alone. He will remember only that he saw truth and beauty from his position, and expect the time when a vision as broad shall overlook the same field as freely.

A Week on the Concord and Merrimack Rivers, p. 341

There is all the poetry in the world in a name. It is a poem which the mass of men hear and read. What is poetry in the common sense but a string of such jingling names? I want nothing better than a good word. The name of a thing may easily be more than the thing itself to me.

"A Yankee in Canada" in *Excursions*, pp. 93–94

The mass of men are very unpoetic yet that Adam that names things is always a poet.

Written July 30, 1853, in his *Journal*, vol. 6, p. 280

When I stand in a library where is all the recorded wit of the world, but none of the recording, a mere accumulated, and not truly cumulative treasure, where immortal works stand side by side with anthologies that did not survive their month, and cobweb and mildew have already spread from these to the binding of those; and happily I am reminded of what poetry is, I perceive that Shakespeare and Milton did not foresee into what company they were to fall. Alas! that so soon the work of a true poet should be swept into such a dust-hole!

A Week on the Concord and Merrimack Rivers, p. 341

He would be a poet who could impress the winds and streams into his service, to speak for him; who nailed words to their primitive senses, as farmers drive down stakes in the spring which the frost has heaved; who derived his words as often as he used them—transplanted them to his page with earth adhering to their roots;—whose words were so true, and fresh, and natural that they would appear to expand like the buds at the approach of spring, though they lay half smothered between two musty leaves in a library,—aye, to bloom and bear fruit there after their kind annually for the faithful reader, in sympathy with surrounding Nature.

"Walking" in *Excursions*, p. 208

The prosaic mind sees things badly, or with the bodily sense; but the poet sees them clad in beauty, with the spiritual sense.

Written December 9, 1859, in his *Journal*, vol. XIII, p. 18; emended from manuscript Journal (MA 1302, The Morgan Library & Museum, New York)

Most poems, like the fruits, are sweetest toward the blossom end.

Written August 23, 1853, in his *Journal*, vol. 7, p. 16

No man is rich enough to keep a poet in his pay.

Written March 20, 1858, in his *Journal*, vol. X, p. 316

BOOKS

How many a man has dated a new era in his life from the reading of a book.

Walden, p. 107

The book exists for us perchance which will explain our miracles and reveal new ones. The at present unutterable things we may find somewhere uttered. These same questions that disturb and puzzle and confound us have in their turn occurred to all the wise men; not one has been omitted; and each has answered them, according to his ability, by his words and his life.

Walden, p. 108

Books are the treasured wealth of the world and the fit inheritance of generations and nations.

Walden, p. 102

I never read a novel, they have so little real life and thought in them.

A Week on the Concord and Merrimack Rivers, p. 71

A truly good book is something as wildly natural and primitive—mysterious & marvelous, ambrosial & fertile—as a fungus or a lichen.

Written November 16, 1850, in his *Journal*, vol. 3, p. 141

A truly good book is something as natural, and as unexpectedly and unaccountably fair and perfect, as a wild flower discovered on the prairies of the west, or in the jungles of the east.

"Walking" in *Excursions*, pp. 207–208

Read the best books first, or you may not have a chance to read them at all.

A Week on the Concord and Merrimack Rivers, p. 96

A truly good book attracts very little favor to itself. It is so true that it teaches me better than to read it. I must soon lay it down and commence living on its hint.

Written February 19, 1841, in his *Journal*, vol. 1, p. 268

Books, not which afford us a cowering enjoyment, but in which each thought is of unusual daring; such as an idle man cannot read, and a timid one would not be entertained by, which even make us dangerous to existing institutions,—such I call good books.

A Week on the Concord and Merrimack Rivers, p. 96

When I read an indifferent book it seems the best thing I can do, but the inspiring volume hardly leaves me leisure to finish its latter pages. It is slipping out of my fingers while I read. It creates no atmosphere in which it may be perused, but one in which its teachings may be practiced. It confers on me such wealth that I lay it down with the least regret. What I began by reading I must finish by acting.

Written February 19, 1841, in his *Journal*, vol. 1, p. 268

There is a sort of homely truth and naturalness in some books, which is very rare to find, and yet looks quite cheap.

Written March 13, 1841, in his *Journal*, vol. 1, p. 286

Scholars have for the most part a diseased way of looking at the world.

Written April 27, 1843, in his *Journal*, vol. 1, p. 456

It is remarkable, but on the whole, perhaps, not to be lamented, that the world is so unkind to a new book. Any distinguished traveller who comes to our shores, is likely to get more dinners and speeches of welcome than he can well dispose of, but the best books, if noticed at all, meet with coldness and suspicion, or, what is worse, gratuitous, off-hand criticism.

"Thomas Carlyle and His Works" in *Early Essays and Miscellanies*, pp. 223–224

Most books belong to the house and street only, and in the fields their leaves feel very thin. They are bare and obvious, and have no halo or haze about them. Nature lies far and fair behind them all.

A Week on the Concord and Merrimack Rivers, p. 150

You can sometimes catch the sense better by listening than by reading.

Reported by Mary Hosmer Brown in *Memories of Concord*, p. 92

For the most part an author but consults with all who have written before upon any subject and his book is but the advice of so many. But a true book will never have been forestalled but the topic itself will be new and, by consulting with nature, it will consult not only with those who have gone before, but with those who may come after.

Written March 13, 1841, in his *Journal*, vol. 1, p. 288

There is always room and occasion enough for a true book on any subject; as there is room for more light the brightest day and more rays will not interfere with the first.

A Week on the Concord and Merrimack Rivers, p. 109

Books are for the most part willfully and hastily written, as parts of a system, to supply a want real or imagined. Books of natural history aim commonly to be hasty schedules, or inventories of God's property, by some clerk. They do not in the least teach the divine view of nature, but the popular view, or rather the popular method of studying nature, and make haste to conduct the persevering pupil only into that dilemma where the professors always dwell.

A Week on the Concord and Merrimack Rivers, pp. 97–98

A book should contain pure discoveries, glimpses of *terra firma*, though by shipwrecked mariners, and not the art of navigation by those who have never been out of sight of land.

A Week on the Concord and Merrimack Rivers, p. 98

He who resorts to the easy novel, because he is languid, does no better than if he took a nap.

A Week on the Concord and Merrimack Rivers, p. 96

All that are printed and bound are not books; they do not necessarily belong to letters, but are oftener to be ranked with the other luxuries and appendages of civilized life. Base wares are palmed off under a thousand disguises.

A Week on the Concord and Merrimack Rivers, p. 96

By dint of able writing and pen-craft, books are cunningly compiled, and have their run and success even among the learned, as if they were the result of a new man's thinking, and their birth is attended with some natural throes. But in a little while their covers fall off, for no binding will avail, and it appears that they are not Books or Bibles at all. There are new and patented inventions in this shape, purporting to be for the elevation of the race, which many a pure scholar and genius who has learned to read is for a moment deceived by, and finds himself reading a horse-rake, or spinning jenny, or wooden nutmeg, or oak-leaf cigar, or steam-power press, or kitchen range, perchance, when he was seeking serene and biblical truths.

A Week on the Concord and Merrimack Rivers, p. 97

If men were to be destroyed and the books they have written be transmitted to a new race of creatures, in a new world, what kind of record would be found in them of so remarkable a phenomenon as the rainbow?

Written March 13, 1859, in his *Journal*, vol. XII, pp. 44–45; emended from manuscript Journal (MA 1302, The Morgan Library & Museum, New York)

It is necessary to find out exactly what books to read on a given subject. Though there may be a thousand books written upon it, it is only important to read 3 or 4—they will contain all that is essential & a few pages will show which they are. Books which are books are all that you want—& there are but half a dozen in any thousand.

Written March 16, 1852, in his *Journal*, vol. 4, p. 392

We do not learn much from learned books, but from true, sincere, human books, from frank and honest biographies.

A Week on the Concord and Merrimack Rivers, p. 98

It is not all books that are as dull as their readers.

Walden, p. 107

Books must be read as deliberately and reservedly as they were written.

Walden, p. 101

So far as the natural history is concerned, you often have your choice between uninteresting truth and interesting falsehood.

Written March 5, 1860, in his *Journal*, vol. XIII, p. 181

Books can only reveal us to ourselves, and as often as they do us this service we lay them aside.

> To Benjamin Bowen Wiley, April 26, 1857, in *The Correspondence of Henry David Thoreau*, p. 478

Blessed is the man who can have his library at hand, and oft peruse the books, without the fear of a taskmaster! he is far enough from harmful idleness, who can call in and dismiss these friends when he pleases. An honest book's the noblest work of man.

> To his sister, Helen, January 23, 1840, in Latin; English translation by Franklin B. Sanborn in *Familiar Letters*, p. 31

He who cannot read is worse than deaf and blind, is yet but half alive, is still-born.

> Written March 10, 1856, in his *Journal*, vol. VIII, p. 203

I would rather write books than lectures.

> Written December 6, 1854, in his *Journal*, vol. VII, p. 79

The woodchopper reads the wisdom of ages recorded on the paper that holds his dinner, then lights his pipe with it. When we ask for a scrap of paper for the most trivial use, it may have the confessions of Augustine or the sonnets of Shakespeare, and we won't observe it. The student kindles his fire, the editor packs his trunk, the sportsman loads his gun, the traveller wraps his dinner, the Irishman papers his shanty, the schoolboy peppers the plastering, the belle pins up her hair, with the printed thoughts of men. Surely he who can see so large a portion of the earth's surface thus darkened with the record of human thought and experience, and feel no desire to learn to read it, is without curiosity.

Written March 10, 1856, in his *Journal*, vol. VIII, p. 203; emended from manuscript *Journal* (MA 1302, The Morgan Library & Museum, New York)

In a true history or biography, of how little consequence those events of which so much is commonly made! For example, how difficult for a man to remember in what towns or houses he has lived, or when! Yet one of the first steps of his biographer will be to establish these facts, and he will thus give an undue importance to many of them. I find in my Journal that the most important events in my life, if recorded at all, are not dated.

Written December 26, 1855, in his *Journal*, vol. VIII, p. 64

In books, that which is most generally interesting is what comes home to the most cherished private experience of the greatest number. It is not the book of him who has travelled the farthest over the surface of the globe, but of him who has lived the deepest and been the most at home.

Written November 20, 1857, in his *Journal*, vol. X, p. 190

A book should be so true as to be intimate and familiar to all men as the sun to their faces. Such a word as is occasionally uttered to a companion in the woods in summer, and both are silent.

Written September 4, 1841, in his *Journal*, vol. 1, p. 330

LOVE

How insufficient is all wisdom without love.

Written March 25, 1842, in his *Journal*, vol. 1, p. 390

Our life without love is coke and ashes.

A Week on the Concord and Merrimack Rivers, p. 284

It is strange that men will talk of miracles, revelation, inspiration, and the like, as things past, while love remains.

"Chastity & Sensuality" in *Early Essays and Miscellanies*, p. 277

Ignorance and bungling with love are better than wisdom and skill without.

A Week on the Concord and Merrimack Rivers, p. 284

Only lovers know the value and magnanimity of truth.

A Week on the Concord and Merrimack Rivers, p. 267

May we so love as never to have occasion to repent of our love.

"Chastity & Sensuality" in *Early Essays and Miscellanies*, p. 276

Till we have loved we have not imagined the heights of love.

Written September 28, 1843, in his *Journal*, vol. 1, p. 468

The light of the sun is but the shadow of love.

"Paradise (to be) Regained" in *Reform Papers*, p. 46

The heart is forever inexperienced.

A Week on the Concord and Merrimack Rivers, p. 262

The violence of love is as much to be dreaded as that of hate.

A Week on the Concord and Merrimack Rivers, p. 273

The obstacles which the heart meets with are like granite blocks which one alone can not move.

Written October 27, 1851, in his *Journal*, vol. 4, p. 155

I love men with the same distinction that I love woman—as if my friend were of some third sex—some other or stranger and still my friend.

Written May 5, 1846, in his *Journal*, vol. 2, p. 245

What is the singing of birds, or any natural sound, compared with the voice of one we love?

Written April 30, 1851, in his *Journal*, vol. 3, p. 211

My love must be as free
    As is the eagle's wing,
Hovering o'er land and sea
    And everything.

Untitled poem in *Collected Poems of Henry Thoreau*, p. 68

What avails it that another loves you, if he does not understand you? Such love is a curse.

A Week on the Concord and Merrimack Rivers, p. 278

Love.
We two that planets erst had been
Are now a double star,
And in the heavens may be seen,
Where that we fixed are.

Yet whirled with subtle power along,
Into new space we enter,
And evermore with spheral song
Revolve about one centre.

Written January 20, 1839, in his *Journal*, vol. 1, p. 66

To one we love we are related as to nature in the spring.
Our dreams are mutually intelligible. We take the census, and find that there is one.

Written April 30, 1851, in his *Journal*, vol. 3, p. 211

There is no remedy for love but to love more.

Written July 25, 1839, in his *Journal*, vol. 1, p. 81

Love is a thirst that is never slaked.

Written March 28, 1856, in his *Journal*, vol. VIII, p. 231

MANNERS

I often accuse my finest acquaintances of an immense
frivolity; for, while there are manners and compliments we do not meet, we do not teach one another the

lessons of honesty and sincerity that the brutes do, or of steadiness and solidity that the rocks do. The fault is commonly mutual, however; for we do not habitually demand any more of each other.

"Life without Principle" in *Reform Papers*, pp. 168–169

The man who thrusts his manners upon me does as if he were to insist on introducing me to his cabinet of curiosities, when I wished to see himself.

"Life without Principle" in *Reform Papers*, p. 175

For the most part we can only treat one another to our wit, our good manners and equanimity, and though we have eagles to give we demand of each other only coppers.

"Reform and the Reformers" in *Reform Papers*, p. 189

Much of our poetry has the very best manners, but no character.

A Week on the Concord and Merrimack Rivers, pp. 374–375

Nations are possessed with an insane ambition to perpetuate the memory of themselves by the amount of hammered stone they leave. What if equal pains were taken to smooth and polish their manners?

Walden, p. 57

The finest manners in the world are awkwardness & fatuity when contrasted with a finer intelligence.

Written February 16, 1851, in his *Journal*, vol. 3, p. 194

It is possible for a man wholly to disappear & be merged in his manners.

Written July 21, 1851, in his *Journal*, vol. 3, p. 322

To me there is something devilish in manners. The best manners is nakedness of manners.

Written January 31, 1852, in his *Journal*, vol. 4, p. 310

Excuse our hard and cold New England manners, lay it partly to the climate: granite and ice, you know, are our chief exports.

To Thomas Cholmondeley, November 8, 1855, in *The Correspondence of Henry David Thoreau*, p. 399

One man lies in his words and gets a bad reputation— another in his manners and enjoys a good one.

Written June 25, 1852, in his *Journal*, vol. 5, p. 145

My neighbor does not recover from his formal bow so soon as I do from the pleasure of meeting him.

Written February 16, 1851, in his *Journal*, vol. 3, p. 195

With many men their fine manners are a lie all over, a skim-coat or finish of falsehood. They are not brave enough to do without this sort of armor, which they wear night and day.

Written March 29, 1858, in his *Journal*, vol. X, p. 332

The vice of manners is that they are continually deserted by the character. They are castoff clothes or shells claiming the respect of the living creature.

Written February 16, 1851, in his *Journal*, vol. 3, p. 195

I have always found that what is called the best of manners are the worst, for they are simply the shell without the meat. They cover no life at all. . . . They are masks by the help of which the wearers ignore you and remain concealed themselves.

Written October 4, 1859, in his *Journal*, vol. XII, p. 370;
emended from manuscript Journal (MA 1302, The Morgan
Library & Museum, New York)

Men are very generally spoiled by being so civil and well disposed. You can have no profitable conversation with them they are so conciliatory—determined to agree with you.

Written July 21, 1851, in his *Journal*, vol. 3, p. 322

I would not have every man cultivated any more than I would have every acre of earth cultivated.

Written February 13, 1851, in his *Journal*, vol. 3, p. 192

NATURE

Where is the literature which gives expression to Nature?

"Walking" in *Excursions*, p. 208

I wish to speak a word for Nature, for absolute Freedom and Wildness, as contrasted with a Freedom and Culture merely civil,—to regard man as an inhabitant, or a part and parcel of Nature, rather than a member of society.

"Walking" in *Excursions*, p. 185

Flora of Northern United States.

Cornus canadensis, L.

Northern shore of Michigan, opposite Mackinaw.

coll. H. Mann.

FIG. 11. Flora collected by Horace Mann, Jr., when accompanying Thoreau to Minnesota in 1861. The Albert W. Bussewitz Collection at the Thoreau Institute at Walden Woods. Courtesy of the Walden Woods Project.

Once I was part and parcel of nature—now I am observant of her.

Written April 2, 1852, in his *Journal*, vol. 4, p. 416

I love to see that Nature is so rife with life that myriads can be afforded to be sacrificed and suffered to prey on one another; that tender organizations can be so serenely squashed out of existence like pulp,—tadpoles which herons gobble up, and tortoises and toads run over in the road; and that sometimes it has rained flesh and blood! With the liability to accident, we must see how little account is to be made of it.

Walden, p. 318

My pulse must beat with nature. After a hard day's work without a thought turning my very brain in to a mere tool, only in the quiet of evening do I so far recover my senses as to hear the cricket which in fact has been chirping all day. In my better hours I am conscious of the influx of a serene & unquestionable wisdom which partly unfits and if I yielded to it more rememberingly would wholly unfit me for what is called the active business of life—for that furnishes nothing on which the eye of reason can rest. What is that other kind of life to which I am thus continually allured?— which alone I love?

Written June 22, 1851, in his *Journal*, vol. 3, p. 274

There can be no very black melancholy to him who lives in the midst of Nature and has his senses still.

Walden, p. 131

We must go out and re-ally ourselves to Nature every day. We must take root, send out some little fibre at least, even every winter day. I am sensible that I am imbibing health when I open my mouth to the wind. Staying in the house breeds a sort of insanity always. Every house is in this sense a hospital. A night and a forenoon is as much confinement to those wards as I can stand. I am aware that I recover some sanity which I had lost almost the instant that I come abroad.

Written December 29, 1856, in his *Journal*, vol. IX, p. 200

We are wont to forget that the sun looks on our cultivated fields and on the prairies and forests without distinction. They all reflect and absorb his rays alike, and the former make but a small part of the glorious picture which he beholds in his daily course. In his view the earth is all equally cultivated like a garden.

Walden, p. 166

I am refreshed and expanded when the freight train rattles past me, and I smell the stores which go dispensing their odors all the way from Long Wharf to Lake Champlain, reminding me of foreign parts, of coral reefs, and Indian oceans, and tropical climes, and the extent of the globe.

Walden, p. 119

It is difficult to conceive of a region uninhabited by man. We habitually presume his presence and influence everywhere. And yet we have not seen pure Nature, unless we have seen her thus vast, and drear, and inhuman, though in the midst of cities.

The Maine Woods, p. 70

How important is a constant intercourse with nature and the contemplation of natural phenomenon to the preservation of moral & intellectual health.

Written May 6, 1851, in his *Journal*, vol. 3, p. 217

Nature always adopts the simplest modes which will accomplish her end.

"The Dispersion of Seeds" in *Faith in a Seed*, p. 25

I make it my business to extract from nature whatever nutriment she can furnish me though at the risk of endless iteration I milk the sky & the earth.

Written November 3, 1853, in his *Journal*, vol. 7, p. 140

I love nature partly *because* she is not man, but a retreat from him. None of his institutions control or pervade her. There a different kind of right prevails. In her midst I can be glad with an entire gladness. If this world was all man I could not stretch myself—I should lose all hope. He is constraint; she is freedom to me. He makes me wish for another world; she makes me content with this. None of the joy she supplies is subject to his rules & definitions. What he touches he taints. In thought he moralizes. One would think that no free joyful labor was possible to him.

Written January 3, 1853, in his *Journal*, vol. 5, p. 422

I feel slightly complimented when Nature condescends to make use of me without my knowledge as when I help scatter her seeds in my walk or carry burs and cockles on my clothes from field to field. I feel as though I had done something for the commonweal, and were entitled to board and lodging. I take such airs upon me as the boy who holds a horse for the circus company whom all the spectators envy.

Written February 6, 1841, in his *Journal*, vol. 1, p. 253

I have a room all to my self; it is Nature.

Written January 3, 1853, in his *Journal*, vol. 5, p. 422

Nature will bear the closest inspection; she invites us to lay our eye level with the smallest leaf, and take an insect view of its plain. She has no interstices; every part is full of life.

"Natural History of Massachusetts" in *Excursions*, p. 7

Nature would not appear so rich, the profusion so rich, if we knew a use for everything.

Written August 11, 1853, in his *Journal*, vol. 6, p. 297

When we can no longer ramble in the fields of Nature, we ramble in the fields of thought & literature. The old become readers. Our heads retain their strength when our legs have become weak.

Written after January 10, 1851, in his *Journal*, vol. 3, pp. 178–179

Books of natural history make the most cheerful winter reading. I read in Audubon with a thrill of delight, when the snow covers the ground, of the magnolia, and the Florida keys, and their warm sea breezes; of the fence-rail, and the cotton-tree, and the migrations of the rice-bird; of the breaking up of winter in Labrador, and the melting of the snow on the forks of the Missouri; and owe an accession of health to these reminiscences of luxuriant nature.

"Natural History of Massachusetts" in *Excursions*, p. 3

I should like to keep some book of natural history always by me as a sort of elixir—the reading of which would restore the tone of my system and secure me true and cheerful views of life.

Written December 31, 1841, in his *Journal*, vol. 1, p. 354

With man all is uncertainty. He does not confidently look forward to another spring. But examine the root of the savory-leaved aster, and you will find the new shoots, fair purple shoots, which are to curve upward and bear the next year's flowers, already grown half an inch or more in earth. Nature is confident.

Written October 12, 1858, in his *Journal*, vol. XI, pp. 206–207

Nature has left nothing to the mercy of man.

Written March 22, 1861, in his *Journal*, vol. XIV, p. 334

I walk out into a nature such as the old prophets and poets Menu, Moses, Homer, Chaucer, walked in.

"Walking" in *Excursions*, p. 192

Left to herself, nature is always more or less civilized, and delights in a certain refinement; but where the axe has encroached upon the edge of the forest, the dead and unsightly limbs of the pine, which she had concealed with green banks of verdure, are exposed to sight.

"A Walk to Wachusett" in *Excursions*, p. 36

I do not know where to find in any literature whether ancient or modern—any adequate account of that Nature with which I am acquainted. Mythology comes nearest to it of any.

Written after February 9, 1851, in his *Journal*, vol. 3, p. 186

For my part, I feel, that with regard to Nature, I live a sort of border life, on the confines of a world, into which I make occasional and transient forays only, and my patriotism and allegiance to the state into whose territories I seem to retreat are those of a moss-trooper. Unto a life which I call natural I would gladly follow even a will o' the wisp through bogs and sloughs unimaginable.

"Walking" in *Excursions*, p. 217

Nature was here something savage and awful, though beautiful. I looked with awe at the ground I trod on, to see what the Powers had made there, the form and fashion and material of their work. This was that Earth of which we have heard, made out of Chaos and Old Night. Here was no man's garden, but the unhandselled globe. It was not lawn, nor pasture, nor mead, nor woodland, nor lea, nor arable, nor waste-land. It was the fresh and natural surface of the planet Earth, as it was made forever and ever,—to be the dwelling of man, we say,—so Nature made it, and man may use it if he can. Man was not to be associated with it. It was Matter, vast, terrific,—not his Mother Earth that we have heard of, not for him to tread on, or be buried in,—no, it were being too familiar even to let his bones lie there—the home this of Necessity and Fate. There was there felt the presence of a force not bound to be kind to man. It was a place for heathenism and superstitious rites,—to be inhabited by men nearer of kin to the rocks and to wild animals than we. We walked over it with a certain awe, stopping from time to time to pick the blueberries which grew there, and had a smart and spicy taste. Perchance where *our* wild pines stand, and leaves lie on their forest floor in Concord, there were once reapers, and husbandmen planted grain; but here not even the surface had been scarred by man, but it was a specimen of what God saw fit to make this world. What is it to be admitted to a museum, to see a myriad of particular things, compared with being shown some star's surface, some hard matter in its home! I stand in awe of my body, this matter to which I am bound has become so strange to me. I fear not spirits, ghosts, of which I am one,—*that* my body might,—but I fear bodies, I tremble to meet them. What is this Titan that has possession of me? Talk of mysteries!—Think of our life in nature,—daily to be shown matter, to come in contact with it,—rocks, trees, wind on our cheeks! the *solid* earth! the *actual* world! the *common sense*! *Contact*! *Contact*! *Who* are we? *where* are we?

The Maine Woods, pp. 70–71

There are two worlds—the post-office & Nature. I know them both.

Written January 3, 1853, in his *Journal*, vol. 5, p. 422

Ah dear nature—the mere remembrance, after a short forgetfulness, of the pine woods! I come to it as a hungry man to a crust of bread.

Written December 12, 1851, in his *Journal*, vol. 4, p. 201

Man and his affairs, church and state—and school, trade and commerce, and manufactures and agriculture,— even politics, the most alarming of them all,—I am pleased to see how little space they occupy in the landscape.

"Walking" in *Excursions*, p. 191

What is nature unless there is an eventful human life passing within her?

Written November 2, 1853, in his *Journal*, vol. 7, p. 135

Sophia says, bringing company into my sanctum, by way of apology, that I regard the dust on my furniture like the bloom on fruits, not to be swept off. Which reminds me that the bloom on fruits and stems is the only dust which settles on Nature's furniture.

Written September 15, 1856, in his *Journal*, vol. IX, p. 83

In the forenoon commonly I see nature only through a window—in the afternoon my study or apartment in which I sit is a vale.

Written October 8, 1851, in his *Journal*, vol. 4, p. 133

If I am too cold for human friendship, I trust I shall not soon be too cold for natural influences. It appears to be a law that you cannot have a deep sympathy with both man & nature. Those qualities which bring you near to the one estrange you from the other.

Written April 11, 1852, in his *Journal*, vol. 4, p. 435

I sit in my boat on Walden playing the flute this evening and see the perch, which I seem to have charmed, hovering around me, and the moon travelling over the ribbed bottom, and feel that nothing but the wildest imagination can conceive of the manner of life we are living. Nature is a wizard. The Concord nights are stranger than the Arabian nights.

Written May 27, 1841, in his *Journal*, vol. 1, p. 311

There are odors enough in nature to remind you of everything if you had lost every sense but smell.

Written May 6, 1852, in his *Journal*, vol. 5, p. 34

How nicely is Nature adjusted! The least disturbance of her equilibrium is betrayed and corrects itself. As I looked down on the surface of the brook, I was surprised to see a leaf floating, as I thought, up the stream, but I was mistaken. The motion of a particle of dust on the surface of any brook far inland shows which way the earth declines toward the sea, which way lies the constantly descending route, and the only one.

Written December 22, 1859, in his *Journal*, vol. XIII, p. 38

We, too, are out, obeying the same law with all nature. Not less important are the observers of the birds than the birds themselves.

Written March 20, 1858, in his *Journal*, vol. X, p. 315

When I find a new and rare plant in Concord I seem to think it has but just sprung up here,—that it is, and not I am, the newcomer,—while it has grown here for ages before I was born.

Written September 2, 1856, in his *Journal*, vol. IX, p. 56

If any part of nature excites our pity, it is for ourselves we grieve, for there is eternal health and beauty.

Written December 11, 1855, in his *Journal*, vol. VIII, p. 44

How many of our troubles are house-bred!

Written March 28, 1858, in his *Journal*, vol. X, p. 326

Some of our richest days are those in which no sun shines outwardly, but so much the more a sun shines inwardly.

Written November 16, 1850, in his *Journal*, vol. 3, p. 142

Why do precisely these objects which we behold make a world?

Walden, p. 225

The perch swallows the grub-worm, the pickerel swallows the perch, and the fisherman swallows the pickerel; and so all the chinks in the scale of being are filled.

Walden, p. 284

Nature invites fire to sweep her floors for purification.

Written May 5, 1852, in his *Journal*, vol. 5, p. 26

The Maker of this earth but patented a leaf.

Walden, p. 308

The man of Science who is not seeking for expression but for a fact to be expressed merely studies nature as a dead language. I pray for such inward experience as will make nature significant.

Written May 10, 1853, in his *Journal*, vol. 6, p. 105

How happens it that we reverence the stones which fall from another planet, and not the stones which belong to this,—another globe, not this,—heaven, and not earth? Are not the stones in Hodge's wall as good as the aerolite at Mecca? Is not our broad back-door-stone as good as any corner-stone in heaven?

Written August 30, 1856, in his *Journal*, vol. IX, p. 45

Let men tread gently through nature.

Written April 26, 1857, in his *Journal*, vol. IX, p. 344

Nature is a greater and more perfect art, the art of God.

A Week on the Concord and Merrimack Rivers, p. 318

How rarely a man's love for nature becomes a ruling principle with him, like a youth's affection for a maiden, but more enduring! All nature is my bride. That nature which to one is a stark and ghastly solitude is a sweet, tender, and genial society to another.

Written April 23, 1857, in his *Journal*, vol. IX, p. 337

NEWS, NEWSPAPERS, AND THE PRESS

Hardly a man takes a half-hour's nap after dinner, but when he wakes he holds up his head and asks, "What's the news?" as if the rest of mankind had stood his sentinels.

Walden, p. 93

What have we to do with petty rumbling news? We have our own great affairs.

To Lidian Emerson, June 20, 1843, in *The Correspondence of Henry David Thoreau*, p. 120

We rarely meet a man who can tell us any news which he has not read in a newspaper, or been told by his neighbor; and, for the most part, the only difference between us and our fellow is, that he has seen the newspaper, or been out to tea, and we have not.

"Life without Principle" in *Reform Papers*, p. 169

I do not know but it is too much to read one newspaper a week. I have tried it recently, and for so long it seems to me that I have not dwelt in my native region.

"Life without Principle" in *Reform Papers*, p. 169

The newspapers are the ruling power. What Congress does is an after-clap.

Written November 17, 1850, in his *Journal*, vol. 3, p. 144

The news we hear, for the most part, is not news to our genius. It is the stalest repetition.

"Life without Principle" in *Reform Papers*, p. 170

When I have taken up this paper or the Boston *Times* with my cuffs turned up I have heard the gurgling of the sewer through every column—I have felt that I was handling a paper picked out of the public sewers—a leaf from the gospel of the gambling house—the groggery & the brothel—harmonizing with the gospel of the Merchant's exchange.

Written April 26, 1851, in his *Journal*, vol. 3, p. 209

The last new journal thinks that it is very liberal, nay, bold, but it dares not publish a child's thought on important subjects, such as life and death and good books. It requires the sanction of the divines just as surely as the tamest journal does. If it had been published at the time of the famous dispute between Christ and the doctors, it would have published only the opinions of the doctors and suppressed Christ's.

Written March 2, 1858, in his *Journal*, vol. X, pp. 289–290

I have no time to read newspapers. If you chance to live & move and have your being in that thin stratum in which the events which make the news transpire— thinner than the paper on which it is printed—then those things will fill the world for you—but if you soar above or dive below that plain you cannot remember nor be reminded of them.

Written April 3, 1853, in his *Journal*, vol. 6, pp. 65–66

The Church has much improved within a few years; but the Press is almost, without exception, corrupt. I believe that, in this country, the press exerts a greater and a more pernicious influence than the Church did in its worst period.

"Slavery in Massachusetts" in *Reform Papers*, p. 99

Look at your editors of popular magazines. I have dealt with two or three the most liberal of them. They are afraid to print a *whole* sentence, a *sound* sentence, a free-spoken sentence.

Written November 16, 1858, in his *Journal*, vol. XI, p. 325; emended from manuscript Journal (MA 1302, The Morgan Library & Museum, New York)

The editor has . . . no more right to omit a sentiment than to insert one, or put words into my mouth. I do not ask anybody to adopt my opinions, but I do expect that when they ask for them to print, they will print them, or obtain my consent to their alteration or omission.

To James Russell Lowell, editor of the *Atlantic Monthly*, on the omission of a sentence from Thoreau's essay "Chesuncook," June 22, 1858, in *The Correspondence of Henry David Thoreau*, p. 515

I believe that in this country the press exerts a greater and a more pernicious influence than the Church. We are not a religious people but we are a nation of politicians. We do not much care for—we do not read the Bible—but we do care for & we do read the newspaper. It is a bible which we read every morning & every afternoon standing & sitting—riding & walking. It is a bible which lies on every table & counter, which every man carries in his pocket, which the mail & thousands of missionaries are continuously dispersing. It is the only book which America has printed and is capable of exerting an almost inconceivable influence for good or for bad.

Written after 19 April 1851, in his *Journal*, vol. 3, p. 206

I repeat the testimony of many an intelligent traveller as well as my own convictions when I say that probably no country was ever ruled by so mean a class of tyrants as are the editors of the periodical press in *this* country.

. . .—the *free* men of New England have only to—refrain from purchasing & reading these sheets have only to withhold their cents to kill a score of them at once.

Written after 19 April 1851, in his *Journal*, vol. 3, pp. 206–207

I heard a fairer news than the journals ever print. It told of things worthy to hear, and worthy of the electric fluid to carry the news of, not of the price of cotton and flour, but it hinted at the price of the world itself and of things which are priceless, of absolute truth and beauty.

A Week on the Concord and Merrimack Rivers, p. 177

We are eager to tunnel under the Atlantic and bring the old world some weeks nearer to the new; but perchance the first news that will leak through into the broad, flapping American ear will be that the Princess Adelaide has the whooping cough.

Walden, p. 52

To a philosopher all *news*, as it is called, is gossip, and they who edit and read it are old women over their tea.

Walden, p. 94

I am sure that I never read any memorable news in a newspaper. If we read of one man robbed, or murdered, or killed by accident, or one house burned, or one vessel wrecked, or one steamboat blown up, or one cow run over on the Western Railroad, or one mad dog killed, or one lot of grasshoppers in the winter,—we never need read of another. One is enough. If you are acquainted with the principle, what do you care for a myriad instances and applications?

Walden, p. 94

What news! How much more important to know what that is which was never old!

Walden, p. 95

Every day or two I strolled to the village to hear some of the gossip which is incessantly going on there, circulating either from mouth to mouth, or from newspaper to newspaper, and which, taken in homeopathic doses, was really as refreshing in its way as the rustle of leaves and the peeping of frogs.

Walden, p. 167

Blessed are they who never read a newspaper, for they shall see Nature, and through her, God.

To Parker Pillsbury, April 10, 1861, in *The Correspondence of Henry David Thoreau*, p. 611

It is surprising what a tissue of trifles and crudities make the daily news. For one event of interest there are nine hundred and ninety-nine insignificant, but about the same stress is laid on the last as on the first.

Written August 9, 1858, in his *Journal*, vol. XI, p. 87

As for the herd of newspapers, I do not chance to know *one in the country* that will deliberately print anything that will ultimately and permanently reduce the number of its subscribers.

Written October 19, 1859, in his *Journal*, vol. XII, p. 406; emended from manuscript Journal (MA 1302, The Morgan Library & Museum, New York)

OBSERVATION

What I see is mine.

A Week on the Concord and Merrimack Rivers, p. 350

You might say of a philosopher that he was in this world as a spectator.

Written after October 31, 1850, in his *Journal*, vol. 3, p. 130

A man may walk abroad & no more see the sky than if he walked under a shed.

Written August 21, 1851, in his *Journal*, vol. 4, p. 6

From the right point of view, every storm and every drop in it is a rainbow.

Written December 11, 1855, in his *Journal*, vol. VIII, pp. 44–45

I perceive that more or other things are seen in the reflection than in the substance.

Written December 9, 1856, in his *Journal*, vol. IX, p. 172

The question is not what you look at but how you look & whether you see.

Written August 5, 1851, in his *Journal*, vol. 3, pp. 354–355

I am always struck by the centrality of the observer's position. He always stands fronting the middle of the arch & does not suspect at first that a thousand observers on a thousand hills behold the sunset sky from equally favorable positions.

Written July 10, 1851, in his *Journal*, vol. 3, p. 298

I have the habit of attention to such excess that my senses get no rest but suffer from a constant strain. Be not preoccupied with looking. Go not to the object. Let it come to you.

Written September 13, 1852, in his *Journal*, vol. 5, p. 344

It is impossible for the same person to see things from the poet's point of view and that of the man of science.

Written February 18, 1852, in his *Journal*, vol. 4, p. 356

That virtue we appreciate is as much ours as another's. We see so much only as we possess.

Written June 22, 1839, in his *Journal*, vol. 1, p. 74

We must look for a long time before we can see.

"Natural History of Massachusetts" in *Excursions*, p. 28

When I have found myself ever looking down & confining my gaze to the flowers I have thought it might be well to get into the habit of observing the clouds as a corrective—But ha! that study would be just as bad—What I need is not to look at all but a true sauntering of the eye.

Written September 13, 1852, in his *Journal*, vol. 5, p. 344

All distant landscapes seen from hill tops are veritable pictures which will be found to have no actual existence to him who travels to them.

Written May 1, 1851, in his *Journal*, vol. 3, p. 212

I must let my senses wander as my thoughts—my eyes see without looking. Carlyle said that how to observe was to look but I say that it is rather to see & the more you look the less you will observe.

Written September 13, 1852, in his *Journal*, vol. 5, pp. 343–344

From the mountains we do not discern our native hills, but from our native hills we look out easily to the far blue mountains which seem to preside over them. As I look north westward to that summit from a Concord cornfield how little can I realize all the life that is passing between me & it—the retired up country farm houses—the lonely mills—wooded vales—wild rocky pastures—and new clearings on stark mountain sides & rivers gurgling through primitive woods! All these and how much more I *overlook*. I see the very peak—there can be no mistake—but how much I do not see that is between me & it—how much I over-look!

Written September 27, 1852, in his *Journal*, vol. 5, p. 357

As you *see* so at length will you *say*.

Written November 1, 1851, in his *Journal*, vol. 4, p. 158

A man receives only what he is ready to receive, whether physically or intellectually or morally, as animals conceive at certain seasons their kind only. We hear and apprehend only what we already half know. If there is something that does not concern me, which is out of my line, which by experience or by genius my attention is not drawn to, however novel and remarkable it may be, if it is spoken, we hear it not, if it is written, we read it not, or if we read it, it does not detain us. Every man thus *tracks himself* through life, in all his hearing and reading and observation and travelling. His observations make a chain. The phenomenon or fact that cannot in any wise be linked with the rest which he has observed, he does not observe. By and by we may be ready to receive what we cannot receive now.

Written January 5, 1860, in his *Journal*, vol. XIII, p. 77

You cannot see anything until you are clear of it.

Written November 1, 1858, in his *Journal*, vol. XI, p. 273

Many an object is not seen, though it falls within the range of our visual ray, because it does not come within the range of our intellectual ray, *i.e.*, we are not looking for it. So, in the largest sense, we find only the world we look for.

Written July 2, 185, in his *Journal*, vol. IX, p. 466

We cannot see anything unless we are possessed with the idea of it, and then we can hardly see anything else.

Written November 4, 1858, in his *Journal*, vol. XI, p. 285

A man *sees* only what concerns him. A botanist absorbed in the pursuit of grasses does not distinguish the grandest pasture oaks. He as it were tramples down oaks unwittingly in his walks.

Written September 9, 1858, in his *Journal*, vol. XI, p. 153; emended from manuscript Journal (MA 1302, The Morgan Library & Museum, New York)

Sometimes I would rather get a transient glimpse or side view of a thing than stand fronting to it,—as these polypodies. The object I caught a glimpse of as I went by haunts my thoughts a long time, is infinitely suggestive, and I do not care to front it and scrutinize it, for I know that the thing that really concerns me is not there, but in my relation to that.

Written November 5, 1857, in his *Journal*, vol. X, p. 164

Not only different objects are presented to our attention at different seasons of the year, but we are in a frame of body and of mind to appreciate different objects at different seasons. I see one thing when it is cold and another when it is warm.

Written November 17, 1858, in his *Journal*, vol. XI, p. 330

Flowers were made to be seen not overlooked.

Written June 15, 1852, in his *Journal*, vol. 5, p. 96

If we can listen we shall hear.

Written January 26, 1841, in his *Journal*, vol. 1, p. 233

There was a remarkable sunset.... The sunset sky reached quite from west to east, and it was the most varied in its forms and colors of any that I remember to have seen. At one time the clouds were most softly and delicately rippled, like the ripple-marks on sand. But it was hard for me to see its beauty then, when my mind was filled with Captain Brown. So great a wrong as his fate implied overshadowed all the beauty in the world.

Written November 12, 1859, in his *Journal*, vol. XII, p. 443

A fact stated barely is dry. It must be the vehicle of some humanity in order to interest us.... A man has not seen a thing who has not felt it.

Written February 23, 1860, in his *Journal*, vol. XIII, p. 160

OPINION AND ADVICE

Public opinion is a weak tyrant compared with our own private opinion. What a man thinks of himself, that it is which determines, or rather indicates, his fate.

Walden, p. 7

Let us settle ourselves, and work and wedge our feet downward through the mud and slush of opinion, and prejudice, and tradition, and delusion, and appearance, that alluvion which covers the globe.

Walden, p. 97

There is a stronger desire to be respectable to one's neighbors than to one's self.

Written winter 1845–1846, in his *Journal*, vol. 2, p. 220

He unconsciously tells his biography as he proceeds, and we see him early and earnestly deliberating on these subjects, and wisely and bravely, without counsel or consent of any, occupying a ground at first, from which the varying tides of public opinion cannot drive him.

"Wendell Phillips Before Concord Lyceum" in *Reform Papers*, p. 60

What is the value of his esteem who does not justly esteem another?

Written February 15, 1851, in his *Journal*, vol. 3, p. 193

I sometimes despair of getting anything quite simple and honest done in this world by the help of men. They would have to be passed through a powerful press first, to squeeze their old notions out of them, so that they would not soon get upon their legs again, and then there would be some one in the company with a maggot in his head, hatched from an egg deposited there nobody knows when, for not even fire kills these things, and you would have lost your labor.

Walden, p. 25

There are few men who do not love better to give advice than to give assistance.

Written June 4, 1850, in his *Journal*, vol. 3, p. 80

I have lived some thirty years on this planet, and I have yet to hear the first syllable of valuable or even earnest advice from my seniors. They have told me nothing, and probably cannot tell me any thing to the purpose. Here is life, an experiment to a great extent untried by me; but it does not avail me that they have tried it. If I have any experience which I think valuable, I am sure to reflect that this my Mentors said nothing about.

Walden, p. 9

Practically, the old have no very important advice to give the young, their own experience has been so partial, and their lives have been such miserable failures, for private reasons, as they must believe; and it may be that they have some faith left which belies that experience, and they are only less young than they were.

Walden, p. 9

I remembered the story of a conceited fellow, who, in fine clothes, was wont to lounge about the village once, giving advice to workmen. Venturing one day to substitute deeds for words, he turned up his cuffs, seized a plasterer's board, and having loaded his trowel without mishap, with a complacent look toward the lathing overhead, made a bold gesture thitherward; and straightway, to his complete discomfiture, received the whole contents in his ruffled bosom.

Walden, p. 245

It is remarkable that among all the preachers there are so few moral teachers. The prophets are employed in excusing the ways of men. Most reverend seniors, the *illuminati* of the age, tell me, with a gracious, reminiscent smile, betwixt an aspiration and a shudder, not to be too tender about these things,—to lump all that, that is, make a lump of gold of it. The highest advice I have heard on these subjects was grovelling.

"Life without Principle" in *Reform Papers*, pp. 166–167

The preacher's standard of morality is no higher than that of his audience. He studies to conciliate his hearers & never to offend them.

Written February 26, 1852, in his *Journal*, vol. 4, p. 365

And as for advice, the information floating in the atmosphere of society is as evanescent and unserviceable to him as gossamer for clubs of Hercules.

On social reformer John Adolphus Etzler in "Paradise (to be) Regained" in *Reform Papers*, p. 41

I have never known advice to be of use but in trivial and transient matters.

A Week on the Concord and Merrimack Rivers, p. 283

They, methinks, are poor stuff and creatures of a miserable fate who can be advised and persuaded in very important steps.

Written December 27, 1858, in his *Journal*, vol. XI, p. 379

Stuff a cold and starve a cold are but two ways. They are the two practices both always in full blast. Yet you must take advice of the one school as if there was no other.

A Week on the Concord and Merrimack Rivers, p. 256

Others give their advice, he gives his sympathy also.

On Thomas Carlyle in "Thomas Carlyle and His Works" in *Early Essays and Miscellanies*, p. 234

Why should we ever go abroad, even across the way, to ask a neighbor's advice? There is a nearer neighbor within is incessantly telling us how we should behave. But we wait for the neighbor without to tell us of some false, easier way.

To H.G.O. Blake, December 19, 1854, in *The Correspondence of Henry David Thoreau*, p. 355; emended from facsimile of manuscript letter (manuscript location unknown)

He has a hand to shake and to be shaken, and takes a sturdy and unquestionable interest in you, as if he had assumed the care of you, but if you will break your neck, he will even give you the best advice as to the method.

"The Landlord" in *Excursions*, p. 52

When once we thus fall behind ourselves, there is no accounting for the obstacles which rise up in our path, and no one is so wise as to advise, and no one so powerful as to aid us while we abide on that ground.

> To H.G.O. Blake, May 2, 1848, in *The Correspondence of Henry David Thoreau*, p. 221

Do not waste any reverence on my attitude. I merely manage to sit up where I have dropped. I am sure that my acquaintances mistake me. They ask my advice on high matters, but they do not know even how poorly on 't I am for hats and shoes. I have hardly a shift. Just as shabby as I am in my outward apparel, ay, and more lamentably shabby, am I in my inward substance.

> To H.G.O. Blake, August 9, 1850, in *The Correspondence of Henry David Thoreau*, p. 265

If you would convince a man that he does wrong, do right. But do not care to convince him. Men will believe what they see. Let them see.

> To H.G.O. Blake, March 27, 1848, in *Familiar Letters*, p. 163

I beg that the Class will not consider me an object of charity, and if any of them are in want of pecuniary assistance, and will make known their case to me, I will engage to give them some advice of more worth than money.

> To Henry Williams, Jr., secretary of Thoreau's Harvard class of 1837, September 30, 1847, in *The Correspondence of Henry David Thoreau*, p. 186

I would thus from time to time take advice of the birds.

> Written May 12, 1857, in his *Journal*, vol. IX, p. 364

I doubt whether one can give or receive any very pertinent advice.

Written December 27, 1858, in his *Journal*, vol. XI, p. 379

Show me a man who consults his genius, and you have shown me a man who cannot be advised.

Written December 27, 1858, in his *Journal*, vol. XI, p. 379

You may think this harsh advice, but, believe me, it is sincere.

To Samuel Ripley Bartlett, recommending that Bartlett not publish his poem "The Concord Fight," January 19, 1860, in *The Correspondence of Henry David Thoreau*, p. 572

Let us not send to the city for aught more essential than our broadcloths and groceries, or, if we read the opinions of the city, let us entertain opinions of our own.

"Slavery in Massachusetts" in *Reform Papers*, p. 99

What every body echoes or in silence passes by as true to-day may turn out to be a falsehood to-morrow, mere smoke of opinion, which some had trusted for a cloud that would sprinkle fertilizing rain on their fields.

Walden, p. 8

Be fast rooted withal in your native soil of originality and independence, your virgin mould of unexhausted strength and fertility—Nor suffer yourself ever to be transplanted again into the foreign and ungenial regions of tradition and conformity, or the lean and sandy soils of public opinion.

"Reform and the Reformers" in *Reform Papers*, p. 191

As to how to preserve potatoes from rotting, your opinion may change from year to year, but as to how to preserve your soul from rotting, I have nothing to learn but something to practice.

To H.G.O. Blake, February 27, 1853, in *The Correspondence of Henry David Thoreau*, p. 297

There are very few whose opinion I value.

To George Thatcher, December 26, 1848, in *The Correspondence of Henry David Thoreau*, p. 234

Always you have to contend with the stupidity of men. It is like a stiff soil, a hard-pan. If you go deeper than usual, you are sure to meet with a pan made harder even by the superficial cultivation. The stupid you have always with you.

Written February 13, 1860, in his *Journal*, vol. XIII, p. 145

They who merely have a talent for affairs are forward to express their opinions.

A Roman soldier sits there to decide upon the righteousness of Christ.

Written August 19, 1851, in his *Journal*, vol. 3, p. 378

All a man's strength & all his weakness go to make up the authority of any particular opinion which he may utter. He is strong or weak with all his strength & weakness combined.

Written February 16, 1854, in his *Journal*, vol. 8, p. 5

PAST, PRESENT, AND FUTURE

In any weather, at any hour of the day or night, I have been anxious to improve the nick of time, and notch it on my stick too; to stand on the meeting of two eternities, the past and future, which is precisely the present moment; to toe that line.

Walden, p. 17

He is blessed over all mortals who loses no moment of the passing life in remembering the past.

"Walking" in *Excursions,* p. 220

I must live above all in the present.

Written January 7, 1851, in his *Journal,* vol. 3, p. 174

I *live* in the *present.* I only remember the past—and anticipate the future.

To H.G.O. Blake, March 27, 1848, in *The Correspondence of Henry David Thoreau,* p. 216

We should be blessed if we lived in the present always, and took advantage of every accident that befell us, like the grass which confesses the influence of the slightest dew that falls on it; and did not spend our time in atoning for the neglect of past opportunities, which we call doing our duty. We loiter in winter while it is already spring.

Walden, p. 314

I wish to be translated to the future & look at my work as it were at a structure on the plain, to observe what portions have crumbled under the influence of the elements.

Written January 1, 1852, in his *Journal*, vol. 4, p. 235

Hope and the future for me are not in lawns and cultivated fields, not in towns and cities, but in the impervious and quaking swamps.

"Walking" in *Excursions*, p. 204

The prospect of the young is forward and unbounded, mingling the future with the present.

A Week on the Concord and Merrimack Rivers, p. 133

The revelations of nature are infinitely glorious & cheering—hinting to us of a remote future—of possibilities untold.

Written May 21, 1851, in his *Journal*, vol. 3, p. 229

And do we live but in the present? How broad a line is that?

A Week on the Concord and Merrimack Rivers, p. 153

All questions rely on the present for their solution. Time measures nothing but itself.

A Week on the Concord and Merrimack Rivers, p. 312

We go eastward to realize history, and study the works of art and literature, retracing the steps of the race,—

we go westward as into the future, with a spirit of enterprise and adventure.

"Walking" in *Excursions*, p. 196

The past is the canvass on which our idea is painted,— the dim prospectus of our future field. We are dreaming of what we are to do.

"The Service" in *Reform Papers*, p. 17

It would be no reproach to a philosopher, that he knew the future better than the past, or even than the present. It is better worth knowing.

"Thomas Carlyle and His Works" in *Early Essays and Miscellanies*, p. 256

The future is worth expecting.

Written March 21, 1853, in his *Journal*, vol. 6, p. 22

We believe that the possibility of the future far exceeds the accomplishment of the past. We review the past with the common sense but we anticipate the future with transcendental senses.

Written June 7, 1851, in his *Journal*, vol. 3, p. 245

POSSESSIONS

A lady once offered me a mat, but as I had no room to spare within the house, nor time to spare within or without to shake it, I declined it, preferring to wipe my feet on the sod before my door. It is best to avoid the beginnings of evil.

Walden, p. 67

I have as much property as I can command and use.

Written January 26, 1841, in his *Journal*, vol. 1, p. 232

FIG. 12. John Thoreau & Co. Pencil Box. The Walden Woods Project Collection at the Thoreau Institute at Walden Woods. Courtesy of the Walden Woods Project.

I had three pieces of limestone on my desk, but I was terrified to find that they required to be dusted daily, when the furniture of my mind was all undusted still, and threw them out the window in disgust.

Walden, p. 36

I am amused to see from my window here how busily man has divided and staked off his dominion. God must smile at his puny fences running hither and thither everywhere over the land.

Written February 20, 1842, in his *Journal*, vol. 1, p. 365

I bought me a spy-glass some weeks since. I buy but few things and those not till long after I began to want them so that when I do get them I am prepared to make a perfect use of them and extract their whole sweet.

Written April 10, 1854, in his *Journal*, vol. 8, p. 61

The better part of the man is soon ploughed into the soil for compost. By a seeming fate, commonly called necessity, they are employed, as it says in an old book, laying up treasures which moth and rust will corrupt and thieves break through and steal. It is a fool's life, as they will find when they get to the end of it, if not before.

Walden, p. 5

The assessors called me into their office this year and said they wished to get an inventory of my property; asked if I had any real estate. No. Any notes at interest or railroad shares? No. Any taxable property? None that I knew of. "I own a boat," I said; and one of them thought that that might come under the head of a pleasure carriage, which is taxable.

Written November 30, 1855, in his *Journal*, vol. VIII, pp. 36–37

If you mean by hard times, times not when there is no bread, but when there is no cake, I have no sympathy with you.

Written January 28, 1852, in his *Journal*, vol. 4, p. 298

It is glorious to consider how independent man is of all enervating luxuries; and the poorer he is in respect to them, the richer he is.

Written November 22, 1860, in his *Journal*, vol. XIV, p. 259

I know one or two families, at least, in this town, who, for nearly a generation, have been wishing to sell their houses in the outskirts and move into the village, but have not been able to accomplish it, and only death will set them free.

Walden, p. 34

POVERTY AND WEALTH

I am never rich in money, and I am never meanly poor.

A Week on the Concord and Merrimack Rivers, p. 293

Let me see no other conflict but with prosperity.

Written June 25, 1840, in his *Journal*, vol. 1, p. 142

When my eye ranges over some 30 miles of this globe's surface—an eminence—green & waving with sky and mountains to bound it—I am richer than Croesus.

Written after May 12, 1850, in his *Journal*, vol. 3, p. 72

Who will not confess that the necessity to get money has helped to ripen some of his schemes?

Written February 6, 1852, in his *Journal*, vol. 4, p. 331

Merely to come into the world the heir of a fortune is not to be born, but to be still-born, rather.

"Life without Principle" in *Reform Papers*, p. 160

Just in proportion to the outward poverty is the inward wealth.

Written November 13, 1851, in his *Journal*, vol. 4, p. 184

Absolutely speaking, the more money, the less virtue; for money comes between a man and his objects, and obtains them for him; and it was certainly no great virtue to obtain it. It puts to rest many questions which he would otherwise be taxed to answer; while the only new question which it puts is the hard but superfluous one, how to spend it.

"Resistance to Civil Government" in *Reform Papers*, p. 77

A man is rich in proportion to the number of things which he can afford to let alone.

Walden, p. 82

There is a reptile in the throat of the greedy man always thirsting & famishing. It is not his own natural hunger & thirst which he satisfies.

Written September 2, 1851, in his *Journal*, vol. 4, p. 30

Money is not required to buy one necessary of the soul.

Walden, p. 329

You cannot serve two masters. It requires more than a day's devotion to know and to possess the wealth of a day.

"Life without Principle" in *Reform Papers*, p. 169

Poverty was her lot, but she possessed those virtues without which the rich are but poor.

From Thoreau's obituary for Anna Jones in *Early Essays and Miscellanies*, p. 121

You speak of poverty and dependence. Who are poor and dependent? Who are rich and independent? When was it that men agreed to respect the appearance and not the reality?

To H.G.O. Blake, April 3, 1850, in *The Correspondence of Henry David Thoreau*, p. 256

I should like not to exchange *any* of my life for money.

To H.G.O. Blake, December 31, 1856, in *The Correspondence of Henry David Thoreau*, p. 461

The problem of life becomes one cannot say by how many degrees more complicated as our material wealth is increased, whether that needle they tell of was a gateway or not,—since the problem is not merely nor mainly to get life for our bodies, but by this or a similar discipline to get life for our souls; by cultivating the lowland farm on right principles, that is with this view, to turn it into an upland farm. You have so many more talents to account for. If I accomplish as much more in spiritual work as I am richer in worldly goods, then I am just as worthy, or worth just as much as I was before, and no more.

> To H.G.O. Blake, February 27, 1853, in *The Correspondence of Henry David Thoreau*, p. 297

O how I laugh when I think of my vague indefinite riches. No run on my bank can drain it—for my wealth is not possession but enjoyment.

> To H.G.O. Blake, December 6, 1856, in *The Correspondence of Henry David Thoreau*, p. 444

I am grateful for what I am & have. My thanksgiving is perpetual. It is surprising how contented one can be with nothing definite—only a sense of existence.

> To H.G.O. Blake, December 6, 1856, in *The Correspondence of Henry David Thoreau*, p. 444

Again and again I congratulate myself on my so-called poverty. I was almost disappointed yesterday to find thirty dollars in my desk which I did not know that I possessed, though now I should be sorry to lose it.

> Written February 8, 1857, in his *Journal*, vol. IX, pp. 245–246

Superfluous wealth can buy superfluities only.

> *Walden*, p. 329

The best thing a man can do for his culture when he is rich is to endeavor to carry out those schemes which he entertained when he was poor.

> "Resistance to Civil Government" in *Reform Papers*, p. 77

If you wish to give a man a sense of poverty, give him a thousand dollars. The next hundred dollars he gets will not be worth more than ten that he used to get. Have pity on him; withhold your gifts.

In my experience I have found nothing so truly impoverishing as what is called wealth, *i.e.* the command of greater means than you had before possessed, though comparatively few and slight still, for you thus inevitably acquire a more expensive habit of living, and even the very same necessaries and comforts cost you more than they once did. Instead of gaining, you have lost some independence, and if your income should be suddenly lessened, you would find yourself poor, though possessed of the same means which once made you rich.

Men's minds run so much on work and money that the mass instantly associate all literary labor with a pecuniary reward. They are mainly curious to know how much money the lecturer or author gets for his work. They think that the naturalist takes so much pains to collect plants or animals because he is paid for it. An Irishman who saw me in the fields making a minute in my note-book took it for granted that I was casting up my wages and actually inquired what they came to, as if he had never dreamed of any other use for writing. I might have quoted to him that the wages of sin are death, as the most pertinent answer.

The less you get, the happier and richer you are.

Written November 28, 1860, in his *Journal*, vol. XIV, p. 277

Truly this is a world of vain delights. We think that men have a substratum of common sense but sometimes are peculiarly frivolous. But consider what a value is seriously and permanently attached to gold and so-called precious stones almost universally. Day and night, summer and winter, sick or well, in war and in peace, men speak of and believe in gold as a great treasure. . . . Men seriously and, if possible, religiously believe in and worship gold.

Written October 13, 1860, in his *Journal*, vol. XIV, p. 118

It is foolish for a man to accumulate material wealth chiefly, houses and land. Our stock in life, our real estate, is that amount of thought which we have had, which we have thought out. The ground we have thus created is forever pasturage for our thoughts. I fall back on to visions which I have had. What else adds to my possessions and makes me rich in all lands? If you have ever done any work with these finest tools, the imagination and fancy and reason, it is a new creation, independent on the world, and a possession forever. You have laid up something against a rainy day. You have to that extent cleared the wilderness.

Written May 1, 1857, in his *Journal*, vol. IX, p. 350

That man is the richest whose pleasures are the cheapest.

Written March 11, 1856, in his *Journal*, vol. VIII, p. 205

Truly, our greatest blessings are very cheap.

"Thomas Carlyle and His Works" in *Early Essays and Miscellanies*, p. 267

RELIGIOUS CONCERNS

RELIGION AND RELIGIONS

I do not prefer one religion or philosophy to another. I have no sympathy with the bigotry & ignorance which make transient & partial & puerile distinctions between one man's faith or form of faith & another's— as Christian & heathen. I pray to be delivered from narrowness, partiality, exaggeration, bigotry.

Written after April 26, 1850, in his *Journal*, vol. 3, p. 62

In some lyceums they tell me that they have voted to exclude the subject of religion. But how do I know what their religion is, and when I am near to or far from it? I have walked into such an arena and done my best to make a clean breast of what religion I have experienced, and the audience never suspected what I was about.

"Life without Principle" in *Reform Papers*, p. 168

We are grateful when we are reminded by interior evidence, of the permanence of universal laws; for our faith is but faintly remembered, indeed, is not a remembered assurance, but a use and enjoyment of knowledge. It is when we do not have to believe, but come into actual contact with Truth, and are related to her in the most direct and intimate way.

A Week on the Concord and Merrimack Rivers, pp. 291–292

To the philosopher all sects all nations are alike. I like Brahma, Hare, Buddha, the Great Spirit, as well as God.

Written after April 26, 1850, in his *Journal*, vol. 3, p. 62

There are various, nay incredible faiths; why should we be alarmed at any of them?

A Week on the Concord and Merrimack Rivers, p. 66

A man's real faith is never contained in his creed, nor is his creed an article of his faith.

A Week on the Concord and Merrimack Rivers, p. 78

There is no infidelity so great as that which prays and keeps the Sabbath and founds churches.

Written January 1, 1842, in his *Journal*, vol. 1, p. 355

When the husk gets separated from the kernel, almost all men run after the husk and pay their respects to that. It is only the husk of Christianity that is so bruited and wide spread in this world, the kernel is still the very least and rarest of all things. There is not a single church founded on it.

"Huckleberries," pp. 3–4

I am not sure but this Catholic religion would be an admirable one if the priest were quite omitted.

"A Yankee in Canada" in *Excursions*, p. 88

If a man do not revive with nature in the spring, how shall he revive when a white-collared priest prays for him?

Written March 20, 1858, in his *Journal*, vol. X, p. 315

Who are the religious? They who do not differ much from mankind generally, except that they are more conservative and timid and useless, but who in their conversation and correspondence talk about kindness of Heavenly Father.... And because they take His name in vain so often they presume that they are better than you.

Written November 20, 1858, in his *Journal*, vol. XI, p. 338

What is called the religious world very generally deny virtue to all who have not received the Gospel.

Written December 4, 1860, in his *Journal*, vol. XIV, p. 294

If Christ should appear on earth he could on all hands be denounced as a mistaken, misguided man, insane and crazed.

Written October 19, 1859, in his *Journal*, vol. XII, p. 407; emended from manuscript Journal (MA 1302, The Morgan Library & Museum, New York)

FAITH AND SPIRIT

Though I do not believe that a plant will spring up where no seed has been, I have great faith in a seed—a, to me, equally mysterious origin for it. Convince me that you have a seed there, and I am prepared to expect wonders.

"An Address on the Succession of Forest Trees" in *Excursions*, pp. 181–182

Who could believe in prophecies of Daniel or of Miller that the world would end this summer while one Milk-weed with faith matured its seeds!

Written September 24, 1851, in his *Journal*, vol. 4, p. 96

The best scripture after all records but a meager faith. Its saints live reserved and austere. Let a brave devout man spend the year in the woods of Maine or Labra-dor, and see if the Hebrew scripture speak adequately to his condition and experience, from the setting in of winter to the breaking up of the ice.

"A Winter Walk" in *Excursions*, p. 75

The coward wants resolution, which the brave man can do without. He recognizes no faith above a creed, think-ing this straw, by which he is moored, does him good service, because his sheet anchor does not drag.

"The Service" in *Reform Papers*, p. 5

We cannot but respect the vigorous faith of those hea-then, who sternly believed somewhat, and are inclined to say to the critics, who are offended by their superstitious rites,—Don't interrupt these men's prayers. As if we knew more about human life and a God, than the heathen and ancients.

A Week on the Concord and Merrimack Rivers, p. 344

It is not every man who can be a Christian, even in a very moderate sense, whatever education you give him. It is a matter of constitution and temperament, after all. He may have to be born again many times. I have known many a man who pretended to be a Christian, in whom it was ridiculous, for he had no genius for it.

"The Last Days of John Brown" in Reform Papers, pp. 148–149

It is necessary not to be Christian, to appreciate the beauty and significance of the life of Christ.

A Week on the Concord and Merrimack Rivers, p. 67

If it were not for death & funerals I think the institution of the Church would not stand longer.

Written November 16, 1851, in his Journal, vol. 4, p. 189

That nation is not Christian where the principles of humanity do not prevail, but the prejudices of race.

Written September 25, 1851, in his Journal, vol. 4, p. 98

I expect the Christian not to be superstitious but to be distinguished by the clearness of his knowledge, the strength of his faith, the breadth of his humanity.

Written September 25, 1851, in his Journal, vol. 4, p. 98

The bigoted & sectarian forget that without religion or devotion of some kind nothing great was ever accomplished.

Written July 27, 1852, in his *Journal*, vol. 5, p. 261

The bells are particularly sweet this morning. I hear more methinks than ever before. How much more religion in their sound, than they ever call men together to.

Written January 2, 1853, in his *Journal*, vol. 5, p. 420

I suppose that what in other men is religion is in me love of nature.

Written October 30, 1842, in his *Journal*, vol. 2, p. 55

In the last stage of civilization, Poetry, Religion and Philosophy will be one.

Written December 17, 1837, in his *Journal*, vol. 1, p. 19

Faith, indeed, is all the reform that is needed; it is itself a reform.

"Paradise (to be) Regained" in *Reform Papers*, p. 43

It might seem that I had some spite against the priest, but not so, I am on as good terms with him as with another man.

Passage omitted from *A Week on the Concord and Merrimack Rivers* as published in Linck C. Johnson, *Thoreau's Complex Weave*, p. 455

If you take this life to be simply what old religious folks pretend, (I mean the effete, gone to seed in a drought, mere human galls stung by the Devil once), then all your joy & serenity is reduced to grinning and bearing it.

> To H.G.O. Blake, May 20, 1860, in *The Correspondence of Henry David Thoreau*, p. 579

Our religion is where our love is.

> To Isaiah T. Williams, September 8, 1841, in *The Correspondence of Henry David Thoreau*, p. 52

GOD

Every incident is a parable of the great teacher.

> Written April 18, 1852, in his *Journal*, vol. 4, p. 468

The unconsciousness of man is the consciousness of God.

> *A Week on the Concord and Merrimack Rivers*, p. 329

As I stand over the insect crawling amid the pine needles on the forest floor, and endeavoring to conceal itself from my sight, and ask myself why it will cherish those humble thoughts, and hide its head from me who might perhaps be its benefactor, and impart to its race some cheering information, I am reminded of the greater Benefactor and Intelligence that stands over me the human insect.

> *Walden*, p. 332

God himself culminates in the present moment, and will never be more divine in the lapse of all the ages.

> *Walden*, p. 97

God's voice is but a clear bell sound.

Written March 3, 1841, in his *Journal*, vol. 1, p. 277

My desire for knowledge is intermittent but my desire to commune with the spirit of the universe—to be intoxicated even with the fumes, call it, of that divine nectar—to bear my head through atmospheres and over heights unknown to my feet—is perennial & constant.

Written February 9, 1851, in his *Journal*, vol. 3, p. 185

I feel my maker blessing me.

Written June 22, 1851, in his *Journal*, vol. 3, p. 275

The Deity would be reverenced, not feared.

From a college essay, "Sublimity," March 31, 1837, in *Early Essays and Miscellanies*, p. 96

The most glorious fact in my experience is not any thing that I have done or may hope to do, but a transient thought, or vision, or dream, which I have had. I would give all the wealth of the world, and all the deeds of all the heroes, for one true vision. But how can I communicate with the gods who am a pencil-maker on the earth, and not be insane?

A Week on the Concord and Merrimack Rivers, p. 140

The strains of a more heroic faith vibrate through the week days and the fields than through the Sabbath and the Church. To shut the ears to the immediate voice of God, and prefer to know him by report will be the only sin.

To Isaiah T. Williams, September 8, 1841, in *The Correspondence of Henry David Thoreau*, p. 52

When you travel to the celestial city, carry no letter of introduction. When you knock ask to see God—none of the servants.

To H.G.O. Blake, March 27, 1848, in *The Correspondence of Henry David Thoreau*, p. 216

Let *God* alone if need be. Methinks, if I loved him more, I should keep him,—I should keep myself rather,—at a more *respectful* distance. It is not when I am going to meet him, but when I am just turning away and leaving him alone, that I discover that God is. I say God. I am not sure that that is the name. You will know whom I mean.

To H.G.O. Blake, April 3, 1850, in *The Correspondence of Henry David Thoreau*, p. 257; emended from facsimile of manuscript letter (manuscript location unknown)

What if God were to confide in us for a moment! Should we not then be gods?

To Ralph Waldo Emerson, February 12, 1843, in *The Correspondence of Henry David Thoreau*, p. 86

So far as thinking is concerned, surely original thinking is the divinest thing. . . . We check & repress the divinity that stirs within us to fall down & worship the divinity that is dead without us.

Written Sunday, November 16, 1851, in his *Journal*, vol. 4, p. 188

The entertaining a single thought of a certain elevation makes all men of one religion. It is always some base alloy that creates the distinction of sects.

Written August 8, 1852, in his *Journal*, vol. 5, p. 289

I go to see many a good man or good woman so called & utter freely that thought which alone it was given to me to utter but there was a man who lived a long long time ago & his name was Moses, & another whose name was Christ, and if your thought does not or does not appear to coincide with what they said, the good man or the good woman has no ears to hear you.

They think they love God! It is only his old clothes of which they make scarecrows for the children.

Written Sunday, November 16, 1851, in his *Journal*, vol. 4, p. 189

As a mother loves to see her child imbibe nourishment and expand, so God loves to see his children thrive on the nutriment he has furnished them.

Written January 22, 1859, in his *Journal*, vol. XI, p. 424

There is no such thing as sliding up hill. In morals the only sliders are back-sliders.

Written June 17, 1854, in his *Journal*, vol. 8, p. 206

There is more of God, and divine help, in my little finger, than in idle prayer and trust.

Written January 29, 1841, in his *Journal*, vol. 1, p. 236

SCIENCE

One studies books of science merely to learn the language of naturalists—to be able to communicate with them.

Written March 23, 1853, in his *Journal*, vol. 6, p. 28

Science is always brave, for to know, is to know good; doubt and danger quail before her eye.

"Natural History of Massachusetts" in *Excursions*, p. 6

With all your science can you tell how it is & whence it is that light comes into the soul?

Written July 16, 1851, in his *Journal*, vol. 3, p. 306

Science is inhuman.

Written May 1, 1859, in his *Journal*, vol. XII, p. 171

I have just been through the process of killing the cistude for the sake of science but I cannot excuse myself for this murder & see that such actions are inconsistent with the poetic perception—however they may serve science—& will affect the quality of my observations. I pray that I may walk more innocently & serenely through nature. No reasoning whatever reconciles me to this act. It affects my day injuriously. I have lost some self respect.

Written August 18, 1854, in his *Journal*, vol. 8, p. 278

The knowledge of an unlearned man is living & luxuriant like a forest but covered with mosses & lichens and for the most part inaccessible & going to waste. The knowledge of the man of science is like timber collected in yards for public works which stub supports a green sprout here & there—but even this is liable to dry rot.

Written January 7, 1851, in his *Journal*, vol. 3, p. 174

I confess to a little squeamishness on the score of robbing their nests, though I could easily go to the length of abstracting an egg or two gently, now and then, and if the advancement of science obviously demanded it might be carried even to the extreme of deliberate murder.

To Horatio R. Storer, February 15, 1847, in *The Correspondence of Henry David Thoreau*, p. 175

I have become sadly scientific.

To his sister, Sophia, July 13, 1852, in *The Correspondence of Henry David Thoreau*, p. 283

I am an observer of nature generally, and the character of my observations, so far as they are scientific, may be inferred from the fact that I am especially attracted by such books of science as White's Selborne and Humboldt's "Aspects of Nature."

To Spencer F. Baird, in reply to a letter from the Association for the Advancement of Science, December 19, 1853, in *The Correspondence of Henry David Thoreau*, p. 310

I *am* in the lecture field—but my subjects are not *scientific*—rather transcendentalist & aesthetic—

> Draft reply to Charles C. Morse in answer to his query whether Thoreau would deliver two or more scientific lectures before the Athenaeum & Mechanics Association in Rochester, New York, July 12, 1860, in *The Correspondence of Henry David Thoreau*, p. 583; emended from manuscript (MS HM 20592, Houghton Library, Harvard University)

Science never saw a ghost nor does it look for any but it sees everywhere the traces—and it is itself the agent—of a Universal Intelligence.

> Written December 2, 1853, in his *Journal*, vol. 7, p. 186

How little I know of that *arbor-vitae* when I have learned only what science can tell me!

> Written March 5, 1858, in his *Journal*, vol. X, p. 294

I rarely read a sentence in a botany which reminds me of flowers or living plants. Very few indeed write as if they had seen the thing which they pretend to describe.

> Written September 22, 1860, in his *Journal*, vol. XIV, p. 92

If there is not something mystical in your explanation—something unexplainable—some elements of mystery, it is quite insufficient. If there is nothing in it which speaks to my imagination, what boots it? What sort of science is that which enriches the understanding but robs the imagination? Not merely robs Peter to pay Paul but takes from Peter more than it ever gives to Paul.

> Written December 25, 1851, in his *Journal*, vol. 4, p. 222

The old naturalists were so sensitive and sympathetic to nature that they could be surprised by the ordinary events of life. It was an incessant miracle to them, and therefore gorgons and flying dragons were not incredible to them. The greatest and saddest defect is not credulity, but our habitual forgetfulness that our science is ignorance.

Written March 5, 1860, in his *Journal*, vol. XIII, p. 180

A history of animated nature must itself be animated.

Written February 18, 1860, in his *Journal*, vol. XIII, p. 154

As it is important to consider Nature from the point of view of science, remembering the nomenclature and system of men, and so, if possible, go a step further in that direction, so it is equally important often to ignore or forget all that men presume that they know, and take an original and unprejudiced view of Nature, letting her make what impression she will on you, as the first men, and all children and natural men still do.

Written February 28, 1860, in his *Journal*, vol. XIII, pp. 168–169

THE SEASONS

We discover a new world every time that we see the earth again after it has been covered for a season with snow.

Written January 8, 1860, in his *Journal*, vol. XIII, p. 81

Perhaps what most moves us in winter is some reminiscence of far-off summer. How we leap by the side of the open brooks! What beauty in the running brooks! What life! What society!

Written January 12, 1855, in his *Journal*, vol. VII, p. 112

The seasons were not made in vain. Because the fruits of the earth are already ripe, we are not to suppose that there is no fruit left for winter to ripen. It is for man the seasons and all their fruits exist. The winter was made to concentrate & harden & mature the kernel of his brain—to give tone & firmness & consistency to his thought. Then is the great harvest of the year—the harvest of thought.

Written January 30, 1854, in his *Journal*, vol. 7, p. 256

Is not January the hardest month to get through? When you have weathered that you get into the gulf-stream of winter nearer the shores of Spring.

Written February 2, 1854, in his *Journal*, vol. 7, p. 261

The coldest night for a long, long time was last. Sheets froze stiff about the faces. . . . People dreaded to go to bed. The ground cracked in the night as if a powder-mill had blown up, and the timbers of the house also. . . . Every bearded man in the street is a gray-beard.

Written February 7, 1855, in his *Journal*, vol. VII, p. 173

In winter we lead a more inward life. Our hearts are warm and cheery, like cottages under drifts, whose windows and doors are half concealed, but from whose chimneys the smoke cheerfully ascends. The imprisoning drifts increase the sense of comfort which the house affords, and in the coldest days we are content to sit over the hearth, and see the sky through the chimney top, enjoying the quiet and serene life that may be had in a warm corner by the chimney side, or feeling our pulse by listening to the low of cattle in the street, or the sound of the flail in distant barns, all the long afternoon. No doubt a skilful physician could determine our health by observing how these simple and natural sounds affected us.

"A Winter Walk" in *Excursions*, pp. 74–75

Is not January alone pure winter? December belongs to the fall—is a wintery November—February to the spring—it is a snowy March.

Written February 9, 1854, in his *Journal*, vol. 7, p. 279

Never is there so much light in the air as in one of these bright winter afternoons, when all the earth is covered with new-fallen snow and there is not a cloud in the sky. The sky is much the darkest side, like the bluish lining of an egg-shell. There seems nothing left to make night out of. With this white earth beneath & that spot[less] skimmed-milk sky above him, man is but a black speck enclosed in a white egg-shell.

Written February 13, 1859, in his *Journal*, vol. XI, p. 455

We learn by the January thaw that the winter is intermittent and are reminded of other seasons. The back of the winter is broken.

Written February 14, 1851, in his *Journal*, vol. 3, p. 193

I am reminded of spring by the quality of the air. . . . It is a natural resurrection, an experience of immortality.

Written February 24, 1852, in his *Journal*, vol. 4, p. 363

How imperceptibly the first springing takes place!

Written March 3, 1859, in his *Journal*, vol. XII, p. 8

In a pleasant spring morning all men's sins are forgiven.

Walden, p. 314

The first pleasant days of spring come out like a squirrel and go in again.

Written March 7, 1855, in his *Journal*, vol. VII, p. 234

To us snow and cold seem a mere delaying of the spring. How far we are from understanding the value of these things in the economy of Nature!

Written March 8, 1859, in his *Journal*, vol. XII, p. 24

They were pleasant spring days, in which the winter of man's discontent was thawing as well as the earth, and the life that had lain torpid began to stretch itself.

Walden, p. 41

No mortal is alert enough to be present at the first dawn of the spring, but he will presently discover some evidence that vegetation had awaked some days at least before.

Written March 17, 1857, in his *Journal*, vol. IX, p. 295

For the first time I perceive this spring that the year is a circle. I see distinctly the spring arc thus far. It is drawn with a firm line.

Written April 18, 1852, in his *Journal*, vol. 4, p. 468

Is not all the summer akin to a paradise?

Written May 9, 1852, in his *Journal*, vol. 5, p. 47

It seems to take but one summer day to fetch the summer in.

Written May 18, 1851, in his *Journal*, vol. 3, p. 220

The year has many seasons more than are recognized in the Almanac.

Written May 31, 1850, in his *Journal*, vol. 3, p. 74

Each season is but an infinitesimal point. It no sooner comes than it is gone. It has no duration. It simply gives a tone and hue to my thought. Each annual phenomenon is a reminiscence and prompting. Our thoughts and sentiments answer to the revolutions of the seasons, as two cog-wheels fit into each other. We are conversant with only one point of contact at a time, from which we receive a prompting and impulse and instantly pass to a new season or point of contact. A year is made up of a certain series and number of sensations and thoughts which have their language in nature. Now I am ice, now I am sorrel. Each experience reduces itself to a mood of the mind.

Written June 6, 1857, in his *Journal*, vol. IX, pp. 406–407

No one to my knowledge has observed the minute differences in the seasons. Hardly two nights are alike.

Written June 11, 1851, in his *Journal*, vol. 3, p. 253

And so the seasons went rolling on into summer, as rambles into higher and higher grass.

Walden, p. 319

The night of the year is approaching. What have we done with our talent? All nature prompts & reproves us. How early in the year it begins to be late.

Written August 18, 1853, in his *Journal*, vol. 6, p. 306

The seasons do not cease a moment to revolve and therefore nature rests no longer at her culminating point than at any other. If you are not out at the right instant the summer may go by & you not see it. How much of the year is spring & fall—how little can be called summer! The grass is no sooner grown than it begins to wither.

Written August 19, 1851, in his *Journal*, vol. 3, p. 379

The sound of the crickets gradually prevails more and more. I hear the year falling asleep.

Written August 21, 1852, in his *Journal*, vol. 5, p. 304

There is no plateau on which Nature rests at midsummer, but she instantly commences the descent to
winter.

Written August 23, 1858, in his *Journal*, vol. XI, p. 119

Live in each season as it passes—breathe the air, drink
the drink, taste the fruit, & resign yourself to the influences of each.

Written August 23, 1853, in his *Journal*, vol. 7, p. 15

The year is but a succession of days & I see that I could
assign some office to each day which summed up
would be the history of the year. Everything is done in
season and there is no time to spare.

Written August 24, 1852, in his *Journal*, vol. 5, p. 313

The corn stalks are stacked like muskets along the fields.

Written September 17, 1852, in his *Journal*, vol. 5, p. 346

October is the month of painted leaves. Their rich glow
now flashes round the world. As fruits and leaves and
the day itself acquire a bright tint, just before they fall,
so the year near its setting. October is its sunset sky;
November the later twilight.

"Autumnal Tints" in *Excursions*, pp. 224–225

Now the year itself begins to be ripe, ripened by the
frost, like a persimmon.

Written October 4, 1859, in his *Journal*, vol. XII, p. 373

Now, methinks, the autumnal tints are brightest in our
streets and in the woods generally. . . . Stand where half

a dozen large elms droop over a house. It is as if you stood within a ripe pumpkin rind, and you feel as mellow as if you were the pulp.

Written October 6, 1858, in his *Journal*, vol. XI, pp. 199–200

Why do you flee so soon, sir, to the theatres, lecture-rooms, and museums of the city? If you will stay here awhile I will promise you strange sights. You shall walk on water; all these brooks and rivers and ponds shall be your highway. You shall see the whole earth covered a foot or more deep with purest white crystals, in which you slump or over which you glide, and all the trees and stubble glittering in icy armor.

Written October 18, 1859, in his *Journal*, vol. XII, p. 400

It is surprising how any reminiscence of a different season of the year affects us. . . . You only need to make a faithful record of an average summer's day experience & summer mood & read it in the winter & it will carry you back to more than that Summer day alone could show.

Written October 26, 1853, in his *Journal*, vol. 7, p. 115

The seasons and all their changes are in me. I see not a dead eel or floating sucker, or a gull, but it rounds my life and is like a line or accent in its poem. Almost I believe the Concord would not rise and overflow its banks again, were I not here. After a while I learn what my moods and seasons are. I would have nothing subtracted. I can imagine nothing added. My moods are thus *periodical*, not two days in my year alike.

The perfect correspondence of Nature to man, so that he is at home in her!

> Written October 26, 1857, in his *Journal*, vol. X, p. 127; emended from manuscript *Journal* (MA 1302, The Morgan Library & Museum, New York)

Nature now, like an athlete, begins to strip herself in earnest for her contest with her great antagonist Winter. In the bare trees and twigs what a display of muscle!

> Written October 29, 1858, in his *Journal*, vol. XI, p. 260

If the race had never lived through a winter what would they think was coming?

> Written November 8, 1850, in his *Journal*, vol. 3, p. 133

Winter has a concentrated and nutty kernel if you know where to look for it.

> Written November 8, 1858, in his *Journal*, vol. XI, p. 298

The dry grasses are not dead for me. A beautiful form has as much life at one season as another.

> Written November 11, 1850, in his *Journal*, vol. 3, p. 138

Now all that moves migrates, or has migrated. Ducks are gone by. The citizen has sought the town.

> Written November 14, 1858, in his *Journal*, vol. XI, p. 321

October answers to that period in the life of man when he is no longer dependent on his transient moods— when all his experience ripens into wisdom.... He bears his fruit.

> Written November 14, 1853, in his *Journal*, vol. 7, p. 160

Summer is gone with all its infinite wealth, and still nature is genial to man. Though he no longer bathes in the stream, or reclines on the bank, or plucks berries on the hills, still he beholds the same inaccessible beauty around him.

Written November 22, 1860, in his *Journal*, vol. XIV, p. 259

I love the winter, with its imprisonment and its cold, for it compels the prisoner to try new fields and re-sources. I love to have the river closed up for a season and a pause put to my boating, to be obliged to get my boat in. I shall launch it again in the spring with so much more pleasure. This is an advantage in point of abstinence and moderation compared with the seaside boating, where the boat ever lies on the shore. I love best to have each thing in its season only, and enjoy doing without it at all other times.

Written December 5, 1856, in his *Journal*, vol. IX, p. 160

We are hunters pursuing the summer on snow-shoes and skates, all winter long.

Written December 6, 1856, in his *Journal*, vol. IX, p. 164

That grand old poem called Winter is round again without any connivance of mine. . . . It was summer, and now again it is winter. Nature loves this rhyme so well that she never tires of repeating it. . . . What a poem! an epic in blank verse, enriched with a million tinkling rhymes. It is solid beauty.

Written December 7, 1856, in his *Journal*, vol. IX, pp. 167–168

The winter, with its snow and ice, is not an evil to be corrected. It is as it was designed and made to be, for the artist has had leisure to add beauty to use.

Written December 11, 1855, in his *Journal*, vol. VIII, p. 43

If in the winter there are fewer men in the fields & woods ... you see the tracks of those who had preceded you, and so are more reminded of them than in summer.

Written December 12, 1859, in his *Journal*, vol. XIII, p. 21

How completely a load of hay in the winter revives the memory of past summers! Summer in us is only a little dried like it.

Written January 5, 1858, in his *Journal*, vol. X, pp. 237–238

As a child looks forward to the coming of the summer so could we contemplate with quiet joy the circle of the seasons returning without fail eternally.

Written January 6, 1838, in his *Journal*, vol. 1, p. 25

SIMPLICITY

If we would aim at perfection in any thing, simplicity must not be overlooked.

From a college essay on "The ways in which a man's style may be said to offend against simplicity," November 27, 1835, in *Early Essays and Miscellanies*, p. 24

Simplicity is the law of nature for men as well as for flowers.

Written February 29, 1852, in his *Journal*, vol. 4, p. 367

I do believe in simplicity. It is astonishing as well as sad, how many trivial affairs even the wisest thinks he must attend to in a day; how singular an affair he thinks he must omit. When the mathematician would solve a difficult problem, he first frees the equation of all en-cumbrances, and reduces it to its simplest terms. So simplify the problem of life, distinguish the necessary and the real. Probe the earth to see where your main roots run.

To H.G.O. Blake, March 27, 1848, in *The Correspondence of Henry David Thoreau*, p. 215

To what end do I lead a simple life at all, pray? That I may teach others to simplify their lives?—and so all our lives be *simplified* merely, like an algebraic formula? Or not, rather, that I may make use of the ground I have cleared, to live more worthily and profitably?

To H.G.O. Blake, September 26, 1855, in *The Correspondence of Henry David Thoreau*, p. 384

Our life is frittered away by detail. An honest man has hardly need to count more than his ten fingers, or in extreme cases he may add his ten toes, and lump the rest. Simplicity, simplicity, simplicity! I say, let your affairs be as two or three, and not a hundred or a thousand; instead of a million count half a dozen, and keep your accounts on your thumb nail. In the midst of this chopping sea of civilized life, such are the clouds and storms and quicksands and thousand-and-one items to be allowed for, that a man has to live, if he would not founder and go to the bottom and not make his port at all, by dead reckoning, and he must be a great calculator indeed who succeeds. Simplify, simplify.

Walden, p. 91

To be calm to be serene—there is the calmness of the lake when there is not a breath of wind—there is the calmness of a stagnant ditch. So is it with us. Sometimes we are clarified & calmed healthily as we never were before in our lives—not by an opiate but by some unconscious obedience to the all-just laws—so that we become like a still lake of purest crystal and without an effort our depths are revealed to ourselves. All the world goes by us & is reflected in our deeps. Such clarity! obtained by such pure means! By simple living—by honesty of purpose—we live & rejoice.

Written June 22, 1851, in his *Journal*, vol. 3, pp. 274–275

The rule is to carry as little as possible.

Written July 22, 1857, in his *Journal*, vol. IX, p. 488

As for the complex ways of living I love them not however much I practice them. In as many places as possible I will get my feet down to the earth.

Written October 22, 1853, in his *Journal*, vol. 7, pp. 108–109

In proportion as he simplifies his life, the laws of the universe will appear less complex, and solitude will not be solitude, nor poverty poverty, nor weakness weakness.

Walden, p. 324

Every morning was a cheerful invitation to make my life of equal simplicity, and I may say innocence, with Nature herself.

Walden, p. 88

What you call bareness and poverty is to me simplicity. God could not be unkind to me if he should try. . . . It is the greatest of all advantages to enjoy no advantage at all. I find it invariably true, the poorer I am, the richer I am. What you consider my disadvantage, I consider my advantage. While you are pleased to get knowledge and culture in many ways, I am delighted to think that I am getting rid of them.

Written December 5, 1856, in his *Journal*, vol. IX, p. 160

It is well to find your employment and amusement in simple and homely things. These wear best and yield most.

Written October 5, 1856, in his *Journal*, vol. IX, p. 104

The savage lives simply through ignorance & idleness or laziness but the philosopher lives simply through wisdom.

Written September 1, 1853, in his *Journal*, vol. 7, p. 29

By poverty, *i.e.* simplicity of life and fewness of incidents, I am solidified and crystallized, as a vapor or
liquid by cold.

Written February 8, 1857, in his *Journal,* vol. IX, p. 246

Again and again I am surprised to observe what an interval there is, in what is called civilized life, between
the shell and the inhabitant of the shell,—what a dis-
proportion there is between the life of man and his
conveniences and luxuries.

Written September 16, 1859, in his *Journal,* vol. XII, p. 330

We are often reminded that if there were bestowed on
us the wealth of Croesus, our aims must still be the
same, and our means essentially the same. Moreover, if
you are restricted in your range by poverty, if you cannot buy books and newspapers, for instance, you are
but confined to the most significant and vital experiences; you are compelled to deal with the material
which yields the most sugar and the most starch.

Walden, p. 329

There are 2 kinds of simplicity, one that is akin to foolishness—the other to wisdom. The philosopher's style
of living is only outwardly simple but inwardly complex. The savage's style is both outwardly & inwardly
simple. A simpleton can perform many mechanical labors but is not capable of profound thought. It was
their limited view, not in respect to *style* but to the *object* of living. A man who has equally limited views

with respect to the end of living will not be helped by the most complex & refined style of living.

Written September 1, 1853, in his *Journal*, vol. 7, p. 30

SOCIETY

Society is always diseased, and the best is the most so.

"Natural History of Massachusetts" in *Excursions*, p. 4

I am not responsible for the successful working of the machinery of society. I am not the son of the engineer.

"Resistance to Civil Government" in *Reform Papers*, p. 81

In obedience to an instinct of their nature men have pitched their cabins, and planted corn and potatoes within speaking distance of one another, and so formed towns and villages, but they have not associated, they have only assembled, and society has signified only a *convention* of men.

Written March 14, 1838, in his *Journal*, vol. 1, p. 38

I feel that my connection with and obligation to society are still very slight and transient.

"Life without Principle" in *Reform Papers*, p. 160

We pine & starve and lose spirit on the thin gruel of society.

Written after September 11, 1849, in his *Journal*, vol. 3, p. 27

The society which I was made for is not here.

Written July 19, 1851, in his *Journal*, vol. 3, p. 313

May I so live and refine my life as fitting myself for a society ever higher than I actually enjoy.

Written July 16, 1851, in his *Journal*, vol. 3, p. 311

Every proverb in the newspapers originally stood for a truth. Thus the proverb that—Man was made for society—so long as it was not allowed to conflict with another important truth, deceived no one; but now that the same words have come to stand for another thing, it may be for a lie, we are obliged, in order to preserve its significance, to write it anew, so that properly it will read—Society was made for man.

Written March 14, 1838, in his *Journal*, vol. 1, p. 35

But special I remember thee,
Wachusett, who like me
Standest alone without society.

"A Walk to Wachusett" in *Excursions*, p. 30

The mind that perceives clearly any natural beauty is in that instant withdrawn from human society. My desire for society is infinitely increased—my fitness for any actual society is diminished.

Written July 26, 1852, in his *Journal*, vol. 5, p. 251

I see nothing permanent in the society around me & am not quite committed to any of its ways.

Written after July 29, 1850, in his *Journal*, vol. 3, p. 98

The vast majority are men of society. They live on the surface, they are interested in the transient & fleeting. They are like drift wood on the flood. They ask forever & only the news—the froth & scum of the eternal sea.

Written April 24, 1852, in his *Journal*, vol. 4, pp. 486–487

Society is commonly too cheap. We meet at very short intervals, not having had time to acquire any new value for each other.

Walden, p. 136

I perceive that, when an acorn and a chestnut fall side by side, the one does not remain inert to make way for the other, but both obey their own laws, and spring and grow and flourish as best they can, till one, perchance, overshadows and destroys the other. If a plant cannot live according to its nature, it dies; and so a man.

"Resistance to Civil Government" in *Reform Papers*, p. 81

What men call social virtue, good fellowship, is commonly but the virtue of pigs in a litter which lie close together to keep each other warm.

Written October 23, 1852, in his *Journal*, vol. 5, p. 383

Men talk to me about society as if I had none and they had some, as if it were only to be got by going to the sociable or to Boston.

Written March 27, 1857, in his *Journal*, vol. IX, p. 307

Emerson says that his life is so unprofitable and shabby for the most part, that he is driven to all sorts of resources, and, among the rest, to men. I tell him that we differ only in our resources. Mine is to get away from men.

To H.G.O. Blake, August 8, 1854, in *Familiar Letters*, pp. 229–230

I live in an angle of a leaden wall, into whose composition was poured a little alloy of bell metal. Often, in the repose of my mid-day, there reaches my ears a confused *tintinnabulum* from without. It is the noise of my contemporaries.

Walden, p. 329

I was seized and put into jail, because, as I have elsewhere related, I did not pay a tax to, or recognize the authority of, the state which buys and sells men, women, and children, like cattle, at the door of its senate-house. I had gone down to the woods for other purposes. But, wherever a man goes, men will pursue and paw him with their dirty institutions, and, if they can, constrain him to belong to their desperate odd-fellow society. It is true, I might have resisted forcibly with more or less effect, might have run "amok" against society; but I preferred that society should run "amok" against me, it being the desperate party.

Walden, p. 171

As for the dispute about solitude & society any comparison is impertinent. It is an idling down on the plain at the base of a mountain instead of climbing steadily to its top. Of course you will be glad of all the society you can get to go up with. . . . It is not that we love to be alone, but that we love to soar, and when we do soar, the company grows thinner & thinner till there is none at all.

To H.G.O. Blake, May 21, 1856, in *The Correspondence of Henry David Thoreau*, p. 424

As some heads cannot carry much wine, so it would seem that I cannot bear so much society as you can. I have an immense appetite for solitude, like an infant for sleep, and if I don't get enough of it this year I shall cry all the next.

To Daniel Ricketson, September 9, 1857, in *The Correspondence of Henry David Thoreau*, p. 493

I have lately got back to that glorious society called Solitude, where we meet our friends continually, and can imagine the outside world also to be peopled. Yet some of my acquaintance would fain hustle me into the almshouse for *the sake of society*, as if I were pining for that diet, when I seem to myself a most befriended man, and find constant employment. However, they do not believe a word I say.

To H.G.O. Blake, January 1, 1859, in *The Correspondence of Henry David Thoreau*, p. 536

The doctors are all agreed that I am suffering from want of society. Was never a case like it. First, I did not know that I was suffering at all. Secondly, as an Irishman might say, I had thought it was indigestion of the society I got.

To H.G.O. Blake, January 1, 1859, in *The Correspondence of Henry David Thoreau*, p. 537

Use all the society that will abet you.

To H.G.O. Blake, May 21, 1856, in *The Correspondence of Henry David Thoreau*, p. 424

Saturday evening I went to the school room, hall, or what not, to see the children & their teachers & patrons dance. . . . This Sat. eve-dance is a regular thing, & it is thought something strange if you don't attend. They take it for granted that you want *society*!

To his sister, Sophia, November 1, 1856, Perth Amboy, New Jersey, in *The Correspondence of Henry David Thoreau*, p. 439

I dwell as much aloof from society as ever; find it just as impossible to agree in opinion with the most intelligent of my neighbors; they not having improved one jot, nor I either.

To Thomas Cholmondeley, October 20, 1856, in *The Correspondence of Henry David Thoreau*, p. 436

Society seems to have invaded and overrun me.

Written August 13, 1854, in his *Journal*, vol. 8, p. 265

SOLITUDE

I am not alone if I stand by myself.

A Week on the Concord and Merrimack Rivers, p. 184

Happy the man who is furnished with all the advantages to relish solitude; he is never alone, and yet may

be retired in the midst of a crowd; he holds sweet converse with the sages of antiquity, and gathers wisdom
from their discourse—he enjoys the fruit of their labors—their knowledge is his knowledge—their wisdom his inheritance.

> From a college essay on the topic "Speak of the privileges and
> pleasures of a literary man," September 18, 1835, in *Early Essays
> and Miscellanies*, p. 20

It would be better if there were but one inhabitant to a
square mile, as where I live.

> *Walden*, p. 136

Men frequently say to me, "I should think you would
feel lonesome down there, and want to be nearer to
folks, rainy and snowy days and nights especially." I am
tempted to reply to such,—This whole earth which we
inhabit is but a point in space. How far apart, think
you, dwell the two most distant inhabitants of yonder
star, the breadth of whose disk cannot be appreciated
by our instruments? Why should I feel lonely? is not
our planet in the Milky Way?

> *Walden*, p. 133

How alone must our life be lived—We dwell on the
sea-shore and none between us and the sea. Men are
my merry companions—my fellow-pilgrims—who be-
guile the way, but leave me at the first turn in the road—
for none are travelling *one* road so far as myself.

> Written March 13, 1841, in his *Journal*, vol. 1, p. 288

I have a great deal of company in my house; especially in the morning, when nobody calls. Let me suggest a few comparisons, that some one may convey an idea of my situation. I am no more lonely than the loon in the pond that laughs so loud, or than Walden Pond itself. What company has that lonely lake, I pray? And yet it has not the blue devils, but the blue angels in it, in the azure tint of its waters. The sun is alone, except in thick weather, when there sometimes appear to be two, but one is a mock sun. God is alone,—but the devil, he is far from being alone; he sees a great deal of company; he is legion. I am no more lonely than a single mullein or dandelion in a pasture, or a bean leaf, or a sorrel, or a horse-fly, or a humble-bee. I am no more lonely than the Mill Brook, or a weathercock, or the northstar, or the south wind, or an April shower, or a January thaw, or the first spider in a new house.

Walden, p. 137

I find it wholesome to be alone the greater part of the time. To be in company, even with the best, is soon wearisome and dissipating. I love to be alone. I never found the companion that was so companionable as solitude. We are for the most part more lonely when we go abroad among men than when we stay in our chambers. A man thinking or working is always alone, let him be where he will. Solitude is not measured by the miles of space that intervene between a man and his fellows.

Walden, p. 135

What sort of space is that which separates a man from his fellows and makes him solitary? I have found that no exertion of the legs can bring two minds much nearer to one another. What do we want most to dwell near to? Not to many men surely, the depot, the post-office, the bar-room, the meeting-house, the school-house, the grocery, Beacon Hill, or the Five Points, where men most congregate, but to the perennial source of our life, whence in all our experience we have found that to issue, as the willow stands near the water and sends out its roots in that direction. This will vary with different natures, but this is the place where a wise man will dig his cellar.

Walden, p. 133

I was describing the other day my success in solitary and distant woodland walking outside the town. I do not go there to get my dinner, but to get that suste-nance which dinners only preserve me to enjoy, with-out which dinners are a vain repetition.

Written January 11, 1857, in his *Journal*, vol. IX, p. 215

I thrive best on solitude. If I have had a companion only one day in a week, unless it were one or two I could name, I find that the value of the week to me has been seriously affected. It dissipates my days, and often it takes me another week to get over it.

Written December 28, 1856, in his *Journal*, vol. IX, p. 200

I do not know if I am singular when I say that I believe there is no man with whom I can associate who will

not, comparatively speaking, spoil my afternoon. That
society or encounter may at last yield a fruit which I
am not aware of, but I cannot help suspecting that I
should have spent those hours more profitably alone.

Written November 25, 1857, in his *Journal*, vol. X, p. 204

You think that I am impoverishing myself by withdrawing from men, but in my solitude I have woven for
myself a silken web or *chrysalis*, and, nymph-like, shall
ere long burst forth a more perfect creature, fitted for a
higher society.

Written February 8, 1857, in his *Journal*, vol. IX, p. 246

By my intimacy with nature I find myself withdrawn
from man. My interest in the sun & the moon, in the
morning & the evening compels me to solitude.

Written July 26, 1852, in his *Journal*, vol. 5, pp. 250–251

Ah! I need solitude. I have come forth to this hill at
sunset to see the forms of the mountains in the horizon—to behold & commune with something grander
than man. Their mere distance & unprofanedness is an
infinite encouragement. It is with an infinite yearning &
aspiration that I seek solitude—more & more resolved &
strong—but with a certain genial weakness that I seek
society ever.

Written August 14, 1854, in his *Journal*, vol. 8, pp. 267–268

Mrs. A. takes on dolefully on account of the solitude in
which she lives, but she gets little consolation. Mrs. B.
says she envies her that retirement. Mrs. A. is aware

that she does, and says it is as if a thirsty man should envy another the river in which he is drowning. So goes the world. It is either this extreme or that. Of solitude one gets too much and another not enough.

Written March 11, 1859, in his *Journal*, vol. XII, p. 38

It is surprising how much room there is in nature, if a man will follow his proper path. In these broad fields— in these extensive woods—on this stretching river I never meet a walker—passing behind the farmhouses I see no man out.

Written January 26, 1853, in his *Journal*, vol. 5, p. 454

I have found myself as well off when I have fallen into a quagmire as in an arm chair in the most hospitable house. The prospect was pretty much the same. Without anxiety let us wander on admiring whatever beauty the woods exhibit.

Written after July 29, 1850, in his *Journal*, vol. 3, p. 98

SUCCESS

Even talent is respectable only when it indicates a depth of character unfathomed. Surely, it is better that our wisdom appear in the constant success of our spirits, than in our business or the maxims which fall from our lips merely.

"Sir Walter Raleigh" in *Early Essays and Miscellanies*, p. 216

Every man's success is in proportion to his *average* ability.

Written between 1842 and 1844, in his *Journal*, vol. 2, p. 61

Undoubtedly, in the most brilliant successes, the first rank is always sacrificed.

"Paradise (to be) Regained" in *Reform Papers*, p. 23

Regard not your past failures nor successes. All the past is equally a failure & a success. It is a success in as much as it offers you the present opportunity.

Written after July 29, 1850, in his *Journal*, vol. 3, p. 95

Those slight labors which afford me a livelihood, and by which it is allowed that I am to some extent service-able to my contemporaries, are as yet commonly a pleasure to me, and I am not often reminded that they are a necessity. So far I am successful.

"Life without Principle" in *Reform Papers*, p. 160

I foresee, that, if my wants should be much increased, the labor required to supply them would become a drudgery. If I should sell both my forenoons and after-noons to society, as most appear to do, I am sure, that, for me, there would be nothing left worth living for. I trust that I shall never thus sell my birthright for a mess of pottage.

"Life without Principle" in *Reform Papers*, p. 160

Alas! this is the crying sin of the age, this want of faith in the prevalence of a man. Nothing can be effected but by one man. He who wants help wants everything. True, this is the condition of our weakness, but it can never be the means of our recovery. We must first succeed alone, that we may enjoy our success together.

"Paradise (to be) Regained" in *Reform Papers*, p. 42

In the long run men hit only what they aim at. Therefore, though they should fail immediately, they had better aim at something high.

Walden, p. 27

If one advances confidently in the direction of his dreams, and endeavors to live the life which he has imagined, he will meet with success unexpected in common hours. He will put some things behind, will pass an invisible boundary; new, universal, and more liberal laws will begin to establish themselves around and within him; or the old laws be expanded, and interpreted in his favor in a more liberal sense, and he will live with the license of a higher order of beings.

Walden, pp. 323–324

Men were born to succeed, not to fail.

Written March 21, 1853, in his *Journal*, vol. 6, p. 23

A living dog is better than a dead lion. Shall a man go and hang himself because he belongs to the race of pygmies, and not be the biggest pygmy that he can? Let every one mind his own business, and endeavor to be what he was made.

Walden, pp. 325–326

Nothing memorable was ever accomplished in a prosaic mood.

Cape Cod, p. 95

If the day and the night are such that you greet them with joy, and life emits a fragrance like flowers and sweet-scented herbs, is more elastic, more starry, more immortal,—that is your success.

Walden, p. 216

It has found an audience of excellent character, and quite numerous, some 2000 copies having been dispersed. I should consider it a greater success to interest one wise and earnest soul, than a million unwise & frivolous.

To Calvin Greene, on the reception of *Walden*, February 10, 1856, in *The Correspondence of Henry David Thoreau*, p. 407

If a man has spent all his days about some business, by which he has merely got to be rich, as it is called, *i.e.*, has got much money, many houses and barns and woodlots, then his life has been a failure, I think; but if he has been trying to better his condition in a higher sense than this, has been trying to invent something, to be somebody,—*i.e.*, to invent and get a patent for himself,—so that all may see his originality, though he should never get above board,—and great inventors, you know, commonly die poor,—I shall think him comparatively successful.

Written November 29, 1860, in his *Journal*, vol. XIV, pp. 281–282

I never triumph so as when I have the least success in my neighbor's eyes.

> To H.G.O. Blake, December 31, 1856, in *The Correspondence of Henry David Thoreau*, p. 461

Your success will be in proportion to your devotion to ideas.

> To H.G.O. Blake, May 20, 1860, in *The Correspondence of Henry David Thoreau*, p. 579

TEMPERAMENT AND ATTITUDE

Do not despair of life. You have no doubt force enough to overcome your obstacles.

> Written December 27, 1857, in his *Journal*, vol. X, p. 228

A retreat is rarely well conducted; if it is, then it is an orderly advance in the face of circumstances.

> "Natural History of Massachusetts" in *Excursions*, pp. 6–7

A man is not his hope, nor his despair, nor yet his past deed.

> *A Week on the Concord and Merrimack Rivers*, p. 129

Men will lie on their backs, talking about the fall of man, and never make an effort to get up.

> "Life without Principle" in *Reform Papers*, p. 161

I always see those of whom I have heard well with a slight disappointment.

> To Ralph Waldo Emerson, June 8, 1843, in *The Correspondence of Henry David Thoreau*, p. 111

If there is any one with whom we have a quarrel is it most likely that that one makes some just demand on us which we disappoint.

> Written November 22, 1853, in his *Journal*, vol. 7, p. 171

We too have our thaws. They come to our January moods when our ice cracks & our sluices break loose.

> Written January 31, 1854, in his *Journal*, vol. 7, p. 259

We are more of the earth—farther from heaven these days. We live in a grosser element—are getting deeper into the mists of earth. Even the birds sing with less vigor & vivacity. The season of hope & promise is past—already the season of small fruits has arrived. . . . We are a little saddened, because we begin to see the interval between our hopes & their fulfillment. The prospect of the heavens is taken away and we are presented only with a few small berries.

> Written June 17, 1854, in his *Journal*, vol. 8, pp. 204–205

Methinks that these prosers with their saws & their laws do not know how glad a man can be. What wisdom—what warning can prevail against gladness? There is no law so strong which a little gladness may not transgress.

> Written January 3, 1853, in his *Journal*, vol. 5, p. 422

When we have experienced many disappointments, such as the loss of friends, the notes of birds cease to affect us as they did.

Written February 5, 1859, two days after his father died, in his *Journal*, vol. XI, p. 439

There was a time when the beauty & the music were all within & I sat & listened to my thoughts & there was a song in them. I sat for hours on rocks and wrestled with the melody which possessed me. I sat and listened by the hour to a positive though faint & distant music not sung by any bird nor vibrating any earthly harp. When you walked with a joy which knew not its own origin. When you were an organ of which the world was but one poor broken pipe. I lay long on the rocks foundered like a harp on the sea-shore that knows not how it is dealt with.

Written May 23, 1854, in his *Journal*, vol. 8, p. 147

To live like a philosopher, is to live, not foolishly, like other men, but wisely, and according to universal laws. In this, which was the ancient sense, we think there has been no philosopher in modern times. The wisest and most practical men of recent history, to whom this epithet has been hastily applied, have lived comparatively meagre lives, of conformity and tradition, such as their fathers transmitted to them. But a man may live in what style he can. Between earth and heaven, there is room for all kinds. If he take counsel of fear and prudence, he has already failed.

"Thomas Carlyle and His Works" in *Early Essays and Miscellanies*, p. 256

Men die of fright & live of confidence.

> Written after July 29, 1850, in his *Journal*, vol. 3, p. 96

It is best that reason should govern us and not these blind intimations in which we exalt our fears into a genius.

> Written August 8, 1851, in his *Journal*, vol. 3, p. 360

What danger is there if you don't think of any?

> *Walden*, p. 153

It is true, nothing could originally demand our respect, which was not, at the same time, *capable*, in a greater or less degree, of exciting our fear, but this does not prove fear to be the source of that respect.

> From a college essay, "Sublimity," March 31, 1837, in *Early Essays and Miscellanies*, p. 97

I am required, it is true, to respect the feelings of my neighbor within the limits of his own estate, but the fear of displeasing the world ought not, in the least, to influence my actions; were it otherwise the principal avenue to reform would be closed.

> From a college essay, "Moral Excellence," May 19, 1837, in *Early Essays and Miscellanies*, p. 106

Even the prophets and redeemers have rather consoled the fears than satisfied the free demands and hopes of man!

> "Reform and the Reformers" in *Reform Papers*, p. 192

Our foes are in our midst and all about us. There is hardly a house but is divided against itself, for our foe is the all but universal woodenness of both head and heart, the want of vitality in man, which is the effect of our vice; and hence are begotten fear, superstition, bigotry, persecution, and slavery of all kinds.

"A Plea for Captain John Brown" in *Reform Papers*, p. 120

Fear creates danger, and courage dispels it.

Written November 12, 1859, in his *Journal*, vol. XII, p. 443

Nothing is so much to be feared as fear.

Written September 7, 1851, in his *Journal*, vol. 4, p. 51

Man is the artificer of his own happiness.

Written January 21, 1838, in his *Journal*, vol. 1, p. 25

Oh Happiness—what is the stuff thou art made of? Is it not gossamer and floating spider's webs?—a crumpled sunbeam—a coiled dew line settling on some flower?

Written January 20, 1841, in his *Journal*, vol. 1, p. 224

Notwithstanding a sense of unworthiness which possesses me not without reason—notwithstanding that I regard myself as a good deal of a scamp—yet for the most part the spirit of the universe is unaccountably kind to me and I enjoy perhaps an unusual share of happiness. Yet I question sometimes if there is not some settlement to come.

Written November 16, 1850, in his *Journal*, vol. 3, p. 144

Practical men, who perform the offices of life but with their bodies, their minds, their understandings, and their senses, and forsake the consequence for the purification of their souls; and, although employed, forsake the fruit of action, obtain infinite happiness; whilst the man who is unemployed, being attached to the fruit by the agent desire, is in the bonds of confinement.

Written after June 20, 1846, in his *Journal*, vol. 2, p. 256

The villagers are out in the sun and every man is happy whose work takes him out doors.

Written March 15, 1852, in his *Journal*, vol. 4, p. 390

He is a happy man who is assured that the animal is dying out in him day by day & the spiritual being established.

Written February 28, 1850, in his *Journal*, vol. 3, p. 49

We are made happy when reason can discover no occasion for it.

To Mrs. Lucy Brown, March 2, 1842, in *The Correspondence of Henry David Thoreau*, p. 62

Greater is the depth of Sadness
Than is any height of gladness.

Written September 5, 1841, in his *Journal*, vol. 1, p. 331

As usual, I find it harder to account for the happiness I enjoy, than for the sadness which instructs me occasionally.

> To Mrs. Lucy Brown, January 25, 1843, in *The Correspondence of Henry David Thoreau*, p. 79

This has indeed been a grand winter for me & for all of us. I am not considering how much I have enjoyed it. What matters it how happy or unhappy we have been, if we have minded our business and advanced our affairs.

> To Daniel Ricketson, March 5, 1856, in *The Correspondence of Henry David Thoreau*, p. 412

Happy the man who observes the heavenly and the terrestrial law in just proportion; whose every faculty, from the soles of his feet to the crown of his head, obeys the law of its level; who neither stoops nor goes on tiptoe, but lives a balanced life, acceptable to nature and to God.

> To H.G.O. Blake, August 10, 1849, in *The Correspondence of Henry David Thoreau*, p. 247

I am too easily contented with a slight and almost animal happiness. My happiness is a good deal like that of the woodchucks.

> To H.G.O. Blake, May 2, 1848, in *The Correspondence of Henry David Thoreau*, p. 222

To be active, well, happy, implies rare courage.

> To H.G.O. Blake, May 20, 1860, in *The Correspondence of Henry David Thoreau*, p. 579

Is hope a less powerful incentive to action than fear?

From a college essay on "The comparative moral policy of severe and mild punishments," September 1835, in *Early Essays and Miscellanies*, p. 23

Think of dashing the hopes of a morning with a cup of coffee or of an evening with a dish of tea.

Written after September 19, 1850, in his *Journal*, vol. 3, p. 119

All things in this world must be seen with the morning dew on them. Must be seen with youthful early-opened hopeful eyes.

Written June 13, 1852, in his *Journal*, vol. 5, p. 93

It chanced the other day that I scented a white water-lily, and a season I had waited for had arrived. It is the emblem of purity. It bursts up so pure and fair to the eye, and so sweet to the scent, as if to show us what purity and sweetness reside in, and can be extracted from, the slime and muck of earth. . . . What confirmation of our hopes is in the fragrance of this flower!

"Slavery in Massachusetts" in *Reform Papers*, p. 108

Make the most of your regrets—never smother your sorrow but tend and cherish it till it comes to have a separate and integral interest.

Written November 13, 1839, in his *Journal*, vol. 1, p. 85

You ask if there is no doctrine of sorrow in my philosophy. Of acute sorrow I suppose that I know comparatively little. My saddest and most genuine sorrows are apt to be but transient regrets. The place of sorrow is supplied, perchance, by a certain hard and proportionably barren indifference.

> To H.G.O. Blake, May 2, 1848, in *The Correspondence of Henry David Thoreau*, p. 221

Fools stand on their island opportunities and look toward another land. There is no other land; there is no other life but this, or the like of this. Where the good husbandman is, there is the good soil. Take any other course, and life will be a succession of regrets. Let us see vessels sailing prosperously before the wind, and not simply stranded barks. There is no world for the penitent and regretful.

> Written April 24, 1859, in his *Journal*, vol. XII, pp. 159–160

Our sympathy is a gift whose value we can never know.

> Written February 2, 1841, in his *Journal*, vol. 1, p. 243

I love that one with whom I sympathize.

> Written November 24, 1858, in his *Journal*, vol. XI, p. 342

It is better to have your head in the clouds, and know where you are, if indeed you cannot get it above them, than to breathe the clearer atmosphere below them, and think that you are in paradise.

> To H.G.O. Blake, April 10, 1853, in *The Correspondence of Henry David Thoreau*, p. 303

Surely joy is the condition of life.

> "Natural History of Massachusetts" in *Excursions*, p. 5

THOUGHTS AND THINKING

Perchance the time will come when every house even will have not only its sleeping rooms, and dining room, and talking room or parlor, but its Thinking Room also, and the architects will put it into their plans. Let it be furnished and ornamented with whatever conduces to serious and creative thought.

"A Yankee in Canada" in *Excursions*, p. 89

The greatest compliment that was ever paid me was when one asked me what *I thought*, and attended to my answer.

"Life without Principle" in *Reform Papers*, p. 155

I take it for granted, when I am invited to lecture anywhere,—for I have had a little experience in that business,—that there is a desire to hear what *I think* on some subject, though I may be the greatest fool in the country,—and not that I should say pleasant things merely, or such as the audience will assent to; and I resolve, accordingly, that I will give them a strong dose of myself. They have sent for me, and engaged to pay for me, and I am determined that they shall have me, though I bore them beyond all precedent.

"Life without Principle" in *Reform Papers*, p. 155

He is the rich man, and enjoys the fruits of his riches, who summer and winter forever can find delight in his own thoughts.

A Week on the Concord and Merrimack Rivers, p. 350

If I were confined to a corner of a garret all my days, like a spider, the world would be just as large to me while I had my thoughts about me.

Walden, p. 328

I am surprised as well as delighted when anyone wishes to know what I think. It is such a rare use they would make of me—as if they were acquainted with the tool. Commonly, if men want anything of me, it is only to know how many acres I make of their land—or at most what trivial news I have burdened myself with. They never will go to law for my meat. They prefer the shell.

Written March 23, 1853, in his *Journal*, vol. 6, p. 31

I hardly know an *intellectual* man, even, who is so broad and truly liberal that you can think aloud in his society.

"Life without Principle" in *Reform Papers*, p. 167

Nothing was ever so unfamiliar and startling to me as my own thought.

Written July 10, 1840, in his *Journal*, vol. 1, p. 154

As the wild duck is more swift and beautiful than the tame, so is the wild—the mallard—thought, which, 'mid falling dews wings its way above the fens.

"Walking" in *Excursions*, p. 207

So there is one *thought* for the field, another for the house. I would have my thoughts, like wild apples, to be food for walkers, and will not warrant them to be palatable, if tasted in the house.

"Wild Apples" in *Excursions*, p. 282

Great thoughts hallow any labor.

Written April 20, 1841, in his *Journal*, vol. 1, p. 302

Great thoughts make great men.

Written February 7, 1841, in his *Journal*, vol. 1, p. 256

My loftiest thought is somewhat like an eagle that suddenly comes into the field of view, suggesting great things and thrilling the beholder, as if it were bound hitherward with a message for me; but it comes no nearer, but circles and soars away, growing dimmer, disappointing me, till it is lost behind a cliff or a cloud.

Written October 26, 1857, in his *Journal*, vol. X, pp. 128–129

I am surprised that my affirmations or utterances come to me ready-made,—not fore-thought,—so that I occasionally awake in the night simply to let fall ripe a statement which I had never consciously considered before, and as surprising and novel and agreeable to me as anything can be.

Written April 1, 1860, in his *Journal*, vol. XIII, p. 238

There is no more Herculean task than to think a thought about this life and then get it expressed.

Written May 6, 1858, in his *Journal*, vol. X, p. 405

How many fine thoughts has every man had! how few fine thoughts are expressed! Yet we never have a fantasy so subtle and ethereal, but that *talent merely*, with more resolution and faithful persistency, after a thousand failures, might fix and engrave it in distinct and enduring words, and we should see that our dreams are the solidest facts that we know.

To H.G.O. Blake, March 27, 1848, in *The Correspondence of Henry David Thoreau*, p. 216

Somebody shut the cat's tail in the door just now & she made such a catewaul as has driven two whole worlds out of my mind. . . I saw unspeakable things in the sky & looming in the horizon of my mind and now they are all reduced to a cat's tail.

Written November 16, 1850, in his *Journal*, vol. 3, pp. 141–142

I would fain keep a journal which should contain those thoughts & impressions which I am most liable to forget that I have had, which would have, in one sense the greatest remoteness, in another the greatest nearness, to me.

Written after January 10, 1851, in his *Journal*, vol. 3, p. 178

A wakeful night will yield as much thought as a long journey. If I try thoughts by their quality—not their quantity—I may find that a restless night will yield more than the longest journey.

Written January 30, 1852, in his *Journal*, vol. 4, p. 309

The pleasures of the intellect are permanent—the pleasures of the heart are transitory.

Written January 22, 1852, in his *Journal*, vol. 4, p. 276

While I am abroad the ovipositors plant their seeds in me. I am fly blown with thought & go home to hatch & brood over them.

Written July 23, 1851, in his *Journal*, vol. 3, p. 330

I am freighted with thought.

Written October 26, 1853, in his *Journal*, vol. 7, p. 117

How rarely I meet a man who can be free, even in thought!

Written May 12, 1857, in his *Journal*, vol. IX, p. 362

Our thoughts are wont to run in muddy or dusty ruts.

Written May 12, 1850, in his *Journal*, vol. 3, p. 65

I take my neighbor, an intellectual man, out into the woods and invite him to take a new and absolute view of things, to empty clean out of his thoughts all institutions of men and start again; but he can't do it, he sticks to his traditions and his crotchets.

Written May 12, 1857, in his *Journal*, vol. IX, p. 362

Associate reverently and as much as you can with your loftiest thoughts.

Written January 22, 1852, in his *Journal*, vol. 4, p. 277

The thinker, he who is serene and self-possessed, is the brave, not the desperate soldier.

Written May 6, 1858, in his *Journal*, vol. X, p. 404

Cars go by & we know their substance as well as their shadow. They stop & we get into them. But those sublime thoughts passing on high do not stop & we never get into them. Their conductor is not like one of us.

Written February 27, 1851, in his *Journal*, vol. 3, p. 200

Walking in the woods it may be some afternoon the shadow of the wings of a thought flits across the landscape of my mind and I am reminded how little eventful is our lives. What have been all these wars & survivors of wars and modern discoveries & improvements so called a mere irritation in the skin. But this shadow which is so soon past & whose substance is not detected suggests that there are events of importance whose interval is to us a true historic period.

Written February 27, 1851, in his *Journal*, vol. 3, p. 200

Is not he hospitable who entertains thoughts?

Written June 12, 1851, in his *Journal*, vol. 3, p. 259

The mind tastes but few flavors in the course of a year. We are visited by but few thoughts which are worth

entertaining, and we chew the cud of these unceas-
ingly. What ruminant spirits we are!

Written August 9, 1858, in his *Journal*, vol. XI, p. 89

If I am visited by a thought, I chew that cud each suc-
cessive morning, as long as there is any flavor in it.
Until my keepers shake down some fresh fodder. Our
genius is like a brush which only once in many months
is freshly dipped into the paint-pot. It becomes so dry
that though we apply it incessantly, it fails to tinge our
earth and sky. Applied to the same spot incessantly, it
at length imparts no color to it.

Written August 9, 1858, in his *Journal*, vol. XI, p. 89

Thoughts of different dates will not cohere.

Written February 8, 1852, in his *Journal*, vol. 4, p. 336

Hold fast to your most indefinite, waking dream. The
very green dust on the walls is an organized vegetable;
the atmosphere has its fauna and flora floating in it;
and shall we think that dreams are but dust and ashes,
are always disintegrated and crumbling thoughts, and
not dust-like thoughts trooping to their standard with
music,—systems beginning to be organized?

To H.G.O. Blake, February 27, 1853, in *Familiar Letters*, p. 216

You *fail* in your thoughts, or you *prevail* in your
thoughts only.

To H.G.O. Blake, September 26, 1859, in *The Correspondence of
Henry David Thoreau*, p. 558

When I was young and compelled to pass my Sunday in the house without the aid of interesting books, I used to spend many an hour till the wished-for sun-down watching the martins soar (from an attic window) and fortunate indeed did I deem myself when a hawk appeared in the heavens though far toward the horizon against a downy cloud and I searched for hours till I had found his mate. They at least took my thoughts from earthly things.

Written April 17, 1852, in his *Journal*, vol. 4, pp. 458–459

I pine for one to whom I can speak my *first thoughts*—thoughts which represent me truly, which are no better & no worse than I—thoughts which have the bloom on them—which alone can be sacred and divine.

Written August 24, 1852, in his *Journal*, vol. 5, p. 311

What philosopher can estimate the different values of a waking thought & a dream?

Written March 31, 1852, in his *Journal*, vol. 4, p. 408

You must walk like a camel, which is said to be the only beast which ruminates while walking.

Written after October 31, 1850, in his *Journal*, vol. 3, p. 130

You conquer fate by thought.

Written May 6, 1858, in his *Journal*, vol. X, p. 405

My thoughts are my company.

Written January 22, 1852, in his *Journal*, vol. 4, p. 277

Our thoughts are the epochs in our lives: all else is but as a journal of the winds that blew while we were here.

To H.G.O. Blake, August 9, 1850, in *The Correspondence of Henry David Thoreau*, p. 265

All I can say is that I live & breathe & have my thoughts.

Written after July 29, 1850, in his *Journal*, vol. 3, p. 97

Each thought that is welcomed and recorded is a nest egg by the side of which more will be laid.

Written January 22, 1852, in his *Journal*, vol. 4, p. 277

The more you have thought and written on a given theme, the more you can still write. Thought breeds thought.

Written February 13, 1860, in his *Journal*, vol. XIII, p. 145

Do not seek expressions—seek thoughts to be expressed.

Written December 25, 1851, in his *Journal*, vol. 4, p. 223

TIME

Take time by the forelock. Now or never! You must live in the present, launch yourself on every wave, find your eternity in each moment.

Written April 24, 1859, in his *Journal*, vol. XII, p. 159

Time is but the stream I go a-fishing in. I drink at it; but while I drink I see the sandy bottom and detect how shallow it is. Its thin current slides away, but eternity remains. I would drink deeper; fish in the sky, whose bottom is pebbly with stars.

Walden, p. 98

I delight to come to my bearings,—not walk in procession with pomp and parade, in a conspicuous place, but to walk even with the Builder of the universe, if I may,—not to live in this restless, nervous, bustling, trivial Nineteenth Century, but stand or sit thoughtfully while it goes by.

Walden, pp. 329–330

Nothing can be more useful to a man than a determination not to be hurried.

Written March 22, 1842, in his *Journal*, vol. 1, p. 385

Be not in haste; mind your private affairs. Consider the turtle. A whole summer—June, July, and August—is not too good nor too much to hatch a turtle in. Perchance you have worried yourself, despaired of the world, meditated the end of life, and all things seemed rushing to destruction; but nature has steadily and serenely advanced with a turtle's pace.

Written August 28, 1856, in his *Journal*, vol. IX, pp. 32–33

Keep the time. Observe the hours of the universe—not of the cars.

Written December 28, 1852, in his *Journal*, vol. 5, p. 412

He that is not behind his time is swift.

Written September 13, 1852, in his *Journal*, vol. 5, p. 343

We are inclined to think of all Romans who lived within five hundred years B.C. as *contemporaries* to each other. Yet Time moved at the same deliberate pace then as now.

Written December 8, 1859, in his *Journal*, vol. XIII, p. 16

Both for bodily & mental health court the present.

Written December 28, 1852, in his *Journal*, vol. 5, p. 412

A man who is not prompt affects me as a creature covered with slime, crawling through mud and lying dormant a great part of the year.

Written September 16, 1859, in his *Journal*, vol. XII, p. 330

Time hides no treasures. We want not its then, but its now.

Written August 9, 1841, and transcribed in 1842 in his *Journal*, vol. 1, p. 414

Time is cheap and rather insignificant. It matters not whether it is a river which changes from side to side in a geological period or an eel that wriggles past in an instant.

Written March 24, 1855, in his *Journal*, vol. VII, pp. 268–269

When I see a stone which it must have taken many yoke of oxen to move lying in a bank wall which was built 200 years ago, I am curiously surprised because it suggests an energy & force of which we have no memorials. Where are the traces of the corresponding moral and intellectual energy?

Written after May 12, 1850, in his *Journal*, vol. 3, p. 71

I do not remember any page which will tell me how to spend this afternoon. I do not so much wish to know how to economize time as how to spend it—by what means to grow rich.

Written September 7, 1851, in his *Journal*, vol. 4, p. 52

If time is short then you have no time to waste.

Written November 16, 1851, in his *Journal*, vol. 4, p. 191

As if you could kill time without injuring eternity.

Walden, p. 8

TRAVEL AND HOME

A man is worth most to himself and to others, whether as an observer, or poet, or neighbor, or friend, where he is most himself, most contented and at home.

Written November 20, 1857, in his *Journal*, vol. X, p. 190

I am afraid to travel much or to famous places lest it might completely dissipate the mind.

Written January 30, 1852, in his *Journal*, vol. 4, p. 309

Fig. 13. Thoreau's house at Walden Pond, based on a sketch by Sophia
Thoreau. Reproduced from the title page of the first edition of *Walden, or,
Life in the Woods* (Boston: Ticknor and Fields, 1854). The Walter Harding
Collection (The Thoreau Society* Collections at the Thoreau Institute).
Courtesy of the Thoreau Society.

Pursue some path, however solitary and narrow and
crooked, in which you can walk with love and reverence. Wherever a man separates from the multitude
and goes his own way, there indeed is a fork in the
road, though the ordinary travellers may along the
high way see only a gap in the paling.

Written October 18, 1855, in his *Journal*, vol. VII, p. 492;
emended from manuscript Journal (MA 1302, The Morgan
Library & Museum, New York)

We only need travel enough to give our intellects an airing.

Written November 20, 1857, in his *Journal*, vol. X, p. 191

A Traveller! I love his title. A Traveller is to be reverenced as such. His profession is the best symbol of our life. Going from—toward—

Written July 2, 1851, in his *Journal*, vol. 3, p. 283

Our life should be so active and progressive as to be a journey.

Written January 28, 1852, in his *Journal*, vol. 4, p. 297

I would say then to my vagrant countrymen—Go not to any foreign theater for spectacles, but consider first that there is nothing which can delight or astonish the eyes, but you may discover it all in yourselves.

"Reform and the Reformers" in *Reform Papers*, p. 194

The question is not where did the traveller go? What places did he see? It would be difficult to choose between places. But who was the traveller? How did he travel? How genuine an experience did he get? For travelling is in the main like as if you staid at home, & then the question is how do you live & conduct yourself at home?

Written January 11, 1852, in his *Journal*, vol. 4, p. 246

We are shown far scenes in order that we may be tempted to inhabit them, and not simply tell what we have seen.

Written November 24, 1857, in his *Journal*, vol. X, p. 202

It is not worth the while to go round the world to count the cats in Zanzibar.

Walden, p. 322

When you are starting away—leaving your more familiar fields for a little adventure like a walk—you look at every object with a traveller's or at least with historical eyes—you pause on the first bridge, where an ordinary walk hardly commences, & begin to observe & moralize like a traveller. It is worth the while to see your native village thus sometimes—as if you were a traveller passing through it—commenting on your neighbors as strangers.

Written September 4, 1851, in his *Journal*, vol. 4, p. 37

There would be this advantage in travelling in your own country even in your own neighborhood, that you would be so thoroughly prepared to understand what you saw.

Written June 12, 1851, in his *Journal*, vol. 3, p. 259

To travel and "descry new lands" is to think new thoughts, and have new imaginings.

Written August 13, 1840, in his *Journal*, vol. 1, p. 171

The deepest and most original thinker is the farthest travelled.

Written August 13, 1840, in his *Journal*, vol. 1, p. 171

I have travelled a good deal in Concord.

Walden, p. 4

It takes a man of genius to travel in his own country—
in his native village—to make any progress between his
door & his gate.

> Written August 6, 1851, in his *Journal*, vol. 3, p. 357

I have a real genius for staying at home.

> To Daniel Ricketson, February 1, 1855, in *The Correspondence of
> Henry David Thoreau*, p. 369

He who rides and keeps the beaten track studies the
fences chiefly.

> *The Maine Woods*, p. 86

Far travel, very *far* travel, or travail, comes near to the
worth of staying at home—

> To Isaac Hecker, after August 15, 1844, in *The Correspondence of
> Henry David Thoreau*, p. 158

Take the shortest way round and stay at home.

> Written November 1, 1858, in his *Journal*, vol. XI, p. 275

Cleave to the simplest ever—Home—home—home.

> To H.G.O. Blake, September 27, 1855, in *The Correspondence of
> Henry David Thoreau*, p. 386

Here I am at home. In the bare and bleached crust of
the earth I recognize my friend.

> Written November 1, 1858, in his *Journal*, vol. XI, p. 275

You must love the crust of the earth on which you
dwell more than the sweet crust of any bread or
cake. You must be able to extract nutriment out of a

sand-heap. You must have so good an appetite as this, else you will live in vain.

Written January 25, 1858, in his *Journal*, vol. X, p. 258

Here, of course, is all that you love, all that you expect, all that you are. Here is your bride elect, as close to you as she can be got. Here is all the best and all the worst you can imagine. What more do you want? Bear here-away then! Foolish people imagine that what they imagine is somewhere else. That stuff is not made in any factory but your own.

Written November 1, 1858, in his *Journal*, vol. XI, p. 275

Only that travelling is good which reveals to me the value of home and enables me to enjoy it better.

Written March 11, 1856, in his *Journal*, vol. VIII, p. 205

Today you may write a chapter on the advantages of travelling & to-morrow you may write another chapter on the advantages of not travelling.

Written November 11, 1851, in his *Journal*, vol. 4, p. 177

One says to me, "I wonder that you do not lay up money; you love to travel; you might take the cars and go to Fitchburg to-day and see the country." But I am wiser than that. I have learned that the swiftest travel-ler is he who goes afoot. I say to my friend, Suppose we try who will get there first. The distance is thirty miles; the fare ninety cents. That is almost a day's wages. I remember when wages were sixty cents a day for labor-ers on this very road. Well, I start now on foot, and get there before night; I have travelled at that rate by the week together. You will in the mean while have earned your fare, and arrive there some time to-morrow, or possibly this evening, if you are lucky enough to get a job in season. Instead of going to Fitchburg, you will be working here the greater part of the day. And so, if the railroad reached round the world, I think that I should keep ahead of you; and as for seeing the country and getting experience of that kind, I should have to cut your acquaintance altogether.

Walden, p. 53

A traveller who looks at things with an impartial eye may see what the oldest inhabitant has not observed.

Written August 20, 1851, in his *Journal*, vol. 3, p. 384

The discoveries which we make abroad are special and particular—those which we make at home are general & significant. The further off the nearer the surface. The nearer home the deeper.

Written September 7, 1851, in his *Journal*, vol. 4, p. 54

This is a common experience in my travelling. I plod along, thinking what a miserable world this is and what miserable fellows we that inhabit it, wondering what it is tempts men to live in it; but anon I leave the town behind and am lost in some boundless heath, and life becomes gradually more tolerable, if not even glorious.

Written June 17, 1857, in his *Journal*, vol. IX, p. 432

It is far more independent to travel on foot. You have to sacrifice so much to the horse. You cannot choose the most agreeable places in which to spend the noon, commanding the finest views, because commonly there is no water there, or you cannot get there with your horse.

Written July 4, 1858, in his *Journal*, vol. XI, p. 7

A man must generally get away some hundreds or thousands of miles from home before he can be said to begin his travels. Why not begin his travels at home! Would he have to go far or look very closely to discover novelties? The traveller who in this sense pursues his travels at home, has the advantage at any rate of a long residence in the country to make his observations correct & profitable. Now the American goes to England while the Englishman comes to America in order to describe the country. No doubt there some advantages in this kind of mutual criticism, but might there not be invented a better way of coming at the truth than this scratch my back and I'll scratch yours method?

Written August 6, 1851, in his *Journal*, vol. 3, pp. 356–357

When it was proposed to me to go abroad, rub off some rust, and *better my condition* in a worldly sense, I fear lest my life will lose some of its homeliness. If these fields and streams and woods, the phenomena of nature here, and the simple occupations of the inhabitants should cease to interest and inspire me, no culture or wealth would atone for the loss. I fear the dissipation that travelling, going into society, even the best, the enjoyment of intellectual luxuries, imply.

Written March 11, 1856, in his *Journal*, vol. VIII, p. 204

I cannot but regard it as a kindness in those who have the steering of me that by the want of pecuniary wealth I have been nailed down to this my native region so long & steadily and made to study & love this spot of earth more & more. What would signify in comparison a thin & diffused love and knowledge of the whole earth instead, got by wandering? The traveller's is but a barren & comfortless condition.

Written November 12, 1853, in his *Journal*, vol. 7, p. 156

I want nothing new, if I can have but a tithe of the old secured to me. I will spurn all wealth beside. Think of the consummate folly of attempting to go away from *here*! When the constant endeavor should be to get nearer and nearer *here*.

Written November 1, 1858, in his *Journal*, vol. XI, p. 275

The man who is often thinking that it is better to be somewhere else than where he is excommunicates himself.

Written November 20, 1857, in his *Journal*, vol. X, pp. 190–191

TREES AND WOODS

What shall we do with a man who is afraid of the woods—their solitude & darkness? What salvation is there for him? God is silent & mysterious.

Written November 16, 1850, in his *Journal*, vol. 3, p. 142

When the chopper would praise a pine, he will commonly tell you, that the one he cut was so big that a yoke of oxen stood on its stump. As if that were what the pine had grown for—to become the footstool of oxen!

The Maine Woods, p. 229

The civilized man regards the pine tree as his enemy. He will fell it & let in the light—grub it up & raise wheat or rye there. It is no better than a fungus to him.

Written February 2, 1852, in his *Journal*, vol. 4, p. 320

Nothing stands up more free from blame in this world than a pine tree.

Written December 20, 1851, in his *Journal*, vol. 4, p. 212

Nothing is so beautiful as the tree tops.

"A Winter Walk" in Excursions, p. 60

The fruit of a tree is neither in the seed or in the full grown tree (the timber) but it is simply the highest use to which it can be put.

Written March 7, 1859, in his *Journal*, vol. XII, p. 24; emended from manuscript Journal (MA 1302, The Morgan Library & Museum, New York)

Every larger tree which I knew and admired is being gradually culled out and carried to mill. . . . I miss them as surely and with the same feeling that I do the old inhabitants out of the village street.

Written December 3, 1855, in his *Journal*, vol. VIII, p. 38

This winter they are cutting down our woods more seriously than ever—Fair Haven Hill—Walden—Lin-
naea Borealis wood &c &c. Thank God they cannot cut
down the clouds!

Written January 21, 1852, in his *Journal*, vol. 4, p. 273

These are the remnants of the primitive wood methinks. We are a young people & have not learned by
experience the consequence of cutting off the forest.

Written September 5, 1854, in his *Journal*, vol. 4, p. 45

The invigorating scent of the recently cut pines refreshes
us—if that is any atonement for this devastation.

Written January 2, 1853, in his *Journal*, vol. 5, p. 418

Though they are cutting off the woods at Walden it is
not all loss. It makes some new & unexpected
prospects.

Written January 30, 1852, in his *Journal*, vol. 4, p. 307

What though the woods be cut down, this emergency
was long ago foreseen and provided for by Nature, and
the interregnum is not allowed to be a barren one. She
is full of resources: she not only begins instantly to heal
that scar, but she consoles (compensates?) and refreshes
us with fruits such as the forest did not produce. To
console us she heaps our baskets with berries.

Written December 30, 1860, in his *Journal*, vol. XIV, p. 301

Methinks the town should have more supervision &
control over its parks than it has. It concerns us all

whether these proprietors choose to cut down all the woods this winter or not.

Written January 22, 1852, in his *Journal*, vol. 4, p. 276

These woods! Why do I not feel their being cut more sorely? Does it not affect me nearly? The axe can deprive me of much. Concord is sheared of its pride. I am certainly the less attached to my native town in consequence. One & a main link is broken. I shall go to Walden less frequently.

Written January 24, 1852, in his *Journal*, vol. 4, p. 283

I do not know but a pine wood is as substantial and as memorable a fact as a friend. I am more sure to come away from it cheered than from those who come nearest to being my friends.

Written December 17, 1851, in his *Journal*, vol. 4, pp. 207–208

How beautiful when a whole tree is like one great scarlet fruit, full of ripe juices, every leaf, from lowest limb to topmost spire, all a-glow, especially if you look toward the sun. What more remarkable object can there be in the landscape?

"Autumnal Tints" in *Excursions*, p. 232

Well may the tender buds attract us at this season, no less than partridges, for they are the hope of the year, the spring rolled up. The summer is all packed in them.

Written January 12, 1855, in his *Journal*, vol. VII, p. 114

The scarlet oak leaf! What a graceful and pleasing outline! a combination of graceful curves and angles. . . .
If I were a drawing-master, I would set my pupils to
copying these leaves, that they might learn to draw
firmly and gracefully. It is a shore to the aerial ocean,
on which the windy surf beats.

Written November 11, 1858, in his *Journal*, vol. XI, p. 314

I should not be ashamed to have a shrub oak for my
coat-of-arms.

Written January 7, 1857, in his *Journal*, vol. IX, p. 207

Many times I thought that if the particular tree, commonly an elm, under which I was walking or riding
were the only one like it in the country, it would be
worth a journey across the continent to see it. Indeed,
I have no doubt that such journies would be under-
taken on hearing a true account of it.

Written January 18, 1859, in his *Journal*, vol. XI, p. 405;
emended from manuscript Journal (MA 1302, The Morgan
Library & Museum, New York)

In the twilight when you can see only the outlines of
the trees in the horizon—the elm tops indicate where
the houses are.

Written September 6, 1850, in his *Journal*, vol. 3, p. 111

There was reason enough for the first settlers selecting
the elm out of all the trees of the forest with which to
ornament his villages. It is beautiful alike by sunlight &
moonlight and the most beautiful specimens are not
the largest. I have seen some only 25 or 30 years old,

more graceful and healthy I think than any others. It is almost become a villageous tree—like martins & blue birds.

Written after July 29, 1850, in his *Journal*, vol. 3, p. 102

See how artfully the seed of a cherry is placed in order that a bird may be compelled to transport it. It is placed in the very midst of a tempting pericarp, so that the creature that would devour a cherry must take a stone into its mouth. The bird is bribed with the pericarp to take the stone with it and do this little service for Nature.

Written September 1, 1860, in his *Journal*, vol. XIV, p. 70

The cars on our railroad, and all their passengers, roll over the trunks of trees *sleeping* beneath them which were planted years before the first white man settled in New England.

Written November 21, 1860, in his *Journal*, vol. XIV, p. 257

The farmer sometimes talks of "brushing up," simply as if bare ground looked better than clothed ground, than that which wears its natural vesture,—as if the wild hedges, which, perhaps, are more to his children than his whole farm beside, were *dirt*. I know of one who deserves to be called the Tree-hater, and, perhaps, to leave this for a new patronymic to his children. You would think that he had been warned by an oracle that he would be killed by the fall of a tree, and so was resolved to anticipate them.

The Maine Woods, p. 154

It is not in vain perhaps that every winter the forest is brought to our doors shaggy with lichens. Even in so humble a shape as a wood-pile it contains sermons for us.

Written September 26, 1852, in his *Journal*, vol. 5, p. 354

Is it the lumberman then who is the friend and lover of the pine—stands nearest to it and understands its nature best? Is it the tanner who has barked it, or he who has boxed it for turpentine, whom posterity will fable to have been changed into a pine at last? No! no! it is the poet; he it is who makes the truest use of the pine— who does not fondle it with an axe, nor tickle it with a saw, nor stroke it with a plane; who knows whether its heart is false without cutting into it; who has not bought the stumpage of the township on which it stands. All the pines shudder and heave a sigh when *that* man steps on the forest floor. No, it is the poet, who loves them as his own shadow in the air, and lets them stand.

The Maine Woods, pp. 121–122

I have been into the lumber yard, and the carpenter's shop, and the tannery, and the lampblack factory, and the turpentine clearing; but when at length I saw the tops of the pines waving and reflecting the light at a distance high over all the rest of the forest, I realized that the former were not the highest use of the pine. It is not their bones or hide or tallow that I love most. It is the living spirit of the tree, not its spirit of turpentine, with which I can sympathize, and which heals my cuts. It is as immortal as I am, and perchance will go to as high a heaven, there to tower above me still.

The Maine Woods, p. 122

All trees covered this morning with a hoar frost, very handsome looking toward the sun,—the ghosts of trees.

Written February 12, 1855, in his *Journal,* vol. VII, p. 179

TRUTH AND SINCERITY

It takes two to speak the truth,—one to speak, and another to hear.

A Week on the Concord and Merrimack Rivers, p. 267

In accumulating property for ourselves or our posterity, in founding a family or a state, or acquiring fame even, we are mortal; but in dealing with truth we are immortal, and need fear no change nor accident.

Walden, p. 99

Any truth is better than make-believe.

Walden, p. 327

What is truth? That which we know not—

"Sir Walter Raleigh" second draft manuscript (Walden Woods Project Collection at the Thoreau Institute at Walden Woods)

Rather than love, than money, than fame, give me truth. I sat at a table where were rich food and wine in abundance, and obsequious attendance, but sincerity and truth were not; and I went away hungry from the inhospitable board.

Walden, pp. 330–331

No face which we can give to a matter will stead us so well at last as the truth. This alone wears well.

Walden, p. 327

If we dealt only with the false and dishonest, we should at last forget how to speak truth.

A Week on the Concord and Merrimack Rivers, p. 267

They who know of no purer sources of truth, who have traced up its stream no higher, stand, and wisely stand, by the Bible and the Constitution, and drink at it there with reverence and humility; but they who behold where it comes trickling into this lake or that pool, gird up their loins once more, and continue their pilgrimage toward its fountain-head.

"Resistance to Civil Government" in *Reform Papers*, p. 88

Men esteem truth remote, in the outskirts of the system, behind the farthest star, before Adam and after the last man.

Walden, pp. 96–97

We do not learn by inference and deduction, and the application of mathematics to philosophy, but by direct intercourse and sympathy. It is with science as with ethics, we cannot know truth by contrivance and method.

"Natural History of Massachusetts" in *Excursions*, p. 28

Men are making speeches . . . all over the country, but each expresses only the thought or the want of thought of the multitude. No man stands on truth.

Written May 4, 1852, in his *Journal*, vol. 5, p. 24

In our science and philosophy, even, there is commonly no true and absolute account of things.

"Life without Principle" in *Reform Papers*, p. 167

All perception of truth is the detection of an analogy.

Written September 5, 1851, in his *Journal*, vol. 4, p. 46

There are innumerable avenues to a perception of the truth.

Written September 4, 1851, in his *Journal*, vol. 4, p. 41

It is a rare qualification to be ably to state a fact simply & adequately. To digest some experience cleanly. To say yes and no with authority. To make a square edge. To conceive & suffer the truth to pass through us living & intact.

Written November 1, 1851, in his *Journal*, vol. 4, p. 157

It is remarkable that the highest intellectual mood which the world tolerates is the perception of the truth of the most ancient revelations, now in some respects out of date, but any direct revelation, any original thoughts it hates like virtue.

> Written November 16, 1851, in his *Journal*, vol. 4, p. 188

As the least drop of wine tinges the whole goblet, so the least particle of truth colors our whole life.

> Written December 31, 1837, in his *Journal*, vol. 1, p. 24

Not that I do not stand on all I have written—but what am I to the truth I feebly utter!

> To Calvin Greene, February 10, 1856, in *The Correspondence of Henry David Thoreau*, p. 407

It is a great satisfaction to find that your oldest convictions are permanent. With regard to essentials, I have never had occasion to change my mind. The aspect of the world varies from year to year, as the landscape is differently clothed, but I find that the *truth* is still *true*, and I never regret any emphasis which it may have inspired.

> To H.G.O. Blake, August 18, 1857, in *The Correspondence of Henry David Thoreau*, p. 491

Let us make distinctions, call things by the right names.

> Written November 28, 1860, in his *Journal*, vol. XIV, p. 278

Nothing is so sure to make itself known as the truth— for what else waits to be known?

> Written December 12, 1851, in his *Journal*, vol. 4, p. 203

I love to weigh, to settle, to gravitate toward that which most strongly and rightfully attracts me;—not hang by the beam of the scale and try to weigh less,—not suppose a case, but take the case that is; to travel the only path I can, and that on which no power can resist me.

> *Walden*, p. 330

The lawyer's truth is not Truth, but consistency, or a consistent expediency.

> "Resistance to Civil Government" in *Reform Papers*, p. 87

I am sorry to think that you do not get a man's most effective criticism until you provoke him. Severe truth is expressed with some bitterness.

> Written March 15, 1854, in his *Journal*, vol. 8, p. 43

A world in which there is a demand for ice creams but not for truths.

> Written August 24, 1852, in his *Journal*, vol. 5, p. 310

Truth is ever returning into herself. I glimpse one feature to-day—another to-morrow—and the next day they are blended.

> Written November 13, 1837, in his *Journal*, vol. 1, p. 11

I fear chiefly lest my expression may not be *extra-vagant* enough, may not wander far enough beyond the narrow limits of my daily experience, so as to be adequate to the truth of which I have been convinced.

> *Walden*, p. 324

It is remarkable how long men will believe in the bot-
tomlessness of a pond without taking the trouble to
sound it.

Walden, p. 285

I too would fain set down something beside facts. Facts
should only be as the frame to my pictures. They
should be material to the mythology which I am writing. Not facts to assist men to make money—farmers
to farm profitably in any common sense. Facts to tell
who I am—and where I have been—or what I have
thought.

Written November 9, 1851, in his *Journal*, vol. 4, p. 170

Truth strikes us from behind, and in the dark, as well
as from before and in broad day-light.

Written November 5, 1837, in his *Journal*, vol. 1, p. 10

I care not whether my vision of truth is a waking thought
or dream remembered, where it is seen in the light or in
the dark. It is the subject of the vision, the truth alone,
that concerns me. The philosopher for whom rainbows,
etc., can be explained away never saw them.

Written November 5, 1857, in his *Journal*, vol. X, p. 165

The settled lecturers are as tame as the settled minis-
ters. The audiences do not want to hear any prophets;
they do not wish to be stimulated and instructed, but
entertained. They, their wives and daughters, go to the
Lyceum to suck a sugar-plum. The little of medicine

they get is disguised with sugar. It is never the re-former they hear there, but a faint and timid echo of him only. They seek a pass-time merely. . . . They ask for orators that will entertain them and leave them where they found them.

Written November 16, 1858, in his *Journal*, vol. XI, pp. 327–328

It is not enough that we are truthful; we must cherish and carry out high purposes to be truthful about.

"Love" in *Early Essays and Miscellanies*, p. 272

Sincerity is a great but rare virtue.

To H.G.O. Blake, September 26, 1855, in *The Correspondence of Henry David Thoreau*, p. 383

What I was learning in college was chiefly, I think, to express myself, and I see now, that as the old orator pre-scribed, 1st, action; 2nd, action; 3d, action; my teachers should have prescribed to me, 1st, sincerity; 2nd, sin-cerity; 3d, sincerity. . . . I mean sincerity in our dealings with ourselves mainly; any other is comparatively easy.

To Richard Fuller, at Harvard, April 2, 1843, in *The Correspon-dence of Henry David Thoreau*, p. 94

To live in relations of truth & sincerity with men is to dwell in a frontier country.

Written January 12, 1852, in his *Journal*, vol. 4, p. 249

Would not men have something to communicate if they were sincere?

Written August 24, 1852, in his *Journal*, vol. 5, p. 310

Deep are the foundations of sincerity.

A Week on the Concord and Merrimack Rivers, p. 329

WALKING

Fig. 14. Old Marlborough Road, Concord, Massachusetts. Photographer: Herbert W. Gleason. Reproduced from *The Writings of Henry D. Thoreau*. The Walden Woods Project Collection at the Thoreau Institute at Walden Woods. Courtesy of the Walden Woods Project.

It is a great art to saunter.

Written April 26, 1841, in his *Journal*, vol. 1, p. 304

I think that I cannot preserve my health and spirits unless I spend four hours a day at least—and it is commonly more than that—sauntering through the woods and over the hills and fields absolutely free from all worldly engagements.

"Walking" in *Excursions*, p. 187

An early morning walk is a blessing for the whole day.

Written April 20, 1840, in his *Journal*, vol. 1, p. 122

Men have cleared some of the earth which no doubt is an advantage to the walker.

Written January 26, 1853, in his *Journal*, vol. 5, p. 454

I am alarmed when it happens that I have walked a mile into the woods bodily, without getting there in spirit. In my afternoon walk I would fain forget all my morning occupations, and my obligations to society. But it sometimes happens that I cannot easily shake off the village. The thought of some work will run in my head, and I am not where my body is; I am out of my senses. In my walks I would fain return to my senses. What business have I in the woods, if I am thinking of something out of the woods?

"Walking" in *Excursions*, p. 190

Walking may be a science so far as the direction of a walk is concerned. I go again to the great meadows to improve this remarkably dry season & walk where in ordinary times I cannot go. There is no doubt a particular season of the year when each place may be visited with most profit & pleasure and it may be worth the while to consider what that season is in each case.

Written August 22, 1854, in his *Journal*, vol. 8, p. 288

You must walk sometimes perfectly free—not prying nor inquisitive—not bent upon seeing things—Throw away a whole day for a single expansion.

Written August 21, 1851, in his *Journal*, vol. 4, p. 6

I must walk more with free senses.

Written September 13, 1852, in his *Journal*, vol. 5, p. 343

I set out once more to climb the mountain of the earth for my steps are symbolical steps & in all my walking I have not reached the top of the earth yet.

Written March 21, 1853, in his *Journal*, vol. 6, p. 22

I wonder that I even get 5 miles on my way the walk is so crowded with events & phenomena.

Written June 7, 1851, in his *Journal*, vol. 3, p. 245

1½ AM. Full moon. Arose and went to the river and bathed, stepping very carefully not to disturb the household and still carefully in the street not to disturb the neighbors. I did not walk naturally & freely till I had got over the wall.

Written August 12, 1851, in his *Journal*, vol. 3, p. 362

I have met with but one or two persons in the course of my life who understood the art of Walking, that is, of taking walks, who had a genius, so to speak, for *saun-tering*; which word is beautifully derived "from idle people who roved about the country, in the middle ages, and asked charity, under pretence of going *à la sainte terre*"—to the holy land, till the children exclaimed, "There goes a *sainte-terrer*", a saunterer—a holy-lander. They who never go to the holy land in their walks, as they pretend, are indeed mere idlers and vagabonds, but they who do go there are saunterers in the good sense, such as I mean.

"Walking" in *Excursions*, p. 185

My walks were full of incidents. I attended not to the affairs of Europe but to my own affairs in Concord fields.

Written January 20, 1852, in his *Journal*, vol. 4, p. 270

I trust that the walkers of the present day are conscious of the blessings which they enjoy in the comparative freedom with which they can ramble over the country & enjoy the landscape.

Written February 12, 1851, in his *Journal*, vol. 3, pp. 189–190

I do not know how to entertain one who can't take long walks. The first thing that suggests itself is to get a horse to draw them, and that brings us at once into contact with stablers and dirty harness, and I do not get over my ride for a long time. I give up my forenoon to them and get along pretty well, the very elasticity of the air and promise of the day abetting me, but they are as heavy as dumplings by mid-afternoon.

Written October 7, 1857, in his *Journal*, vol. X, p. 74

After walking by night several times, I now walk by day, but I am not aware of any crowning advantage in it. I see small objects better, but it does not enlighten me any. The day is more trivial.

Written June 15, 1851, in his *Journal*, vol. 3, p. 272

It requires considerable skill in crossing a country to avoid the houses & too cultivated parts— . . . For that route which most avoids the houses is not only the one in which you will be least molested but it is by far the most agreeable.

Written June 19, 1852, in his *Journal*, vol. 5, p. 114

A turtle walking is as if a man were to try to walk by sticking his legs & arms merely out the windows.

Written May 27, 1853, in his *Journal*, vol. 6, p. 154

WATER: RIVERS, PONDS, AND OCEANS

Who hears the rippling of the rivers will not utterly despair of anything.

Written December 12, 1841, in his *Journal*, vol. 1, p. 342

Every rill is a channel for the juices of the meadow.

"Natural History of Massachusetts," in *Excursions*, p. 18

The water sleeps with stars in its bosom.

Written May 5, 1852, in his *Journal*, vol. 5, p. 29

How cheering it is to behold a full spring bursting forth directly from the earth. . . . I lie almost flat resting my hands on what offers to drink at this water where it bubbles at the very udders of nature for man is never weaned from her breast while this life lasts. How many times in a single walk does he stoop for a draught.

Written July 5, 1852, in his *Journal*, vol. 5, p. 186

For the first time it occurred to me this afternoon what a piece of wonder a river is.—A huge volume of matter ceaselessly rolling through the fields and meadows of this substantial earth making haste from the high places, by stable dwellings of men and Egyptian pyramids, to its restless reservoir. One would think that, by a very natural impulse, the dwellers upon the headwaters of the Mississippi and Amazon would follow in the trail of their waters to see the end of the matter.

Written September 5, 1838, in his *Journal*, vol. 1, p. 55

I should prefer that my farm be bounded by a river—It is to live on the outside of the world and to be well flanked on one side.

Written April 19, 1843, in his *Journal*, vol. 1, p. 454

The river is my own highway the only wild & unfenced part of the world hereabouts.

Written May 30, 1852, in his *Journal*, vol. 5, p. 76

A lake is the landscape's most beautiful and expressive feature. It is earth's eye; looking into which the beholder measures the depth of his own nature.

Walden, p. 186

To go to the sea! Why, it is to have the experience of Noah,—to realize the deluge. Every vessel is an ark.

Cape Cod, p. 149

A field of water betrays the spirit that is in the air. It is continually receiving new life and motion from above. It is intermediate in its nature between land and sky.

Walden, pp. 188–189

Nothing so fair, so pure, and at the same time so large, as a lake, perchance, lies on the surface of the earth. Sky water.

Walden, p. 188

The sea-shore is a sort of neutral ground, a most advantageous point from which to contemplate this world.

Cape Cod, p. 147

I am made to love the pond & the meadow as the wind to ripple the water.

Written November 21, 1850, in his *Journal*, vol. 3, p. 148

I think that I speak impartially when I say that I have never met with a stream so suitable for boating and botanizing as the Concord, and fortunately nobody knows it. I know of reaches which a single country-seat would spoil beyond remedy, but there has not been any important change here since I can remember.

Written August 6, 1858, in his *Journal*, vol. XI, p. 77

We pass haymakers in every meadow, who may think that we are idlers. But nature takes care that every nook and crevice is explored by some one. While they look after the open meadows, we farm the tract between the river's brinks and behold the shores from that side. We, too, are harvesting an annual crop with our eyes, and think you Nature is not glad to display her beauty to us?

Written August 6, 1858, in his *Journal*, vol. XI, p. 77

It is pleasant to embark on a voyage—if only for a short river excursion—the boat to be your home for the day— especially if it is neat & dry—a sort of moving studio it becomes—you can carry so many things with you. It is almost as if you put oars out at your windows & moved your house along.

Written August 31, 1852, in his *Journal*, vol. 5, pp. 319–320

No wonder men love to be sailors, to be blown about the world sitting at the helm, to shave the capes & see the islands disappear under their sterns—gubernators to a piece of wood. It disposes to contemplation & is to me instead of smoking.

Written August 30, 1853, in his *Journal*, vol. 7, pp. 23–24

I like to remember that at the end of half a day's walk I can stand on the bank of the Merrimack. It is just wide enough to interrupt the land and lead my eye and thought down its channel to the sea. A river is superior to a lake in its liberating influence. It has motion and indefinite length. A river touching the back of a town is like a wing, it may be unused as yet, but ready to waft it over the world. With its rapid current it is a slightly fluttering wing. River towns are winged towns.

Written July 2, 1858, in his *Journal*, vol. XI, pp. 4–5

Again, rivers appear to have travelled back and worn into the meadows of their creating, and then they become more meandering than ever. Thus in the course of ages the rivers wriggle in their beds, till it feels comfortable under them.

Written March 24, 1855, in his *Journal*, vol. VII, p. 268

What can be more impressive than to look up a noble river just at evening—one perchance which you have never explored—& behold its placid waters reflecting the woods & sky lapsing inaudibly toward the ocean—to behold as a lake but know it as a river—tempting the beholder to explore it & his own destiny at once.

Written July 9, 1851, in his *Journal*, vol. 3, p. 297

Rivers must have been the guides which conducted the footsteps of the first travellers. They are the constant lure, when they flow by our doors, to distant enterprise and adventure, and, by a natural impulse, the dwellers on their banks will at length accompany their currents to the lowlands of the globe, or explore at their invitation the interior of continents. They are the natural highways of all nations, not only levelling the ground, and removing obstacles from the path of the traveller, quenching his thirst, and bearing him on their bosoms, but conducting him through the most interesting scenery, the most populous portions of the globe, and where the animal and vegetable kingdoms attain their greatest perfection.

A Week on the Concord and Merrimack Rivers, p. 12

WEATHER: RAIN, SNOW, AND WIND

In keeping a journal of one's walks and thoughts it seems to be worth the while to record those phenomena which are most interesting to us at the time, such as the weather.

Written January 25, 1860, in his *Journal*, vol. XIII, p. 106; emended from manuscript *Journal* (MA 1302, The Morgan Library & Museum, New York)

It makes a material difference whether it is *foul* or *fair*, affecting surely our mood and thoughts.

Written January 25, 1860, in his *Journal*, vol. XIII, p. 106; emended from manuscript *Journal* (MA 1302, The Morgan Library & Museum, New York)

I will call the weather fair, if it does not threaten rain or snow or hail; foul, if it rains or snows or hails, or is so overcast that we expect one or the other from hour to hour.

Written January 25, 1860, in his *Journal*, vol. XIII, p. 107

There is no better fence to put between you and the village than a storm into which the villagers do not venture out.

Written March 8, 1859, in his *Journal*, vol. XII, p. 27

This morning it was considerably colder than for a long time, and by noon very much colder than heretofore, with a pretty strong northerly wind. . . . You need greatcoat and buffalo and gloves now, if you ride. I find my hands stiffened and involuntarily finding their way to my pockets. No wonder that the weather is a standing subject of conversation, since we are so sensitive.

Written November 14, 1857, in his *Journal*, vol. X, pp. 177–178

How admirable it is that we can never foresee the weather—that that is always novel. Yesterday nobody dreamed of to-day—nobody dreams of to-morrow. Hence the weather is ever the news. What a fine & measureless joy the gods grant us thus, letting us know nothing about the day that is to dawn. This day yesterday was as incredible as any other miracle.

Written December 29, 1851, in his *Journal*, vol. 4, p. 227

This first spring rain is very agreeable. I love to hear the pattering of the drops on my umbrella, and I love also the wet scent of the umbrella.

Written March 21, 1858, in his *Journal*, vol. X, p. 316

I too revive as does the grass after rain.

Written May 12, 1850, in his *Journal*, vol. 3, p. 65

Clouds are our mountains & the child who had lived on a plain always & had never seen a mountain, would find that he was prepared for the sight of them by his familiarity with clouds.

Written January 14, 1852, in his *Journal*, vol. 4, p. 253

Is not the dew but a humbler gentler rain—the nightly rain—above which we raise our heads & unobstructedly behold the stars?

Written November 21, 1853, in his *Journal*, vol. 7, p. 171

Pray what things interest me at present?
A long soaking rain—the drops trickling down the stubble—while I lay drenched on a last year's bed of wild oats, by the side of some bare hill, ruminating. These things are of moment.

Written March 30, 1840, in his *Journal*, vol. 1, p. 120

Walk often in drizzly weather for then the small weeds (especially if they stand on bare ground) covered with rain drops like beads appear more beautiful than ever.

Written September 3, 1851, in his *Journal*, vol. 4, p. 36

It is worth the while to walk in wet weather—the earth & leaves are strewn with pearls.

Written August 7, 1853, in his *Journal*, vol. 6, p. 288

We look to windward for fair weather.

Written April 4, 1840, in his *Journal*, vol. 1, p. 121

This rain is good for thought. It is especially agreeable to me as I enter the wood and hear the soothing dripping on the leaves. It domiciliates me in nature.

Written May 17, 1858, in his *Journal*, vol. X, p. 427

No weather interfered fatally with my walks, or rather my going abroad, for I frequently tramped eight or ten miles through the deepest snow to keep an appointment with a beech-tree, or a yellow-birch, or an old acquaintance among the pines.

Walden, p. 265

It is because I am allied to the elements that the sound of the rain is thus soothing to me. The sound soaks into my spirit, as the water into the earth, reminding me of the season when snow and ice will be no more, when the earth will be thawed and drink up the rain as fast as it falls.

Written February 15, 1855, in his *Journal*, vol. VII, p. 186

Some of my pleasantest hours were during the long rain storms in the spring or fall, which confined me to the house for the afternoon as well as the forenoon, soothed by their ceaseless roar and pelting; when an early twilight ushered in a long evening in which many thoughts had time to take root and unfold themselves.

Walden, p. 132

A rain which is as serene as fair weather, suggesting fairer weather than was ever seen. You could hug the clods that defile you. You feel the fertilizing influence of you of the rain in your mind. The part that is wettest is fullest of life, like the lichens. You discover evidences of immortality not known to divines. You cease to die.

Written January 27, 1858, in his *Journal*, vol. X, p. 262

And then the rain comes thicker and faster than before, thawing the remaining frost in the ground, detaining the migrating bird; and you turn your back to it, full of serene, contented thought, soothed by the steady dropping on the withered leaves, more at home for being abroad, more comfortable for being wet.

Written January 27, 1858, in his *Journal*, vol. X, pp. 262–263

There is nothing handsomer than a snowflake and a dewdrop. I may say that the maker of the world exhausts his skill with each snowflake and dewdrop that he sends down.

Written January 6, 1858, in his *Journal*, vol. X, p. 239

What a world we live in! where myriads of these little disks, so beautiful to the most prying eye, are whirled down on every traveller's coat, the observant and the unobservant.

Written January 5, 1856, in his *Journal*, vol. VIII, p. 89

Young white pines often stood draped in robes of purest white, emblems of purity, like a maiden that has taken the veil, with their heads slightly bowed and their main stems slanting to one side, like travellers bending to meet the storm with their heads muffled in their cloaks.

Written January 19, 1855, in his *Journal*, vol. VII, p. 118

The snow is the great betrayer. It not only shows tracks of mice, otters &c &c which else we should rarely if ever see, but the tree sparrows are more plainly seen against its white ground and they in turn are attracted by the dark weeds which it reveals. It also drives the crows & other birds out of the woods to the villages for food. We might expect to find in the snow the footprint of a life superior to our own of which no zoology takes cognizance.

Written January 1, 1854, in his *Journal*, vol. 7, pp. 218–219

The effect of the snow is to press down the forest—confound it with the grasses & create a new surface to the earth above—shutting us in with it. And we go along somewhat like moles through our galleries. The sight of the pure and trackless road up Brister's Hill with branches & trees supporting snowy burdens bending over it on each side would tempt us to begin life again.

Written December 26, 1853, in his *Journal*, vol. 7, pp. 205–206

All day a steady, warm, imprisoning rain carrying off the snow, not unmusical on my roof. It is a rare time for the student and reader who cannot go abroad in the afternoon, provided he can keep awake, for we are wont to be drowsy as cats in such weather. Without, it is not walking but wading. It is so long since I have heard it that the steady, soaking, rushing sound of the rain on the shingles is musical.

Written February 15, 1855, in his *Journal*, vol. VII, p. 186

A driving east or northeast storm. I can see through the drisk only one mile. The river is getting partly over the meadows at last, and my spirits rise with it. Methinks this rise of the waters must affect every thought and deed in the town. It qualifies my sentence and life.

Written October 26, 1857, in his *Journal*, vol. X, p. 126; emended from manuscript *Journal* (MA 1302, The Morgan Library & Museum, New York)

A storm is a new, and in some respects more active, life in nature.

Written October 26, 1857, in his *Journal*, vol. X, p. 126

WILDNESS

I wish my neighbors were wilder.

Written March 30, 1851, in his *Journal*, vol. 3, p. 201

In Wildness is the preservation of the World.

"Walking" in *Excursions*, p. 202

Whatever has not come under the sway of man is wild. In this sense original & independent men are wild— not tamed & broken by society.

Written September 3, 1851, in his *Journal*, vol. 4, p. 34

What we call wildness is a civilization other than our own.

Written February 16, 1859, in his *Journal*, vol. XI, p. 450

The era of the Wild Apple will soon be past. It is a fruit which will probably become extinct in New England.

"Wild Apples" in *Excursions*, p. 288

Life consists with Wildness. The most alive is the wildest.

"Walking" in *Excursions*, p. 203

We need the tonic of wildness,—to wade sometimes in marshes where the bittern and the meadow-hen lurk, and hear the booming of the snipe; to smell the whispering sedge where only some wilder and more solitary fowl builds her nest, and the mink crawls with its belly close to the ground.

Walden, p. 317

Trench says a wild man is a *willed* man. Well then a man of will who does what he wills—or wishes—a man of hope and of the future tense—for not only the obstinate is willed but far more the constant & persevering. The obstinate man properly speaking is one who will not. The perseverance of the saints is positive willedness—not a mere passive willingness. The fates are wild for they *will* & the Almighty is wild above all.

Written January 27, 1853, in his *Journal*, vol. 5, pp. 457–458

As I came home through the woods with my string of fish, trailing my pole, it being now quite dark, I caught a glimpse of a woodchuck stealing across my path, and felt a strange thrill of savage delight, and was strongly tempted to seize and devour him raw; not that I was hungry then, except for that wildness which he represented.

Walden, p. 210

Men come tamely home at night only from the next field or street, where their household echoes haunt, and their life pines because it breathes its own breath over again; their shadows morning and evening reach farther than their daily steps. We would come home from far, from adventures, and perils, and discoveries every day, with new experience and character.

Walden, p. 208

I should be pleased to meet man in the woods. I wish he were to be encountered like wild caribous and moose.

Written June 18, 1840, in his *Journal*, vol. 1, p. 131

We would not always be soothing and taming nature, breaking the horse and the ox, but sometimes ride the horse wild and chase the buffalo.

A Week on the Concord and Merrimack Rivers, p. 56

To see wild life you must go forth at a wild season. When it rains & blows keeping men in-doors then the lover of nature must forth.

Written April 19, 1852, in his *Journal*, vol. 4, p. 473

Let a slight snow come and cover the earth, and the tracks of men will show how little the woods and fields are frequented.

Written February 3, 1857, in his *Journal*, vol. IX, p. 236

There are some intervals which border the strain of the wood-thrush, to which I would migrate—wild lands where no settler has squatted; to which, methinks, I am already acclimated.

"Walking" in *Excursions*, p. 203

The red-bird which I saw on my companion's string on election days, I thought but the outmost sentinal of the wild immortal camp of the wild & dazzling infantrie of the wilderness—that the deeper woods abounded with redder birds still—but now that I have threaded all our woods & waded the swamps I have never yet met with his compeer—still less his wilder kindred.

Written May 23, 1854, in his *Journal*, vol. 8, p. 146

It is in vain to dream of a wildness distant from ourselves. There is none such. It is the bog in our brain and bowels, the primitive vigor of Nature in us, that inspires that dream. I shall never find in the wilds of Labrador any greater wildness than in some recess in Concord, *i.e.* than I import into it.

Written August 30, 1856, in his *Journal*, vol. IX, p. 43

Ah, bless the Lord, O my soul! bless him for wildness, for crows that will not alight within gunshot! and bless him for hens, too, that croak and cackle in the yard!

Written January 12, 1855, in his *Journal*, vol. VII, p. 113

I long for wildness—a nature which I cannot put my foot through.

> Written June 22, 1853, in his *Journal*, vol. 6, p. 236

We can never have enough of nature. We must be re-freshed by the sight of inexhaustible vigor, vast and Titanic features, the sea-coast with its wrecks, the wil-derness with its living and its decaying trees, the thun-der cloud, and the rain which lasts three weeks and produces freshets. We need to witness our own limits transgressed, and some life pasturing freely where we never wander.

> *Walden*, p. 318

Some rarely go outdoors—most are always at home at night—very few indeed have stayed out all night once in their lives—fewer still have gone behind the world of humanity—seen its institutions like toad-stools by the way-side.

> Written April 2, 1852, in his *Journal*, vol. 4, p. 420

I enter some glade in the woods, perchance, where a few weeds and dry leaves alone lift themselves above the surface of snow, and it is as if I had come to an open window. I see out and around myself. Our *skylights* are thus far away from the ordinary resorts of men. I am not satisfied with ordinary windows. I must have a true *skylight*.

> Written January 7, 1857, in his *Journal*, vol. IX, p. 209

I love the wild not less than the good.

> *Walden*, p. 210

WISDOM AND IGNORANCE

The title *wise* is, for the most part, falsely applied. How can one be a wise man, if he does not know any better how to live than other men?

"Life without Principle" in *Reform Papers*, p. 162

The community has no bribe that will tempt a wise man. You may raise money enough to tunnel a mountain, but you cannot raise enough to hire a man who is minding *his own* business.

"Life without Principle" in *Reform Papers*, p. 159

The wisest man preaches no doctrines; he has no scheme; he sees no rafter, not even a cobweb, against the heavens. It is clear sky.

A Week on the Concord and Merrimack Rivers, p. 70

A wise man sees as clearly the heathenism & barbarity of his own countrymen as clearly as those of the nations to whom his countrymen send missionaries.

Written January 16, 1852, in his *Journal*, vol. 4, p. 258

Men do not fail commonly for want of knowledge, but for want of prudence to give wisdom the preference.

A Week on the Concord and Merrimack, p. 127

We have heard of a Society for the Diffusion of Useful Knowledge. It is said that Knowledge is power; and the like. Methinks there is equal need of a Society for the Diffusion of Useful Ignorance, what we call Beautiful Knowledge, a knowledge in a higher sense; for what is most of our boasted so-called knowledge but a conceit that we know something, which robs us of the advantage of our actual ignorance? What we call knowledge is often our positive ignorance; ignorance our negative knowledge.

"Walking" in *Excursions*, pp. 214–215

Which is the best man to deal with, he who knows nothing about a subject, and what is extremely rare, knows that he knows nothing,—or he who really knows something about it, but thinks that he knows all?

"Walking" in *Excursions*, p. 215

A man is wise with the wisdom of his time only & ignorant with its ignorance. Observe how the greatest minds yield in some degree to the superstitions of their age.

Written January 31, 1853, in his *Journal*, vol. 5, p. 461

I fear that the character of my knowledge is from year to year becoming more distinct & scientific—That in exchange for views as wide as heaven's cope I am being narrowed down to the field of the microscope. I see details not wholes nor the shadow of the whole. I count some parts & say "I know."

Written August 19, 1851, in his *Journal*, vol. 3, p. 380

We shall see but little way if we require to understand what we see. How few things can a man measure with the tape of his understanding—how many greater things might he be seeing in the meanwhile.

Written February 14, 1851, in his *Journal*, vol. 3, p. 192

I find it to be the height of wisdom not to endeavor to over-see myself and live a life of prudence and common sense but to see over & above myself—entertain sublime conjectures to make myself the thoroughfare of thrilling thoughts—live all that can be lived.

Written November 23, 1850, in his *Journal*, vol. 3, pp. 149–150

Why level downward to our dullest perception always, and praise that as common sense? The commonest sense is the sense of men asleep, which they express by snoring.

Walden, p. 325

We are acquainted with a mere pellicle of the globe on which we live. Most have not delved six feet beneath the surface, nor leaped as many above it. We know not where we are. Beside, we are sound asleep nearly half our time.

Walden, p. 332

I know many men who, in common things, are not to be deceived; who trust no moonshine; who count their money correctly, and know how to invest it; who are said to be prudent and knowing, who yet will stand at a desk the greater part of their lives, as cashiers in banks, and glimmer and rust and finally go out there. If they *know* anything, what under the sun do they do that for? Do they know what *bread* is? or what it is for? Do they know what life is? If they *knew* something, the places which know them now would know them no more forever.

> To H.G.O. Blake, March 27, 1848, in *The Correspondence of Henry David Thoreau*, p. 215

Woe be to the generation that lets any higher faculty in its midst go unemployed.

> Written December 22, 1853, in his *Journal*, vol. 7, p. 201

I have always been regretting that I was not as wise as the day I was born.

> *Walden*, p. 98

Who shall distinguish between the *law* by which a brook finds its river—the *instinct* a bird performs its migrations—& the *knowledge* by which a man steers his ship around the globe?

> Written May 17, 1854, in his *Journal*, vol. 8, pp. 132–133

WOMEN

The society of young women is the most unprofitable I have ever tried.

They are so light & flighty that you can never be sure whether they are there or not there. I prefer to talk with the more staid & settled—*settled for life,* in every sense.

Last night I heard Mrs Oakes Smith lecture on Womanhood. The most important fact about the lecture was that a woman said it and in that respect it was suggestive.

Went to see her afterward. But the interview added nothing to the previous impression, rather subtracted. She was a woman in the too common sense after all. . . . You had to substitute courtesy for sense & argument. It requires nothing less than a chivalric feeling to sustain a conversation with a lady. I carried her lecture for her in my pocket wrapped in her handkerchief—my pocket exhales cologne to this moment. The championness of woman's rights still asks you to be a ladies' man.

Some of my friends make singular blunders. They go out of their way to talk with certain young women of whom they think or have heard that they are pretty and take pains to introduce me to them. That may be a reason why they should look at them, but it is not a reason why they should talk with them. I confess that I am lacking a sense perchance in this respect & I derive no pleasure from talking with a young woman half an hour simply because she has regular features.

Every maiden conceals a fairer flower and more lus-
cious fruit than any calix in the field.

Written November 12, 1841, in his *Journal*, vol. 1, p. 341

The other day I rowed in my boat a free—even lovely
young lady—and as I plied the oars she sat in the stern
and there was nothing but she between me and the sky.
So might all our lives be picturesque if they were free
enough.

Written June 19, 1840, in his *Journal*, vol. 1, p. 132

Man is continually saying to woman, Why will you not
be more wise? Woman is continually saying to man,
Why will you not be more loving?

"Love" in *Early Essays and Miscellanies*, p. 268

I saw at Ricketson's a young woman, Miss Kate Brady,
twenty years old. . . . She was born at the Brady house,
I think in Freetown. . . . I never heard a girl or woman
express so strong a love for nature. She purposes to return to that lonely ruin, and dwell there alone, since
her mother and sister will not accompany her; says
that she knows all about farming and keeping sheep
and spinning and weaving, though it would puzzle her
to shingle the old house. There she thinks she can "live
free." I was pleased to hear of her plans, because they
were quite cheerful & original. . . . A strong love for
outward nature is singularly rare among both men and
women. The scenery immediately about her home-
stead is quite ordinary, yet she appreciates and can use

that part of the universe as no other being can. Her own sex, so tamely bred, only jeer at her for entertaining such an idea, but she has a strong head and a love for good reading, which may carry her through. I would by no means discourage, nor yet particularly encourage her, for I would have her so strong as to succeed in spite of all ordinary discouragements.

It is very rare that I hear one express a strong and imperishable attachment to a particular scenery, or to the whole of nature. . . . They alone are naturalized. . . . The dead earth seems animated at the prospect of their coming, as if proud to be trodden on by them. . . . When I hear of such an attachment in a reasonable, a divine, creature to a particular portion of the earth, it seems as if then first the earth succeeded and rejoiced, as if it had been made and existed only for such a use.

Written April 23, 1857, in his *Journal*, vol. IX, pp. 335–337

We soon began to see women and girls at work in the fields, digging potatoes alone, or bundling up the grain which the men cut. They appeared in rude health with a great deal of color in their cheeks, and if their occupation had made them coarse, it impressed me as better in its effects than making shirts at four-pence apiece, or doing nothing at all, unless it be chewing slate-pencils, with still smaller results. They were much more agreeable objects with their great broad-brimmed hats and flowing dresses, than the men and boys.

"A Yankee in Canada" in *Excursions*, p. 106

The fragrance of the apple blossom reminds me of a pure & innocent & unsophisticated country girl bedecked for church.

Written May 17, 1853, in his *Journal*, vol. 6, p. 134

WORK AND BUSINESS

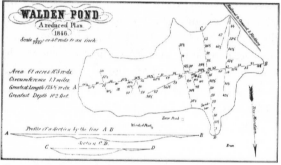

FIG. 15. Thoreau's survey of Walden Pond. Reproduced from the first edition of *Walden, or, Life in the Woods* (Boston: Ticknor and Fields, 1854). The Walter Harding Collection (The Thoreau Society* Collections at the Thoreau Institute). Courtesy of the Thoreau Society.

It is remarkable that there is little or nothing to be remembered written on the subject of getting a living: how to make getting a living not merely honest and honorable, but altogether inviting and glorious; for if getting a living is not so, then living is not. One would think, from looking at literature, that this question had never disturbed a solitary individual's musings. Is it that men are too much disgusted with their experience to speak of it?

"Life without Principle" in *Reform Papers*, p. 161

Do your work, and finish it. If you know how to begin, you will know when to end.

"A Plea for Captain John Brown" in *Reform Papers*, p. 134

What is a day if the day's work be not done?

Written August 30, 1841, in his *Journal*, vol. 1, p. 325

For more than five years I maintained myself thus solely by the labor of my hands, and I found, that by working about six weeks in a year, I could meet all the expenses of living. The whole of my winters, as well as most of my summers, I had free and clear for study.

Walden, p. 69

If a man walk in the woods for love of them half of each day, he is in danger of being regarded as a loafer; but if he spends his whole day as a speculator, shearing off those woods and making earth bald before her time, he is esteemed an industrious and enterprising citizen. As if a town had no interest in its forests but to cut them down!

"Life without Principle" in *Reform Papers*, p. 157

There is a coarse and boisterous money-making fellow in the outskirts of our town, who is going to build a bank-wall under the hill along the edge of his meadow. The powers have put this into his head to keep him out of mischief, and he wishes me to spend three weeks digging there with him. The result will be that he will perhaps get some more money to hoard, and leave for his heirs to spend foolishly. If I do this, most will commend me as an industrious and hard-working man; but if I choose to devote myself to certain labors which yield more real profit, though but little money, they may be inclined to look on me as an idler. Nevertheless, as I do not need the police of meaningless labor to regulate me, and do not see anything absolutely praiseworthy in this fellow's undertaking, any more than in many an enterprise of our own or foreign governments, however amusing it may be to him or them, I prefer to finish my education at a different school.

"Life without Principle" in *Reform Papers*, pp. 156–157

All the world complain now a days of a press of trivial duties & engagements which prevents their employing themselves on some higher ground they know of,—but undoubtedly if they were made of the right stuff to work on that higher ground, provided they were released from all those engagements—they would now at once fulfill the superior engagement, and neglect all the rest, as naturally as they breathe. They would never be caught saying that they had no time for this when the dullest man knows that this is all that he has time for. No man who acts from a sense of duty ever puts the lesser duty above the greater. No man has the desire and the ability to work on high things but he has also the ability to build himself a high staging.

To H.G.O. Blake, July 21, 1852, in *The Correspondence of Henry David Thoreau*, pp. 285–286

I am invited to take some party of ladies or gentlemen on an excursion,—to walk or sail, or the like,—but by all kinds of evasions I omit it, and am thought to be rude and unaccommodating therefore. They do not consider that the wood-path and the boat are my studio, where I maintain a sacred solitude and cannot admit promiscuous company. I will see them occasionally in the evening or at the table, however. They do not think of taking a child away from its school to go a-huckleberrying with them. Why should not I, then, have my school and school hours to be respected? Ask me for a certain number of dollars if you will, but do not ask me for my afternoons.

Written September 16, 1859, in his *Journal*, vol. XII, pp. 332–333

We are determined to be starved before we are hungry. Men say that a stitch in time saves nine, and so they take a thousand stitches to-day to save nine to-morrow.

Walden, p. 93

It may be the fairest day in all the year & you shall not know it—one little chore to do—one little commission to fulfill—one message to carry would spoil heaven itself.

Written July 21, 1851, in his *Journal*, vol. 3, p. 321

Winter has come unnoticed by me, I have been so busy writing. This is the life most lead in respect to Nature. How different from my habitual one! It is hasty, coarse, and trivial, as if you were a spindle in a factory. The other is leisurely, fine, and glorious like a flower. In the first case you are merely getting your living; in the second you live as you go along. You travel only on roads of the proper grade without jar or running off the track, and sweep round the hills by beautiful curves.

Written December 8, 1854, in his *Journal*, vol. VII, p. 80

I have found out a way to live without what is commonly called employment or industry attractive or otherwise. Indeed my steadiest employment, if such it can be called, is to keep myself at the top of my condition, and ready for whatever may turn up in heaven or on earth.

To Henry Williams, Jr., secretary of Thoreau's Harvard class of 1837, September 30, 1847, in *The Correspondence of Henry David Thoreau*, p. 186

The truly efficient laborer will not crowd his day with work, but will saunter to his task, surrounded by a wide halo of ease and leisure, and then do but what he loves best. He is anxious only about the fruitful kernels of time. Though the hen should sit all day, she could lay only one egg, and, besides, would not have picked up materials for another. Let a man take time enough for the most trivial deed, though it be but the paring of his nails.

A Week on the Concord and Merrimack Rivers, pp. 107–108

Of all the duties of life it is hardest to be in earnest. It implies a good deal both before and behind. I sit here in the barn this flowing afternoon weather, while the school bell is ringing in the village, and find that all the things immediate to be done are very trivial. I could postpone them to hear this locust sing.

Written August 18, 1841, in his *Journal*, vol. 1, p. 321

What are 3 score years & ten hurriedly & coarsely lived to moments of divine leisure, in which your life is coincident with the life of the Universe.

Written December 28, 1852, in his *Journal*, vol. 5, p. 412

Do not hire a man who does your work for money, but him who does it for love of it.

"Life without Principle" in *Reform Papers*, p. 159

This spending of the best part of one's life earning money in order to enjoy a questionable liberty during the least valuable part of it reminds me of the Englishman who went to India to make a fortune first, in order that he might return to England and live the life of a poet. He should have gone up garret at once.

Walden, p. 54

We are made to exaggerate the importance of what work we do.

Walden, p. 11

A man had better starve at once than lose his innocence in the process of getting his bread.

Written October 26, 1853, in his *Journal*, vol. 7, p. 115

The weapons with which we have gained our most important victories, which should be handed down as heirlooms from father to son, are not the sword and the lance, but the bush-whack—the turf-cutter, the spade, and the bog-hoe, rusted with the blood of many a meadow, and begrimed with the dust of many a hard-fought field.

"Walking" in *Excursions*, p. 207

There are certain current expressions and blasphemous moods of viewing things as when we say "he is doing a good business" which is more prophane than cursing and swearing. There is death and sin in such words. Let not the children hear them.

Written April 20, 1841, in his *Journal*, vol. 1, p. 302

If a man was tossed out of a window when an infant, and so made a cripple for life, or scared out of his wits by the Indians, it is regretted chiefly because he was thus incapacitated for—business! I think that there is nothing, not even crime, more opposed to poetry, to philosophy, ay, to life itself, than this incessant business.

"Life without Principle" in *Reform Papers*, p. 156

I once invented a rule for measuring cord-wood, and tried to introduce it in Boston; but the measurer there told me that the sellers did not wish to have their wood measured correctly,—that he was already too accurate for them, and therefore they commonly got their wood measured in Charlestown before crossing the bridge.

"Life without Principle" in *Reform Papers*, pp. 158–159

The momentous topics of human life are always of secondary importance to the business in hand, just as carpenters discuss politics between the strokes of the hammer, while they are shingling a roof.

Written January 23, 1841, in his *Journal*, vol. 1, p. 229

How trivial uninteresting & wearisome & unsatisfactory are all employments for which men will pay you money.

Written August 7, 1853, in his *Journal*, vol. 6, p. 288

I thus from time to time break off my connection with eternal truths and go with the shallow stream of human affairs, grinding at the mill of the Phillistines.

Written January 4, 1857, in his *Journal*, vol. IX, p. 205

As for my own business, even that kind of surveying which I could do with most satisfaction my employers do not want. They would prefer that I should do my work coarsely and not too well, ay, not well enough. When I observe that there are different ways of surveying, my employer commonly asks which will give him the most land, not which is most correct.

"Life without Principle" in *Reform Papers*, p. 158

We admire more the man who can use an axe or adze skillfully than him who can merely tend a machine. When labor is reduced to turning a crank it is no longer amusing nor truly profitable.

Written October 19, 1858, in his *Journal*, vol. XI, pp. 227–228

Most men are engaged in business the greater part of their lives, because the soul abhors a vacuum & they have not discovered any continuous employment for man's nobler faculties.

Written April 27, 1854, in his *Journal*, vol. 8, p. 89

Trade curses every thing it handles; and though you trade in messages from heaven, the whole curse of trade attaches to the business.

Walden, p. 70

After having some business dealings with men I am occasionally chagrined & feel as if I had done some wrong & it is hard to forget the ugly circumstance. I see that such intercourse long continued would make me thoroughly prosaic hard & coarse but the longest inter-course with Nature though in her rudest moods does not thus harden & make coarse. A hard insensible man whom we liken to a rock is indeed much harder than a rock. From hard coarse insensible men with whom I have no sympathy I go to commune with the rocks whose hearts are comparatively soft.

Written November 15, 1853, in his *Journal*, vol. 7, pp. 163–164

The ways in which most men get their living, that is, live, are mere make-shifts, and a shirking of the real business of life,—chiefly because they do not know, but partly because they do not mean, any better.

"Life without Principle" in *Reform Papers*, p. 162

We know not yet what we have done, still less what we are doing. Wait till evening, and other parts of our day's work will shine than we had thought at noon, and we shall discover the real purport of our toil. As when the farmer has reached the end of the furrow and looks back, he can best tell where the pressed earth shines most.

A Week on the Concord and Merrimack Rivers, p. 129

Most men would feel insulted, if it were proposed to employ them in throwing stones over a wall, and then in throwing them back, merely that they might earn their wages. But many are no more worthily employed now.

"Life without Principle" in *Reform Papers*, p. 157

If it were not that I desire to do something here (accomplish some work) I should certainly prefer to suffer and die rather than be at the pains to get a living by the modes men propose.

Written February 18, 1851, in his *Journal*, vol. 3, p. 196

How happens it that there are few men so well employed,—so much to their minds, but that a little money or fame would buy them off from their present pursuits?

Written September 7, 1851, in his *Journal*, vol. 4, p. 55

The farmer is endeavoring to solve the problem of a livelihood by a formula more complicated than the problem itself. To get his shoestrings he speculates in herds of cattle. With consummate skill he has set his trap with a hair spring to catch comfort and independence, and then, as he turned away, got his own leg into it.

Walden, p. 33

I would not be one of those who will foolishly drive a nail into mere lath and plastering; such a deed would keep me awake nights. Give me a hammer, and let me feel for the furring. Do not depend on the putty. Drive a nail home and clinch it so faithfully that you can wake up in the night and think of your work with satisfaction,—a work at which you would not be ashamed to invoke the Muse. So will help you God, and so only. Every nail driven should be as another rivet in the machine of the universe, you carrying on the work.

Walden, p. 330

It is not enough to be industrious; so are the ants. What are you industrious about?

To H.G.O. Blake, November 16, 1857, in *The Correspondence of Henry David Thoreau*, p. 496

The ways by which you may get money almost without exception lead downward. To have done anything by which you earned money *merely* is to have been truly idle or worse. If the laborer gets no more than the wages which his employer pays him, he is cheated, he cheats himself.

"Life without Principle" in *Reform Papers*, p. 158

For more than two years past I have lived alone in the woods, in a good plastered and shingled house entirely of my own building, earning only what I wanted, and sticking to my proper work.

To Horace Greeley, May 19, 1848, in *The Correspondence of Henry David Thoreau*, p. 224

I am convinced, both by faith and experience, that to maintain one's self on this earth is not a hardship but a pastime, if we will live simply and wisely; as the pursuits of the simpler nations are still the sports of the more artificial. It is not necessary that a man should earn his living by the sweat of his brow, unless he sweats easier than I do.

Walden, pp. 70–71

There is a certain Irish woodchopper who, when I come across him at his work in the woods in the winter, never fails to ask me what time it is, as if he were in haste to take his dinner-pail and go home. This is not as it should be. Every man, and the woodchopper among the rest, should love his work as much as the poet does his.

Written December 12, 1859, in his *Journal*, vol. XIII, p. 20

I hate the present modes of living and getting a living. Farming and shopkeeping and working at a trade or profession are all odious to me. I should relish getting my living in a simple, primitive fashion. . . . I believe in the infinite joy and satisfaction of helping myself and others to the extent of my ability.

Written November 5, 1855, in his *Journal*, vol. VIII, pp. 7–8

Work your vein till it is exhausted, or conducts you to a broader one.

> To Daniel Ricketson, March 5, 1856, in *The Correspondence of Henry David Thoreau*, p. 412

ON MISCELLANEOUS SUBJECTS

FIG. 16. Bust by Walton Ricketson (1898). Photographer: Alfred W. Hosmer. The Lewis C. Dawes Collection at the Thoreau Institute at Walden Woods. Courtesy of the Walden Woods Project.

Alertness

No method nor discipline can supersede the necessity of being forever on the alert.

Walden, p. 111

America

I would remind my countrymen, that they are to be men first, and Americans only at a late and convenient hour.

"Slavery in Massachusetts" in *Reform Papers*, p. 102

America is said to be the arena on which the battle of freedom is to be fought; but surely it cannot be freedom in a merely political sense that is meant. Even if we grant that the American has freed himself from a political tyrant, he is still the slave of an economical and moral tyrant.

"Life without Principle" in *Reform Papers*, p. 174

If the moon looks larger here than in Europe, probably the sun looks larger also. If the heavens of America appear infinitely higher, the stars brighter, I trust that these facts are symbolical of the height to which the philosophy and poetry and religion of her inhabitants may one day soar.

"Walking" in *Excursions*, p. 200

As a true patriot I should be ashamed to think that Adam in paradise was more favorably situated on the whole than the backwoodsman in this country.

"Walking" in *Excursions*, p. 201

Amusement

FIG. 17. Thoreau's signature, written with eyes closed. The Raymond Adams
Collection (The Thoreau Society* Collections at the Thoreau Institute).
Courtesy of the Thoreau Society.

The cheaper your amusements, the safer and saner.

Written November 18, 1857, in his *Journal*, vol. X, p. 188

The Animal in Us

We are conscious of an animal in us, which awakens in
proportion as our higher nature slumbers. It is reptile
and sensual, and perhaps cannot be wholly expelled;
like the worms which, even in life and health, occupy
our bodies. Possibly we may withdraw from it, but
never change its nature.

Walden, p. 219

Architecture

But it should not be by their architecture but by their
abstract thoughts that a nation should seek to commemorate itself. How much more admirable the
Baghavat geeta than all the ruins of the East. Methinks
there are few specimens of architecture so perfect as a
verse of poetry. Architectural remains are beautiful not
intrinsically & absolutely, but from association.

Written June 26, 1852, in his *Journal*, vol. 5, p. 154

Consider the beauty of New York architecture and there is no very material difference between this & Baalbec. A vulgar adornment of what is vulgar. To what end pray is so much stone hammered? An insane ambition to perpetuate the memory of themselves by the amount of hammered stone they leave. Such is the glory of nations. . . . I love better to see stones in place.

> Written June 26, 1852, in his *Journal*, vol. 5, pp. 154–155

Art

Art is not tame, and Nature is not wild, in the ordinary sense. A perfect work of man's art would also be wild or natural in a good sense. Man tames Nature only that he may at last make her more free even than he found her, though he may never yet have succeeded.

> *A Week on the Concord and Merrimack Rivers*, p. 316

The highest condition of art is artlessness.

> Written June 26, 1840, in his *Journal*, vol. 1, p. 143

The artist cannot be in a hurry.

> Written September 24, 1859, in his *Journal*, vol. XII, p. 344; emended from manuscript *Journal* (MA 1302, The Morgan Library & Museum, New York)

Aspiration

We hug the earth—how rarely we mount! Methinks we might elevate ourselves a little more.

> "Walking" in Excursions, p. 219

We avoid all the calamities that may occur in a lower sphere by abiding perpetually in a higher.

> Written April 27, 1854, in his *Journal*, vol. 8, p. 89

If you aspire to anything better than politics, expect no coöperation from men. They will not further anything good. You must prevail of your own force, as a plant springs and grows by its own vitality.

Written April 3, 1858, in his *Journal*, vol. X, p. 351

We forget to strive and aspire to do better ever than is expected of us.

Written January 13, 1852, in his *Journal*, vol. 4, p. 252

It would be vain for us to be looking ever into promised lands toward which in the meanwhile we were not steadily and earnestly travelling, whether the way led over a mountain-top or through a dusky valley. . . . We are shown far scenes in order that we may be tempted to inhabit them, and not simply tell what we have seen.

Written November 24, 1857, in his *Journal*, vol. X, p. 202

Autumn Leaves

It is pleasant to walk over the beds of these fresh, crisp, and rustling leaves. How beautifully they go to their graves! how gently lay themselves down and turn to mould!—painted of a thousand hues, and fit to make the beds of us living.

"Autumnal Tints" in *Excursions*, p. 241

Awakedness

To be awake is to be alive. I have never yet met a man who was quite awake.

Walden, p. 90

The millions are awake enough for physical labor; but only one in a million is awake enough for effective intellectual exertion, only one in a hundred millions to a poetic or divine life.

Walden, p. 90

Banks

The merchants and banks are suspending and failing all the country over, but not the sand-banks, solid and warm, and streaked with bloody blackberry vines. You may run upon them as much as you please. . . . In these banks, too, and such as these, are my funds deposited, a fund of health and enjoyment. Their (the crickets') prosperity and happiness and, I trust, mine do not depend on whether the New York banks suspend or no. We do not rely on such slender security as the thin paper of the Suffolk Bank. To put your trust in such a bank is to be swallowed up and under go suffocation. Invest, I say, in these country banks. Let your capital be simplicity and contentment. . . . I have no compassion for, nor sympathy with, this miserable state of things. Banks built of granite, after some Grecian or Roman style, with their porticoes and their safes of iron, are not so permanent, and cannot give me so good security for capital invested in them, as the heads of withered hardhack in the meadow. I do not suspect the solvency of these. I know who is their president and cashier.

Written October 14, 1857, in his *Journal,* vol. X, pp. 92–93

Bathing

Bathing is an undescribed luxury.

Written July 9, 1852, in his *Journal*, vol. 5, p. 205

I got up early and bathed in the pond; that was a religious exercise, and one of the best things which I did.

Walden, p. 88

Beer

I would exchange my immortality for a glass of small beer this hot weather.

To his sister, Sophia, July 13, 1852, in *The Correspondence of Henry David Thoreau*, p. 284

Instead of water we got here a draught of beer, which, it was allowed, would be better; clear and thin, but strong and stringent as the cedar sap. It was as if we sucked at the very teats of Nature's pine-clad bosom in these parts—the sap of all Millinocket botany commingled— the topmost most fantastic and spiciest sprays of the primitive wood, and whatever invigorating and stringent gum or essence it afforded, steeped and dissolved in it—a lumberer's drink, which would acclimate and naturalize a man at once—which would make him see green, and, if he slept, dream that he heard the wind sough among the pines.

The Maine Woods, pp. 27–28

Borrowing

It is difficult to begin without borrowing.

Walden, pp. 40–41

Boundaries

Individuals, like nations, must have suitable broad and natural boundaries, even a considerable neutral ground, between them.

Walden, p. 141

Castles in the Air

If you have built castles in the air, your work need not be lost; that is where they should be. Now put the foundation under them.

Walden, p. 324

His castles in the air fall to the ground, because they are not built lofty enough; they should be secured to heaven's roof.

On social reformer John Adolphus Etzler in "Paradise (to be) Regained" in *Reform Papers*, pp. 44–45

Circumstantial Evidence

Some circumstantial evidence is very strong, as when you find a trout in the milk.

Written November 11, 1850, in his *Journal*, vol. 3, p. 139

Color

It is remarkable that no pains is taken to teach children to distinguish colors. I am myself uncertain about the names of many.

Written January 28, 1852, in his *Journal*, vol. 4, p. 300

The color shows fairest & brightest in the bud.

Written June 25, 1852, in his *Journal*, vol. 5, p. 145

The heavens were blue when I was young and that is their color still.

Written January 26, 1852, in his *Journal*, vol. 4, p. 292

The grass there is delightfully green. . . . It is the most refreshing of all colors.

Written April 2, 1852, in his *Journal*, vol. 4, p. 416

Brown is the color for me, the color of our coats and our daily lives, the color of the poor man's loaf. The bright tints are pies and cakes, good only for October feasts, which would make us sick if eaten every day.

Written March 28, 1859, in his *Journal*, vol. XII, pp. 97–98

This plain sheet of snow which covers the ice of the pond, is not such a blankness as is unwritten, but such as is unread. All colors are in white.

Written December 19, 1840, in his *Journal*, vol. 1, p. 207

Common Sense

There is absolutely no common sense; it is common nonsense.

"Paradise (to be) Regained" in *Reform Papers*, p. 41

I am sane only when I have risen above my common sense—when I do not take the foolish view of things which is commonly taken, when I do not live for the low ends for which men commonly live. Wisdom is not common. To what purpose have I senses if I am thus absorbed in affairs?

Written June 22, 1851, in his *Journal*, vol. 3, p. 274

Compensation

If we will be quiet and ready enough, we shall find compensation in every disappointment.

Written September 23, 1838, in his *Journal*, vol. 1, p. 56

Compliments

Compliments and flattery oftenest excite my contempt by the pretension they imply, for who is he that assumes to flatter me? To compliment often implies an assumption of superiority in the complimenter. It is, in fact, a subtle detraction.

Written March 27, 1857, in his *Journal*, vol. IX, p. 307

Conformity

All the community may scream because one man is born who will not do as it does, who will not conform because conformity to him is death,—he is so constituted. They know nothing about his case; they are fools when they presume him to advise. The man of genius knows what he is driving at; nobody else knows. And he alone knows when something comes between him and his object.

Written December 27, 1858, in his *Journal*, vol. XI, p. 380; emended from manuscript *Journal* (MA 1302, The Morgan Library & Museum, New York)

Consistency

A man of settled views, whose thoughts are few and hardened like his bones, is truly mortal, and his only resource is to say his prayers.

Written December 19, 1859, in his *Journal*, vol. XIII, p. 35

Even consistency though it is much abused is sometimes a virtue.

Written after April 19, 1851, in his *Journal*, vol. 3, p. 204

Criticism

We are enabled to criticise others only when we are different from & in a given particular superior to them
ourselves. By our aloofness from men and their affairs
we are enabled to overlook & criticise them.

Written June 22, 1851, in his *Journal*, vol. 3, p. 274

Deliberation

Let us spend one day as deliberately as Nature, and not
be thrown off the tracks by every nutshell and mos-
quito's wing that falls on the rails.

Walden, p. 97

I have come out this afternoon a-cranberrying. . . . I
expected little of this walk, yet it did pass through the
side of my mind that somehow, on this very account
(my small expectation), it would turn out well, as also
the advantage of having some purpose, however small,
to be accomplished—of letting your deliberate wisdom
and foresight in the house to some extent direct and
control your steps.

Wild Fruits, p. 165

Resolve to read no book—to take no walk—to undertake no enterprise but such as you can endure to give

an account of to yourself. Live thus deliberately for the most part.

Written August 23, 1851, in his *Journal*, vol. 4, p. 10

We would have more pause and deliberation.

"Herald of Freedom" in *Reform Papers*, p. 51

What he says of poetry is rapidly uttered, and suggestive of a thought, rather than the deliberate development of any.

"Thomas Carlyle and His Works" in *Early Essays and Miscellanies*, p. 246

Dreams

Dreams are the touchstones of our characters. We are scarcely less afflicted when we remember some unworthiness in our conduct in a dream, than if it had been actual, and the intensity of our grief, which is our atonement, measures the degree by which this is separated from an actual unworthiness. For in dreams we but act a part which must have been learned and rehearsed in our waking hours, and no doubt could discover some waking consent thereto.

A Week on the Concord and Merrimack Rivers, p. 297

In dreams we see ourselves naked and acting out our real characters, even more clearly than we see others awake.

A Week on the Concord and Merrimack Rivers, p. 297

The nearest approach to discovering what we are is in dreams.

Written April 27, 1841, in his *Journal*, vol. 1, pp. 304–305

Echoes

I am surprised that we make no more ado about echoes. They are almost the only kindred voices that I hear.

Written February 11, 1853, in his *Journal*, vol. 5, p. 466

Emergencies

In all emergencies there is always one step which you may take on firm ground where gravity will assure you footing.

Written February 5, 1841, in his *Journal*, vol. 1, p. 250

Enthusiasm

What was *enthusiasm* in the young man must become *temperament* in the mature man.

Written November 1, 1851, in his *Journal*, vol. 4, p. 158

Epitaphs

The rarest quality in an epitaph is truth.

A Week on the Concord and Merrimack Rivers, p. 170

Friends and contemporaries should supply only the name and date, and leave it to posterity to write the epitaph.

A Week on the Concord and Merrimack Rivers, p. 170

Exaggeration

Exaggeration! Was ever any virtue attributed to a man without exaggeration? Was ever any vice, without infinite exaggeration?

"Thomas Carlyle and His Works" in *Early Essays and Miscellanies*, p. 264

Facts

Let us not underrate the value of a fact; it will one day flower in a truth.

"Natural History of Massachusetts" in *Excursions*, p. 27

Of what moment are facts that can be lost,—which need to be commemorated?

"Dark Ages" in *Early Essays and Miscellanies*, p. 143

Fame

Fame itself is but an epitaph; as late, as false, as true.

A Week on the Concord and Merrimack Rivers, p. 170

In some cases fame is perpetually false and unjust. Or rather I should say that she *never* recognizes the simple heroism of an action, but only as connected with its apparent consequence. It praises the interested energy of the Boston tea party, but will be comparatively silent about the more bloody & disinterestedly heroic attack on the Boston Court House—simply because the latter was unsuccessful. Fame is not just. It never finely or discriminatingly praises, but coarsely hurrahs. The truest acts of heroism never reach her ear, are never published by her trumpet.

Written June 4, 1854, in his *Journal*, vol. 8, p. 175

The Family of Man

All nations love the same jests and tales, Jews, Christians, and Mahometans, and the same translated suffice for all. All men are children, and of one family.

A Week on the Concord and Merrimack Rivers, p. 59

Fate

Ninety-nine one-hundredths of our lives we are mere hedgers and ditchers, but from time to time we meet with reminders of our destiny.

Written January 13, 1857, in his Journal, vol. IX, p. 218

The principal, the only thing a man makes is his condition, or fate.

To H.G.O. Blake, May 20, 1860, in The Correspondence of Henry David Thoreau, p. 579

Talk of fate! How little one can know what is fated to another!—what he can do and what he can not do!

Written December 27, 1858, in his Journal, vol. XI, p. 379

Who can doubt that men are by a certain fate what they are, contending with unseen and unimagined difficulties, or encouraged and aided by equally mysterious auspicious circumstances?

Written January 23, 1858, in his Journal, vol. X, p. 251

Fathers

No people ever lived by cursing their fathers, however great a curse their fathers may have been to them.

Cape Cod, p. 17

Commonly men will only be brave as their fathers were brave, or timid.

Walden, p. 164

Fault

The fault-finder will find faults even in paradise.

Walden, p. 328

Faults are not the less faults because they are invariably balanced by corresponding virtues.

A Week on the Concord and Merrimack Rivers, p. 282

Some would find fault with the morning-red, if they ever got up early enough.

Walden, p. 325

Gardening

Gardening is civil and social, but it wants the vigor and freedom of the forest and the outlaw.

A Week on the Concord and Merrimack Rivers, p. 55

Graves

Why should they begin digging their graves as soon as they are born?

Walden, p. 5

Nothing but great antiquity can make grave-yards interesting to me. I have no friends there.

A Week on the Concord and Merrimack Rivers, pp. 170–171

Haste

The fruitless enterprise of some persons who rush helter-skelter, carrying out their crazy scheme,—merely "putting it through," as they phrase it,—reminds me of those thistle-downs which, not being detained nor steadied by any seed at the base, are blown away at the first impulse and go rolling over all obstacles. They may indeed go fastest and farthest, but where they rest at last not even a thistle springs.

Written November 18, 1858, in his *Journal*, vol. XI, pp. 332–333

The longer the lever the less perceptible its motion. It is the slowest pulsation which is most vital. The hero then will know how to wait, as well as to make haste. All good abides with him who waiteth *wisely*; we shall sooner overtake the dawn by remaining here than by hurrying over the hills of the west.

A Week on the Concord and Merrimack Rivers, pp. 128–129

Heaven on Earth

Heaven is the inmost place.

Written December 29, 1841, in his *Journal*, vol. 1, p. 349

Heaven is under our feet as well as over our heads.

Walden, p. 283

Here or nowhere is our heaven.

A Week on the Concord and Merrimack Rivers, p. 380

The flowing sail—the running stream—the waving tree—the roving wind—whence else their infinite health and freedom?

I can see nothing so holy as unrelaxed play and frolic in this bower God has built for us. The suspicion of sin never comes to this thought.

Oh if men felt this they would never build temples even of marble or diamond, but it would be sacrilege and prophane, but disport them forever in this paradise.

Written December 29, 1841, in his *Journal*, vol. 1, p. 350

Do I not live in a garden—in paradise? I can go out each morning before breakfast & do & gather these flowers, with which to perfume my chamber where I read & write all day.

Written June 16, 1854, in his *Journal*, vol. 8, p. 202

History

Most events recorded in history are more remarkable than important, like eclipses of the sun and moon, by which all are attracted, but whose effects no one takes the trouble to calculate.

A Week on the Concord and Merrimack Rivers, p. 129

Critical acumen is exerted in vain to uncover the past; the *past* cannot be *presented*; we cannot know what we are not. But one veil hangs over past, present, and future, and it is the province of the historian to find out, not what was, but what is. Where a battle has been fought, you will find nothing but the bones of men and beasts; where a battle is being fought, there are hearts beating.

A Week on the Concord and Merrimack Rivers, p. 155

Wherever men have lived there is a story to be told, and it depends chiefly on the story-teller or historian whether it is interesting or not.

Written March 18, 1861, in his *Journal*, vol. XIV, p. 330

It will soon be forgotten, in these days of stoves, that we used to roast potatoes in the ashes after the Indian fashion of cooking.

Written March 2, 1852, in his *Journal*, vol. 4, p. 371

Consider what stuff history is made of,—that for the most part it is merely a story agreed on by posterity.

Cape Cod, p. 197

Humor

Especially the transcendental philosophy needs the leaven of humor to render it light and digestible.

"Thomas Carlyle and His Works" in *Early Essays and Miscellanies*, p. 235

Improvements

Men are the inveterate foes of all improvement.

Written April 3, 1858, in his *Journal*, vol. X, p. 351

Almost all our improvements, so called, tend to convert the country into the town.

Written August 22, 1860, in his *Journal*, vol. XIV, p. 57

Inspiration

Improve each occasion when thy soul is reached— drain the cup of inspiration to its last dregs.

Written January 24, 1852, in his *Journal*, vol. 4, p. 281

Integrity

The times may change, but the laws of integrity and magnanimity are immutable.

"Sir Walter Raleigh" in *Early Essays and Miscellanies*, p. 185

The Invitation

It is not the invitation which I hear, but which I feel, that I obey.

Written April 22, 1851, in his *Journal*, vol. 3, p. 208

Justness

It costs us nothing to be just.

Written October 21, 1859, in his *Journal*, vol. XII, p. 414

Leisure

A broad margin of leisure is as beautiful in a man's life as in a book.

Written December 28, 1852, in his *Journal*, vol. 5, p. 412

Sometimes, in a summer morning, having taken my accustomed bath, I sat in my sunny doorway from sunrise till noon, rapt in a revery, amidst the pines and hickories and sumachs, in undisturbed solitude and stillness, while the birds sang around or flitted noiseless through the house, until by the sun falling in at my west window, or the noise of some traveller's wagon on the distant highway, I was reminded of the lapse of time. I grew in those seasons like corn in the night, and they were far better than any work of the hands would have been. They were not time subtracted from my life, but so much over and above my usual allowance.

Walden, pp. 111–112

I thought with what more than princely, with what poetical, leisure I had spent my years hitherto, without care or engagement, fancy-free. I have given myself up to nature; I have lived so many springs and summers and autumns and winters as if I had nothing else to do but to *live* them, and imbibe whatever nutriment they had for me; I have spent a couple of years, for instance, with the flowers chiefly, having none other so binding engagement as to observe when they opened; I could have afforded to spend a whole fall observing the changing tints of the foliage.

Written September 19, 1854, in his *Journal*, vol. VII, p. 46; emended from manuscript *Journal* (MA 1302, The Morgan Library & Museum, New York)

Many a forenoon have I stolen away, preferring to spend thus the most valued part of the day; for I was rich, if not in money, in sunny hours and summer days, and spent them lavishly; nor do I regret that I did not waste more of them in the workshop or the teacher's desk.

Walden, pp. 191–192

Letter Writing

An echo makes me enunciate distinctly. So the sympathy of a friend gives plainness and point to my speech. This is the advantage of letter writing.

Written December 29, 1840, in his *Journal*, vol. 1, p. 211

Letterwriting too often degenerates into a communicating of facts, & not of truths; of other men's deeds, & not our thoughts.

To his sister, Helen, October 27, 1837, in *The Correspondence of Henry David Thoreau*, p. 15

Libraries

The library is a wilderness of books.

Written March 16, 1852, in his *Journal*, vol. 4, p. 392

Though books are to some extent my stock and tools, I have not the usual means with which to purchase them. I therefore regard myself as one whom especially the library was created to serve.

To Jared Sparks, president of Harvard College, September 17, 1849, asking permission to borrow books from the college library, in *The Correspondence of Henry David Thoreau*, p. 249

I have sometimes imagined a library, i.e. a collection of the works of true poets philosophers naturalists &c deposited not in a brick and marble edifice in a crowded & dusty city, guarded by cold-blooded & methodical officials & preyed on by bookworms, in which you own no share, and are not likely to, but rather far away in the depths of a primitive forest—like the ruins of central America—where you can trace a series of crumbling alcoves, the older books protecting the more modern from the elements—partially buried by the luxuriance of nature—which the heroic student could reach only after adventures in the wilderness, amid wild beasts & wild men. That to my imagination seems a fitter place for these interesting relics, which owe no small part of their interest to their antiquity.

Written February 3, 1852, in his *Journal*, vol. 4, pp. 321–322

Life Misspent

Men think foolishly they may abuse & misspend life as they please and when they get to heaven turn over a new leaf.

Written July 21, 1851, in his *Journal*, vol. 3, pp. 321–322

I wish to suggest that a man may be very industrious, and yet not spend his time well. There is no more fatal blunderer than he who consumes the greater part of life getting his living.

"Life without Principle" in *Reform Papers*, p. 160

Lost and Found

If a person lost would conclude that after all he is not lost, he is not beside himself, but standing in his own old shoes on the very spot where he is, and that for the time being he will live there; but the places that have known him, *they* are lost,—how much anxiety and danger would vanish.

A Week on the Concord and Merrimack Rivers, p. 184

It is a surprising and memorable, as well as valuable experience, to be lost in the woods any time.

Walden, p. 170

Majesty

Majesty is in the imagination of the beholder.

Written December 20, 1851, in his *Journal*, vol. 4, p. 210

Maps

How little there is on an ordinary map! How little, I mean, that concerns the walker and the lover of nature. . . . The waving woods, the dells and glades and green banks and smiling fields, the huge boulders, etc., etc., are not on the map, nor to be inferred from the map.

Written November 10, 1860, in his *Journal*, vol. XIV, pp. 228–229

Marriage

The marriage which the mass of men comprehend is but little better than the marriage of the beasts.

Written August 11, 1853, in his *Journal*, vol. 6, p. 297

I hear a man laughed at because he went to Europe twice in search of an imaginary wife who, he thought, was there, though he had never seen nor heard of her. But the majority have gone further while they stayed in America, have actually allied themselves to one whom they thought their wife and found out their mistake too late to mend it.

Written October 14, 1859, in his *Journal*, vol. XII, p. 384

I have had a tragic correspondence, for the most part all on one side, with Miss Ford. She did really wish to—I hesitate to write—marry me. That is the way they spell it. Of course I did not write a deliberate answer. How could I deliberate upon it? I sent back as distinct a *no* as I have learned to pronounce after considerable practice, and I trust that this *no* has succeeded. Indeed,

I wished that it might burst, like hollow shot, after it had struck and buried itself and make itself felt there. *There was no other way.* I really had anticipated no such foe as this in my career.

> To Ralph Waldo Emerson, November 14, 1847, in *The Corre-spondence of Henry David Thoreau*, pp. 190–191

Memory

The men and things of to-day are wont to lie fairer and truer in to-morrow's memory.

> Written March 27, 1857, in his *Journal*, vol. IX, p. 306

Miracles

Men talk about bible miracles because there is no miracle in their lives. Cease to gnaw that crust. There is ripe fruit over your head.

> Written June 9, 1850, in his *Journal*, vol. 3, p. 84

Misery

If misery loves company, misery has company enough.

> Written September 1, 1851, in his *Journal*, vol. 4, p. 26

Misfortune

Misfortunes occur only when a man is false to his Genius.

> Written April 27, 1854, in his *Journal*, vol. 8, p. 89

Mistakes

The best way to correct a mistake is to make it right.

> To Ralph Waldo Emerson, January 24, 1843, in *The Correspon-dence of Henry David Thoreau*, p. 76

An honest misunderstanding is often the ground of future intercourse.

Written March 6, 1841, in his *Journal*, vol. 1, p. 279

The Mysterious and Unexplored

At the same time that we are earnest to explore and learn all things, we require that all things be mysterious and unexplorable, that land and sea be infinitely wild, unsurveyed and unfathomed by us because unfathomable.

Walden, pp. 317–318

Names

A familiar name cannot make a man less strange to me.

"Walking" in *Excursions*, p. 213

New Day

With what infinite faith & promise & moderation begins each new day.

Written August 12, 1851, in his *Journal*, vol. 3, p. 363

New Year

Each new year is a surprise to us.

Written March 18, 1858, in his *Journal*, vol. X, p. 304

Woe be to us when we cease to form new resolutions on the opening of a new year.

Written March 31, 1852, in his *Journal*, vol. 4, p. 406

Novelty

Our appetite for novelty is insatiable. We do not attend to ordinary things, though they are most important, but to extra-ordinary ones. While it is only moderately hot or cold, or wet or dry, nobody attends to it, but when Nature goes to an extreme in any of these directions we are all on the alert with excitement.

> Written March 19, 1859, in his *Journal*, vol. XII, pp. 65–66; emended from manuscript *Journal* (MA 1302, The Morgan Library & Museum, New York)

Do not trouble yourself much to get new things, whether clothes or friends. Turn the old; return to them. . . . Sell your clothes and keep your thoughts.

> *Walden*, p. 328

A man goes to the end of his garden, inverts his head, and does not know his own cottage. The novelty is in us, and it is also in nature.

> Written February 9, 1852, in his *Journal*, vol. 4, p. 339

I do not know that I am very fond of novelty. I wish to get a clearer notion of what I have already some inkling.

> Written August 6, 1851, in his *Journal*, vol. 3, p. 357

I am perchance most & most profitably interested in the things which I already know a little about—a mere & utter novelty is a mere monstrosity to me.

> Written August 6, 1851, in his *Journal*, vol. 3, p. 357

Nudity

Boys are bathing at Hubbard's Bend playing with a boat. . . . The color of their bodies in the sun at a distance is pleasing—the not often seen flesh color. I hear the sound of their sport borne over the water. As yet we have not man in nature. What a singular fact for an angel visitant to this earth to carry back in his note book that men were forbidden to expose their bodies under the severest penalties.

Written June 11, 1852, in his *Journal*, vol. 5, p. 90

Originality

It is for want of original thought that one man's style is like another's.

Written September 8, 1851, in his *Journal*, vol. 4, p. 61

Patience

It is by patient and unanxious labor at the anvil that fairer mornings are to be compelled.

Written October 5, 1840, in his *Journal*, vol. 1, p. 184

Praise

Praise should be spoken as simply & naturally as a flower emits its fragrance.

Written January 31, 1852, in his *Journal*, vol. 4, p. 310

Prayer

How can any man suffer long? For a sense of want is a prayer, and all prayers are answered.

Written December 1, 1856, in his *Journal*, vol. IX, p. 146

May I dare as I have never done. May I persevere as I have never done. May I purify myself anew as with fire & water—soul & body. May my melody not be wanting to the season. May I gird myself to be a hunter of the beautiful that naught escape me. May I attain to a youth never attained. I am eager to report the glory of the universe,—may I be worthy to do it—to have got through with regarding human values so as not to be distracted from regarding divine values. It is reasonable that a man should be something worthier at the end of the year than he was at the beginning.

Written March 15, 1852, in his *Journal*, vol. 4, p. 390

Let me forever go in search of myself—never for a moment think that I have found myself—be as a stranger to myself, never a familiar, seeking acquaintance still.

Written July 16, 1851, in his *Journal*, vol. 3, p. 312

Prejudice

It is never too late to give up our prejudices.

Walden, p. 8

Preparation

I have found my account in travelling in having prepared beforehand a list of questions which I would get answered, not trusting to my interest at the moment, and can then travel with the most profit.

Written August 30, 1856, in his *Journal*, vol. IX, pp. 37–38

I think we may detect that some sort of preparation and faint expectation preceded every discovery we have made.

Written September 2, 1856, in his *Journal*, vol. IX, p. 53

One moment of life costs many hours—hours not of business but of preparation & invitation. Yet the man who does not betake himself at once & desperately to sawing is called a loafer—though he may be knocking at the doors of heaven all the while which shall surely be opened to him. That aim in life is highest which requires the highest & finest discipline. How much—What infinite leisure it requires—as of a lifetime, to appreciate a single phenomenon! You must camp down beside it as for life—having reached your land of promise & give yourself wholly to it. It must stand for the whole world to you—symbolical of all things.

Written December 28, 1852, in his *Journal*, vol. 5, pp. 412–413

Presents

I know many children to whom I fain would make a present on some one of their birthdays, but they are so far gone in the luxury of presents—have such perfect museums of costly ones—that it would absorb my entire earnings for a year to buy them something which would not be beneath their notice.

Written November 5, 1855, in his *Journal*, vol. VIII, p. 8

Private Property and Public Land

Among the Indians, the earth and its productions generally were common and free to all the tribe, like the air and water—but among us who have supplanted the Indians, the public retain only a small yard or common in the middle of the village, with perhaps a graveyard beside it, and the right of way, by sufferance, by a particular narrow route, which is annually becoming narrower, from one such yard to another.

"Huckleberries," p. 30

At present, in this vicinity, the best part of the land is not private property; the landscape is not owned, and the walker enjoys comparative freedom. But possibly the day will come when it will be partitioned off into so-called pleasure grounds, in which a few will take a narrow and exclusive pleasure only,—when fences shall be multiplied, and man traps and other engines invented to confine men to the *public* road; and walking over the surface of God's earth, shall be construed to mean trespassing on some gentleman's grounds. To enjoy a thing exclusively is commonly to exclude yourself from the true enjoyment of it. Let us improve our opportunities then before the evil days come.

"Walking" in *Excursions*, pp. 194–195

It is true, as is said, that we have as good a right to make berries private property as to make grass and trees such; but what I chiefly regret is the, in effect, dog-in-the-manger result, for at the same time that we exclude mankind from gathering berries in our field, we exclude them from gathering health and happiness and inspiration and a hundred other far finer and nobler fruits than berries, which yet we shall not gather ourselves there, nor even carry to market.

Written August 22, 1860, in his *Journal*, vol. XIV, p. 56

What sort of a country is that where the huckleberry fields are private property? When I pass such fields on the highway, my heart sinks within me. I see a blight on the land. Nature is under a veil there.

"Huckleberries," p. 28

As in many countries precious metals belong to the crown, so here natural objects of rare beauty should belong to the public.

Written January 3, 1861, in his *Journal*, vol. XIV, p. 305

Not only the channel but one or both banks of every river should be a public highway.

Written January 3, 1861, in his *Journal*, vol. XIV, p. 305

They who laid out the town should have made the river available as a common possession forever.

"Huckleberries," pp. 31–32

Without being owner of any land I find that I have a civil right in the river—that if I am not a landowner I am a water owner. . . . It is an extensive "common" still left.

Written March 23, 1853, in his *Journal*, vol. 6, p. 30

I think that the top of Mount Washington should not be private property; it should be left unappropriated for modesty and reverence's sake, or if only to suggest that earth has higher uses than we put her to.

Written January 3, 1861, in his *Journal*, vol. XIV, p. 305

Does he chiefly own the land who coldly uses it and gets corn and potatoes out of it, or he who loves it and gets inspiration from it?

Written April 23, 1857, in his *Journal*, vol. IX, p. 337

Profanity

Boys, if you went to talk business with a man, and he persisted in thrusting words having no connection with the subject into all parts of every sentence—Boot-jack, for instance,—wouldn't you think he was taking a liberty with you, and trifling with your time, and wasting his own?

On using profanity, told to his students, as reported by Edward Emerson in *Henry Thoreau as Remembered by a Young Friend*, pp. 128–129

Prophets in the Family

The fathers and the mothers of the town would rather hear the young man or young woman at their tables express reverence for some old statement of the truth than utter a direct revelation themselves. They don't want to have any prophets born into their families. Damn them.

Written November 16, 1851, in his *Journal*, vol. 4, pp 188, 771

Reputation

He is a fortunate man who gets through the world without being burthened by a name and reputation for they are at any rate but his past history and no prophecy and as such concern him no more than another.

Written March 2, 1842, in his *Journal*, vol. 1, p. 368

Responsibility

When I came down-stairs this morning, it raining hard and steadily, I found an Irishman sitting with his coat on his arm in the kitchen, waiting to see me. He wanted to inquire what I thought the weather would be to-day! I sometimes ask my aunt, and she consults the almanac. So we shirk the responsibility.

Written August 12, 1858, in his *Journal*, vol. XI, pp. 94–95

Rest

The wise man is restful—never restless or impatient.

Written September 17, 1839, in his *Journal*, vol. 1, p. 81

Revenge

Revenge is most unheroic.

"Sir Walter Raleigh" in *Early Essays and Miscellanies*, p. 185

Roads

Roads are made for horses and men of business. I do not travel in them much comparatively, because I am not in a hurry to get to any tavern, or grocery, or livery stable, or depot to which they lead.

"Walking" in *Excursions*, p. 192

Saving Our Lives

If we would save our lives we must fight for them.

Written June 16, 1854, in his *Journal*, vol. 8, p. 199

Senses

Employ your senses.

Written June 13, 1851, in his *Journal*, vol. 3, p. 261

Sex

The subject of Sex is a remarkable one, since, though its phenomena concern us so much both directly and indirectly, and, sooner or later it occupies the thoughts of all, yet, all mankind, as it were, agree to be silent about it, at least the sexes commonly one to another.

"Chastity & Sensuality" in *Early Essays and Miscellanies*, p. 274

In a pure society, the subject of copulation would not be so often avoided from shame and not from reverence, winked out of sight, and hinted at only, but treated naturally and simply,—perhaps simply avoided, like the kindred mysteries. If it cannot be spoken of for shame, how can it be acted of?

"Chastity & Sensuality" in *Early Essays and Miscellanies*, p. 274

Love and lust are as far asunder as a flower garden is from a brothel.

"Chastity & Sensuality" in *Early Essays and Miscellanies*, p. 276

The only excuse for reproduction is improvement. Nature abhors repetition.

"Chastity & Sensuality" in *Early Essays and Miscellanies*, p. 278

The intercourse of the sexes, I have dreamed, is incredibly beautiful, too fair to be remembered. I have had thoughts about it, but they are among the most fleeting and irrecoverable in my experience.

"Chastity & Sensuality" in *Early Essays and Miscellanies*, p. 277

I know a man who never speaks of the sexual relation but jestingly, though it is a subject to be approached only with reverence & affection. What can be the character of that man's love?

Written July 5, 1852, in his *Journal*, vol. 5, p. 183

I never had any trouble in all my life, or only when I was about fourteen; then I felt pretty bad a little while on account of my sins, but no trouble since that I know of. That must be the reason why my hair doesn't turn gray faster.

Recalled by Sophia Thoreau in 1863, after "speaking of one's hair turning gray, and to what cause it is sometimes attributed," as related by Calvin Greene in "Memories of Thoreau: Unpublished Anecdotes of New England's Anti-Puritan Author and Naturalist" (*The Truth Seeker*, November 20, 1897), p. 144

Size

Mr Russell showed his microscope at Miss Mackay's. ... The power of this glass was 900 diameters. All the objects were transparent and had a liquid look—crystalline—& reminded me of the moon seen through a telescope. They suggested the significance or insignificance of size & that the moon itself is a microscopic object to us so little it concerns us.

Written August 15, 1854, in his *Journal*, vol. 8, p. 273

Many public speakers are accustomed, as I think foolishly, to talk about what they call *little things* in a patronising way sometimes, advising, perhaps, that they be not wholly neglected; but in making this distinction they really use no juster measure than a ten-foot pole, and their own ignorance. According to this rule a small potatoe is a little thing, a big one a great thing. . . .

A cartwheel is a great thing—a snow flake a little thing. The *Wellingtonia gigantea*—the famous California tree, is a great thing—the seed from which it sprang a little thing—scarcely one traveller has noticed the seed at all—and so with all the seeds or origins of things.

. . . In short, whatever they know and care but *little* about is a little thing.

"Huckleberries," p. 3

The Spur of the Moment

Obey the spur of the moment.

Written January 26, 1852, in his *Journal*, vol. 4, p. 290

Suspicion

There is no rule more invariable than that we are paid for our suspicions by finding what we suspected.

A Week on the Concord and Merrimack Rivers, p. 277

No innocence can quite stand up under suspicion if it is conscious of being suspected. In the company of one who puts a wrong construction upon your actions, they are apt really to deserve a mean construction. While in that society I can never retrieve myself. Attribute to me a great motive, and I shall not fail to have one, but a mean one, and the fountain of virtue will be poisoned by the suspicion.

Written January 28, 1841, in his *Journal*, vol. 1, p. 233

By some obscure law of influence when we are perhaps unconsciously the subject of another's suspicion, we feel a strong impulse, even when it is contrary to our nature to do that which he expects but reprobates.

Written between1842 and 1844, in his *Journal*, vol. 2, p. 45

Transcendentalism

Men are more obedient at first to words than ideas. They mind names more than things. Read them a lecture on "Education," naming that subject, and they will think that they have heard something important, but call it "Transcendentalism," and they will think it moonshine.

Written February 13, 1860, in his *Journal*, vol. XIII, p. 145

I should have told them at once that I was a transcendentalist. That would have been the shortest way of telling them that they would not understand my explanations.

Written March 5, 1853, in his *Journal*, vol. 5, pp. 469–470

Unexplored Lands

Where is the "Unexplored land" but in our own untried enterprises?

To H.G.O. Blake, May 20, 1860, in *The Correspondence of Henry David Thoreau*, p. 580

What was the meaning of that South-Sea Exploring Expedition, with all its parade and expense, but an indirect recognition of the fact, that there are continents and seas in the moral world, to which every man is an isthmus or an inlet, yet unexplored by him, but that it is easier to sail many thousand miles through cold and storm and cannibals, in a government ship, with five hundred men and boys to assist one, than it is to explore the private sea, the Atlantic and Pacific Ocean of one's being alone.

Walden, p. 321

Voting and Elections

I hear of a convention to be held at Baltimore, or elsewhere, for the selection of a candidate for the Presidency, made up chiefly of editors, and men who are politicians by profession; but I think, what is it to any independent, intelligent, and respectable man what decision they may come to, shall we not have the advantage of his wisdom and honesty, nevertheless? Can we not count upon some independent votes? Are there not many individuals in the country who do not attend conventions? But no: I find that the respectable man, so called, has immediately drifted from his position, and despairs of his country, when his country has more reason to despair of him. He forthwith adopts one of the candidates thus selected as the only *available* one, thus proving that he is himself *available* for any purposes of the demagogue. His vote is of no more worth than that of any unprincipled foreigner or hireling native, who may have been bought. Oh for a man who is a *man*, and, as my neighbor says, has a bone in his back which you cannot pass your hand through!

"Resistance to Civil Government" in *Reform Papers*, p. 70

All voting is a sort of gaming, like chequers or backgammon, with a slight moral tinge to it, a playing with right and wrong, with moral questions; and betting naturally accompanies it. The character of the voters is not staked. I cast my vote, perchance, as I think right; but I am not vitally concerned that that right should prevail. I am willing to leave it to the majority. Its obligation, therefore, never exceeds that of expediency. Even voting *for the right* is *doing* nothing for it. It is only expressing to men feebly your desire that it should prevail. A wise man will not leave the right to the mercy of chance, nor wish it to prevail through the power of the majority. There is but little virtue in the action of masses of men. When the majority shall at length vote for the abolition of slavery, it will be because they are indifferent to slavery, or because there is but little slavery left to be abolished by their vote. *They* will then be the only slaves. Only *his* vote can hasten the abolition of slavery who asserts his own freedom by his vote.

"Resistance to Civil Government" in *Reform Papers*, pp. 69–70

Cast your whole vote, not a strip of paper merely, but your whole influence.

"Resistance to Civil Government" in *Reform Papers*, p. 76

War

War is but the compelling of peace.

"The Service" in Reform Papers, p. 9

I do not wish to kill nor to be killed, but I can foresee circumstances in which both these things would be by me unavoidable.

"A Plea for Captain John Brown" in *Reform Papers*, p. 133

Does the threatened war between France & England evince any more enlightenment than a war between two savage tribes—the Irroquois & the Hurons? Is it founded in better reason?

Written February 26, 1852, in his *Journal*, vol. 4, p. 365

The soldier is applauded who refuses to serve in an unjust war by those who do not refuse to sustain the unjust government which makes the war.

"Resistance to Civil Government" in *Reform Papers*, p. 71

We love to fight far from home.

To H.G.O. Blake, December 19, 1854, in *The Correspondence of Henry David Thoreau*, p. 355

The papers are talking about the prospects of a war between England and America. Neither side sees how its country can avoid a long and fratricidal war without sacrificing its honor. Both nations are ready to take a desperate step, to forget the interests of civilization and Christianity and their commercial prosperity and fly at each other's throats. When I see an individual thus beside himself, thus desperate, ready to shoot or be shot, like a blackleg who has little to lose, no serene aims to accomplish, I think he is a candidate for bedlam. What asylum is there for nations to go to?

Written February 27, 1856, in his *Journal*, vol. VIII, p. 189

Weeds

Water the weed till it blossoms; with cultivation it will bear fruit.

Written June 20, 1840, in his *Journal*, vol. 1, p. 134

Shall I not rejoice also at the abundance of the weeds whose seeds are the granary of the birds?

Walden, p. 166

When the farmer cleans out his ditches I mourn the loss of many a flower which he calls a weed.

Written April 9, 1853, in his *Journal*, vol. 6, p. 83

Weeds are uncultivated herbaceous plants which do not bear handsome flowers.

Written September 3, 1856, in his *Journal*, vol. IX, p. 59

The humblest weed is indescribably beautiful.

Written January 11, 1854, in his *Journal*, vol. 7, p. 236

THOREAU DESCRIBES HIS
CONTEMPORARIES

Amos Bronson Alcott

Alcott is a geometer—a visionary.

Written winter 1845–1846, in his *Journal*, vol. 2, p. 223

His attitude is one of greater faith & expectation than that of any man I know.

Written winter 1845–1846, in his *Journal*, vol. 2, pp. 223–224

I have devoted most of my day to Mr Alcott. He is broad & genial but indefinite; some would say feeble; forever feeling about vainly in his speech & touching nothing. But this is a very negative account of him for he thus suggests far more than the sharp & definite practical mind.

Written March 9, 1853, in his *Journal*, vol. 6, p. 101

Alcott spent the day with me yesterday. He spent the day before with Emerson. He observed that he had got his wine & now he had come after his venison.

Written August 10, 1853, in his *Journal*, vol. 6, p. 294

John Brown

A man of rare common sense and directness of speech, as of action; a transcendentalist above all, a man of ideas and principles,—that was what distinguished him. Not yielding to a whim or transient impulse, but carrying out the purpose of a life.

"A Plea for Captain John Brown" in *Reform Papers*, p. 115

Think of him of—his rare qualities! such a man as it takes ages to make, and ages to understand; no mock hero, nor the representative of any party. A man such as the sun may not rise upon again in this benighted land. To whose making went the costliest material, the finest adamant; sent to be the redeemer of those in captivity. And the only use to which you can put him is to hang him at the end of a rope!

"A Plea for Captain John Brown" in *Reform Papers*, p. 136

I rejoice that I live in this age—that I am his contemporary.

"A Plea for Captain John Brown" in *Reform Papers*, p. 126

Thomas Carlyle

We believe that Carlyle has, after all, more readers, and is better known to-day for this very originality of style, and that posterity will have reason to thank him for emancipating the language, in some measure, from the fetters which a merely conservative, aimless, and pedantic literary class had imposed upon it, and setting an example of greater freedom and naturalness.

"Thomas Carlyle and His Works" in *Early Essays and Miscellanies*, pp. 232–233

Carlyle is not a *seer*, but a brave looker-on and *reviewer*; not the most free and catholic observer of men and events, for they are likely to find him preoccupied, but unexpectedly free and catholic when they fall within the focus of his lens.

"Thomas Carlyle and His Works" in *Early Essays and Miscellanies*, p. 246

Thomas De Quincey and Charles Dickens

De Quincey & Dickens have not moderation enough. They never stutter—they flow too readily.

Written September 8, 1851, in his *Journal*, vol. 4, p. 63

Mary Moody Emerson

The wittiest & most vivacious woman that I know— certainly that woman among my acquaintance whom it is most profitable to meet—the least frivolous who will most surely provoke to good conversation and the expression of what is in you. She is singular among

women at least in being really & perseveringly interested to know what thinkers think. She relates herself
surely to the intellectual where she goes.

It is perhaps her greatest praise & peculiarity that
she more surely than any other woman gives her companion occasion to utter his best thought.

In spite of her own biases she can entertain a large
thought with hospitality and is not prevented by any
intellectuality in it as women commonly are. In short
she is a genius.

Written November 13, 1851, in his *Journal*, vol. 4, pp. 183–184

Talking with Miss Mary Emerson this evening, she
said, "It was not the fashion to be so original when I
was young." She is readier to take my view—look
through my eyes for the time—than any young person
that I know in the town.

Written January 26, 1856, when Mary Moody Emerson was
eighty-two, in his *Journal*, vol. VIII, p. 146

Ralph Waldo Emerson

Emerson has special talents unequalled.

... His personal influence upon young persons
greater than any man's.

Written winter 1845–1846, in his *Journal*, vol. 2, p. 224

Of Emerson's Essays I should say that they were not
poetry—that they were not written exactly at the right
crisis though inconceivably near to it.

Written December 2, 1846, in his *Journal*, vol. 2, p. 355

I doubt if Emerson could trundle a wheel barrow through the streets because it would be out of character.

> Written January 30, 1852, in his *Journal*, vol. 4, p. 304

Emerson is too grand for me.

> Written January 31, 1852, in his *Journal*, vol. 4, p. 309

Nathaniel Hawthorne

They say that Mr Pierce the presidential candidate was in town last 5th of July, visiting Hawthorne whose college chum he was, and that Hawthorne is writing a life of him for electioneering purposes.

> To his sister, Sophia, July 13, 1852, in *The Correspondence of Henry David Thoreau*, p. 283

Thomas Wentworth Higginson

Heard Higginson lecture tonight on Mohammed. Why did I not like it better? Can I deny that it was good? . . . I did not like it then, because it did not make me like it—it did not carry me away captive. He is not simple enough. For the most part the manner overbore choked off & stifled.

> Written January 21, 1852, in his *Journal*, vol. 4, p. 274

Henry James, Sr.

I have been to see Henry James, and like him very much. It was a great pleasure to meet him. It makes humanity seem more erect and respectable. I never was more kindly and faithfully catechised. It made me respect myself more to be thought worthy of such wise questions.

To Ralph Waldo Emerson, after having met Henry James, Sr., June 8, 1843, in *The Correspondence of Henry David Thoreau*, p. 110

Horace Mann

Dr. Bartlett handed me a paper to-day, desiring me to subscribe for a statue to Horace Mann. I declined, and said that I thought a man ought not any more to take up room in the world after he was dead. We shall lose one advantage of a man's dying if we are to have a statue of him forthwith.

Written September 18, 1859, in his *Journal*, vol. XII, p. 335

George Minott

Minot is perhaps the most poetical farmer—who most realizes to me the poetry of the farmer's life—that I know. He does nothing (with haste and drudgery) but as if he loved it. He makes the most of his labor and takes infinite satisfaction in every part of it. He is not looking forward to the sale of his crops or any pecuniary profit, but he is paid by the constant satisfaction which his labor yields him. He has not too much land to trouble him—too much work to do—no hired man nor boy—but simply to amuse himself & live. He cares not so much to raise a large crop as to do his work well.

Written October 4, 1851, in his *Journal*, vol. 4, pp. 116–117

Wendell Phillips

It is so rare and encouraging to listen to an orator, who is content with another alliance than with the popular party, or even with the sympathising school of the martyrs, who can afford sometimes to be his own auditor if the mob stay away, and hears himself without reproof, that we feel ourselves in danger of slandering all mankind by affirming, that here is one, who is at the same time an eloquent speaker and a righteous man.

"Wendell Phillips Before Concord Lyceum" in *Reform Papers*, p. 61

Daniel Webster

I should have liked to see Dan. Webster walking about Concord, I suppose the town shook every step he took— But I trust there were some sturdy Concordians who were not tumbled down by the jar, but represented still the upright town.

To his mother, August 29, 1843, in *The Correspondence of Henry David Thoreau*, p. 135

The story is that Webster had appointed to meet some Plymouth gentlemen at Manomet and spend the day fishing with them. After the fishing was [over], he set out to return to Duxbury in his sailboat with Peterson, as he had come, and on the way they saw the seaserpent, which answered to the common account of this creature. It passed directly across their bows only six or seven rods off and then disappeared. On the sail homeward, Webster having had time to reflect on what had occurred, at length said to Peterson, "For God's sake, never say a word about this to any one, for if it should be known that I should have seen the sea-serpent, I should never hear the last of it, but wherever I went should have to tell the story to every one I met."

Written June 14, 1857, in his *Journal*, vol. IX, p. 416

His words are wisdom to those legislators who contemplate no essential reform in the existing government; but for thinkers, and those who legislate for all time, he never once glances at the subject.

"Resistance to Civil Government" in *Reform Papers*, p. 87

Walt Whitman

As for the sensuality in Whitman's "Leaves of Grass," I do not so much wish that it was not written, as that men and women were so pure that they could read it without harm.

Written December 2, 1856, in his *Journal*, vol. IX, p. 149

He is apparently the greatest democrat the world has seen. Kings and aristocracy go by the board at once, as they have long deserved to. A remarkably strong though coarse nature, of a sweet disposition, and much prized by his friends.

To H.G.O. Blake, from Eagleswood, New Jersey, November 19, 1856, in *The Correspondence of Henry David Thoreau*, p. 441

That Walt Whitman, of whom I wrote to you, is the most interesting fact to me at present. I have just read his 2nd edition (which he gave me) and it has done me more good than any reading for a long time. . . . There are 2 or 3 pieces in the book which are disagreeable to say the least, simply sensual. He does not celebrate love at all. It is as if the beasts spoke.

To H.G.O. Blake, from Eagleswood, New Jersey, December 7, 1856, in *The Correspondence of Henry David Thoreau*, p. 444

THOREAU DESCRIBED BY HIS CONTEMPORARIES

Do not dissect a man till he is dead.

Written September 14, 1841, in his *Journal*, vol. 1, p. 333

FIG. 19. Ralph Waldo Emerson. Photographic copy by Alfred W. Hosmer. The Paul Brooks Collection at the Thoreau Institute at Walden Woods. Courtesy of the Walden Woods Project.

Physical Characteristics

My first interview with him was so peculiar that I will venture to state it. . . . I perceived a man walking towards me bearing an umbrella in one hand and a leather travelling-bag in the other. So unlike my ideal Thoreau, whom I had fancied, from the robust nature of his mind and habits of life, to be a man of unusual vigor and size, that I did not suspect, although I had expected him in the morning, that the slight, quaint-looking person before me was the Walden philosopher. There are few persons who had previously read his works that were not disappointed by his personal appearance.

Daniel Ricketson in *Daniel Ricketson and His Friends*, p. 11

In height, he was about the average; in his build, spare, with limbs that were rather longer than usual, or of which he made a longer use. His face, once seen, could not be forgotten. The features were quite marked: the nose aquiline or very Roman, like one of the portraits of Caesar (more like a beak, as was said); large, over-hanging brows above the deepest set blue eyes that could be seen, in certain lights, and in others gray,— eyes expressive of all shades of feeling, but never weak or near-sighted; the forehead not unusually broad or high, full of concentrated energy and purpose; the mouth with prominent lips, pursed up with meaning and thought when silent, and giving out when open a stream of the most varied and unusual and instructive sayings. His hair was a dark brown, exceedingly abundant, fine and soft; and for several years he wore a comely beard. His whole figure had an active earnestness, as if he had no moment to waste. The clenched hand betokened purpose.

William Ellery Channing in *Thoreau: The Poet-Naturalist*, p. 25

He came into the room a quaint, stump figure of a man, whose effect of long trunk and short limbs was heightened by his fashionless trousers being let down

too low. He had a noble face, with tossed hair, a dis-
traught eye, and a fine aquilinity of profile, which made
me think at once of Don Quixote and of Cervantes; but
his nose failed to add that foot to his stature which
Lamb says a nose of that shape will always give a man.

William Dean Howells in *Literary Friends and Acquaintance: A
Personal Retrospect of American Authorship*, p. 59

He is as ugly as sin, long-nosed, queer-mouthed, and
with uncouth and somewhat rustic, although courte-
ous manners, corresponding very well with such an
exterior. But his ugliness is of an honest and agreeable
fashion, and becomes him much better than beauty.

Nathaniel Hawthorne, September 1, 1842, in *The American
Notebooks*, pp. 353–354

We used to bother him a good deal calling him "the
fine scholar with a big nose."

Alfred Munroe, August 8, 1877, quoted in Kenneth Walter
Cameron's "Thoreau's Schoolmate, Alfred Munroe, Remembers
Concord" (*American Transcendental Quarterly* 36), p. 20

He was short of stature, well built, and such a man as I
have fancied Julius Caesar to have been. Every movement was full of courage and repose; the tones of his
voice were those of Truth herself; and there was in his
eye the pure bright blue of the New England sky, as
there was sunshine in his flaxen hair. He had a particularly strong aquiline-Roman nose, which somehow reminded me of the prow of a ship.

Moncure D. Conway in "Thoreau" (*Fraser's Magazine for Town
and Country*, April 1866), p. 461

The touch of his hand was moist and indifferent, as if he had taken up something when he saw your hand coming, and caught your grasp upon it.

John Weiss, a Harvard classmate, in "Thoreau" (Christian Examiner, July 1865), p. 97

Henry retained a particular pronunciation of the letter *r*, with a decided French accent. He says, "September is the first month with a *burr* in it;" and his speech always had an emphasis, a *burr* in it.

William Ellery Channing in *Thoreau: The Poet-Naturalist*, p. 2

He seemed rather less than the medium height, well-proportioned, and noticeably straight and erect. His shoulders were not square but sloping, like those of Mr. Emerson. His head was not large, nor did it strike me as handsome: it was covered with a full growth of rather dark hair somewhat carelessly brushed after no particular style. His face was very striking whether seen in the front or profile view. Large perceptive eyes—blue, I think, large and prominent nose; his mouth concealed by a full dark beard, worn natural but not untrimmed; these features pervaded by a wise, serious and dignified look. The expression of his countenance was not severe or commanding, but it certainly gave no hint of shallowness or trifling.

In speech he was deliberate and positive. The emphatic words seemed to "hang fire" or to be held back for an instant as if to gather force and weight. Although he resembled Emerson in this, there was no appearance of affectation about it; he appeared to be looking at his thought all the time he was selecting and uttering his words.

E. Harlow Russell in an account reported in the *Leominster (Mass.) Daily Enterprise*, December 28, 1899, as quoted in Walter Harding's *Thoreau: Man of Concord*, p. 97

I like to see him come in, he always smells of the pine woods.

James T. Fields in Annie Adams Fields's *James T. Fields: Biographical Notes and Personal Sketches*, p. 102

Henry was the purest-looking man that ever lived.

Mabel Loomis Todd in *The Thoreau Family Two Generations Ago*, p. 19

Conduct and Character

He had a way of his own, and he didn't care much about money; but if there ever was a gentleman alive, he was one.

Barney Mullins, quoted in David Starr Jordan's "Thoreau and John Brown" (*The Current*, April 9, 1887), p. 454

You would find him well worth knowing; he is a man of thought and originality, with a certain iron-poker-ishness, an uncompromising stiffness in his mental character which is interesting, though it grows rather wearisome on close and frequent acquaintance.

Nathaniel Hawthorne to Henry Wadsworth Longfellow, November 21, 1848, quoted in *Final Memorials of Henry Wadsworth Longfellow*, edited by Samuel Longfellow, p. 29

I knew Thoreau well when we were schoolboys together. He was considered by most of us boys as rather stupid, and unsympathetic, though by no means a poor scholar. I suppose we thought him stupid because he did not join heartily in our plays. I cannot recollect that he ever played with us at all. He seemed to have no fun in him.

Alfred Munroe, August 8, 1877, quoted in Kenneth Walter Cameron's "Thoreau's Schoolmate, Alfred Munroe, Remembers Concord" (*American Transcendental Quarterly* 36), p. 20

In college Mr. Thoreau had made no great impression. He was far from being distinguished as a scholar. He was not known to have any literary tastes; was never a contributor to the college periodical, the "Harvardiana"; was not, I think, interested, certainly not conspicuous, in any of the literary or scientific societies of the undergraduates, and, withal, was of an unsocial disposition, and kept himself much aloof from his classmates. At the time we graduated, I doubt whether any of his acquaintances regarded him as giving promise of future distinction.

David Green Haskins in *Ralph Waldo Emerson: His Maternal Ancestors*, pp. 119–120

Those who thought of Thoreau as cold or indifferent little understood the depth of feeling that lay beneath his undemonstrative exterior. During his father's illness his devotion was such that Mrs. Thoreau in recalling it said, "If it hadn't been for my husband's illness, I should never have known what a tender heart Henry had." He mourned deeply for this beloved brother. He laid aside his flute and for years refused to speak his name. A friend told me that twelve years later Thoreau started, turned pale, and could hardly overcome his emotion when some reference to John was made.

Mary Hosmer Brown in *Memories of Concord*, p. 92

Mr. Thorow dined with us yesterday. He is a singular character—a young man with much of wild original nature still remaining in him; and so far as he is sophisticated, it is in a way and method of his own.

Nathaniel Hawthorne, September 1, 1842, in *The American Notebooks*, pp. 353–354

He always reminded me of an eagle, ready to soar to great heights or to swoop down on anything he considered evil.

Anonymous woman, who was his hostess on occasion in Worcester, as reported in Annie R. Marble's *Thoreau: His Home, Friends and Books*, p. 152

Perhaps Thoreau talked rather like one who was accustomed to be listened to than to listen, though this was by no means prominent, and there was not the slightest lack of courtesy in his manner. . . . He gave you a chance to talk, attended to what you said, and then made his reply, but did not come to very close quarters with you or help you out with your thought after the manner of skilled and practiced conversers. Emerson says of him that "he coldly and fully stated his opinion without affecting to believe that it was the opinion of the company." Thoreau was always interesting, often entertaining, but never what you would call charming.

E. Harlow Russell in an account reported in the *Leominster (Mass.) Daily Enterprise*, December 28, 1899, as quoted in Walter Harding's *Thoreau: Man of Concord*, pp. 97–98

Thoreau, the Concord hermit, who lived by himself in the woods, used to come smiling up to his neighbors, to announce that the bluebirds had arrived, with as much interest in the fact as other men take in messages by the Atlantic cable. On certain days, he made long pilgrimages to find

"The sweet rhodora in the wood,"

welcoming the lonely flower like a long-absent friend. He gravely informed us once, that frogs were much more confiding in the spring, than later in the season; for then, it only took an hour to get well acquainted with one of the speckled swimmers, who liked to be tickled with a blade of grass, and would feed from his hand in the most sociable manner.

Louisa May Alcott in "Merry's Monthly Chat with his Friends" (*Merry's Museum*, March 1869), p. 147

In walking, he made a short cut if he could, and when sitting in the shade or by the wall-side seemed merely the clearer to look forward into the next piece of activity.

Ellery Channing in *Thoreau: The Poet Naturalist*, p. 25

I told Thoreau that he would have to come along with me, and he went without any trouble and was locked up. When his tax was paid by some one . . . I told him he was free to go but he would not, until finally I said, "Henry, if you will not go of your own accord I shall put you out, for you cannot stay here any longer." He was the only prisoner that I ever had that did not want to leave when he could.

Sam Staples in "An Evening with Thoreau" as reported in the *Concord High School Voice*, November 15, 1895, p. 23

I do not remember of ever seeing him laugh outright, but he was ever ready to smile at anything that pleased him; and I never knew him to betray any tender emotion except on one occasion, when he was narrating to me the death of his only brother, John Thoreau, from lockjaw, strong symptoms of which, from his sympathy with the sufferer, he himself experienced. At this time his voice was choked, and he shed tears, and went to the door for air. The subject was of course dropped, and never recurred to again.

Daniel Ricketson in *Daniel Ricketson and His Friends*, p. 14

Henry T has built him a house of one room a little distance from Walden pond & in view of the public road. There he lives—cooks, eats, studies & sleeps & is quite happy. He has many visitors, whom he receives with pleasure & does his best to entertain.

Prudence Ward, January 20, 1846, as reported in Henry Seidel Canby's *Thoreau*, p. 216

Mr. Emerson . . . has a friend with him of the name of Henry Thoreau who has come to live with him and be his working-man this year. H. T. is three and twenty, has been through college and kept a school, is very fond of classic studies, and an earnest thinker yet intends being a farmer. He has a great deal of practical sense, and as he has bodily strength to boot, he may look to be a successful and happy man. He has a boat which he made himself, and rows me out on the pond.

> Margaret Fuller to her brother, Richard, May 25, 1841, in *The Letters of Margaret Fuller*, vol. 2, p. 210

If I knew only Thoreau, I should think coöperation of good men impossible. Must we always talk for victory, and never once for truth, for comfort, and joy? Centrality he has, and penetration, strong understanding, and the higher gifts,—the insight of the real, or from the real, and the moral rectitude that belongs to it; but all this and all his resources of wit and invention are lost to me, in every experiment, year after year, that I make, to hold intercourse with his mind. Always some weary captious paradox to fight you with, and the time and temper wasted.

> Ralph Waldo Emerson, written 1856 in *The Journals of Ralph Waldo Emerson*, vol. 8, pp. 15–16

The undersigned very cheerfully hereby introduces to public notice the bearer, Mr. David Henry Thoreau, as a teacher in the higher branches of useful literature. He is a native of this town, and a graduate of Harvard University. He is well disposed and well qualified to instruct the rising generation. His scholarship and moral character will bear the strictest scrutiny. He is modest and mild in his disposition and government, but not wanting in energy of character and fidelity in the duties of his profession. It is presumed his character and usefulness will be appreciated more highly as an acquaintance with him shall be cultivated. Cordial wishes for his success, reputation, and usefulness attend him, as an instructor and gentleman.

Ezra Ripley to the "Friends of Education," May 1, 1838, quoted in Franklin B. Sanborn's *Henry D. Thoreau*, pp. 57–58

We boys used to visit him on Saturday afternoons at his house by Walden, and he would show us interesting things in the woods near by. I did not see the philosophical side. He was never stern or pedantic, but natural and very agreeable, friendly,—but a person you would never feel inclined to fool with. A face that you would long remember. Though short in stature, and inconspicuous in dress, you would not fail to notice him in the street, as more than ordinary.

Edward Emerson in *Henry Thoreau as Remembered by a Young Friend*, p. 129

I recall an occasion when little Edward Emerson, carrying a basket of fine huckleberries, had a fall and spilt them all. Great was his distress, and our offers of berries could not console him for the loss of those gathered by himself. But Thoreau came, put his arm around the troubled child, and explained to him that if the crop of huckleberries was to continue it was necessary that some should be scattered. Nature had provided that little boys should now and then stumble and sow the berries. We shall have a grand lot of bushes and berries on this spot, and we shall owe them to you. Edward began to smile.

Moncure D. Conway in *Autobiography: Memoirs and Experiences*, vol. 1, p. 148

I love Henry, but do not like him.

Elizabeth Hoar, as reported by Ralph Waldo Emerson in 1843 in *The Journals of Ralph Waldo* Emerson, vol. 6, p. 371

He seemed to know what he knew—by no means, I think, the most common of characteristics.

John Witt Randall to Francis Ellingwood Abbot, January 9, 1857, in *Poems of Nature and Life*, p. 109

Anecdotes

Think of it, he stood half an hour today to hear the frogs croak, and he would'nt read the life of Chalmers.

Thoreau's aunt, Maria Thoreau, as recorded by Thoreau on March 28, 1853, in his *Journal*, vol. 6, p. 41

On my birthday, in the early summer, just before I went to take my examination for Harvard, my father and mother invited Thoreau and Channing, both, but especially Thoreau, friends from my babyhood, to dine with us. When we left the table and were passing into the parlour, Thoreau asked me to come with him to our East door—our more homelike door, facing the orchard. It was an act of affectionate courtesy, for he had divined my suppressed state of mind and remembered that first crisis in his own life, and the wrench that it seemed in advance, as a gate leading out into an untried world. With serious face, but with a very quiet, friendly tone of voice, he reassured me, told me that I should be really close to home; very likely should pass my life in Concord. It was a great relief.

Edward Emerson in *Henry Thoreau as Remembered by a Young Friend*, p. 147

I liked Thoreau, though he was morbid. I do not think it was so much a love of woods, streams, and hills that made him live in the country, as from a morbid dislike of humanity. I remember Thoreau saying once, when walking with him in my favorite Brooklyn—"What is there in the people? Pshaw! what do you (a man who sees as well as anybody) see in all this cheering political corruption?"

Walt Whitman as reported in Anne Gilchrist's *Anne Gilchrist: Her Life and Writings*, edited by Herbert Harlakenden Gilchrist, p. 237

Once, when I was nearly seven years old, Thoreau came to the Wayside to make a survey of our land, bringing his surveying apparatus on his shoulder. I watched the short, dark, unbeautiful man with interest and followed him about, all over the place, never losing sight of a movement and never asking a question or uttering a word. The thing must have lasted a couple of hours; when we got back, Thoreau remarked to my father: "Good boy! Sharp eyes, and no tongue!" On that basis I was admitted to his friendship; a friendship or comradeship which began in 1852 and was to last until his death in 1862.

Julian Hawthorne in *The Memoirs of Julian Hawthorne*,
p. 114

Thoreau had his own odd ways. Once he got to the house while I was out—went straight to the kitchen where my dear mother was baking some cakes—took the cakes hot from the oven. He was always doing things of the plain sort—without fuss. I liked all that about him. But Thoreau's great fault was disdain—disdain for men (for Tom, Dick and Harry): inability to appreciate the average life—even the exceptional life: it seemed to me a want of imagination. He couldn't put his life into any other life—realize why one man was so and another man was not so: was impatient with other people on the street and so forth. We had a hot discussion about it—it was a bitter difference: it was rather a surprise to me to meet in Thoreau such a very aggravated case of superciliousness. It was egotistic—into any other not taking that word in its worst sense. . . . Yet he was a man you would have to like—an interesting man, simple, conclusive. When I was at Emerson's Mrs. Emerson told me Thoreau stayed with her during one of Emerson's trips abroad. She said that Thoreau, though odd, was good, equable, assiduous, likeable, throughout. . . . When I lived in Brooklyn—in the suburbs—probably two miles distant from the ferries—

though there were cheap cabs, I always walked to the ferry to get over to New York. Several times when Thoreau was there with me we walked together.

Walt Whitman as reported in Horace Traubel's *With Walt Whitman in Camden (March 28–July 14, 1888)*, pp. 212–213

He tried to place me geographically after he had given me a chair not quite so far off as Ohio, though still across the whole room, for he sat against one wall, and I against the other; but apparently he failed to pull himself out of his revery by the effort, for he remained in a dreamy muse, which all my attempts to say something fit about John Brown and Walden Pond seemed only to deepen upon him. . . . I do not remember that Thoreau spoke of his books or of himself at all, and when he began to speak of John Brown, it was not the warm, palpable, loving, fearful old man of my conception, but a sort of John Brown type, a John Brown ideal, a John Brown principle, which we were somehow (with long pauses between the vague, orphic phrases) to cherish, and to nourish ourselves upon.

William Dean Howells in *Literary Friends and Acquaintance: A Personal Retrospect of American Authorship*, p. 59

I have seen children catch him by the hand, as he was going home from school, to walk with him and hear more.

Dr. Thomas Hosmer as quoted in Edward Emerson's *Henry Thoreau as Remembered by a Young Friend* (Boston: Houghton Mifflin, 1917), p. 128

Mr. Thoreau was always most modest and yet chivalrous in his treatment of women of high or low degree.

Edward Waldo Emerson and Waldo Emerson Forbes in Ralph
Waldo Emerson's *The Journals of Ralph Waldo Emerson*, vol. 6,
p. 371

One of our girls said, that Henry never went through the kitchen without coloring.

Ralph Waldo Emerson, written 1843, in *The Journals of Ralph
Waldo Emerson*, vol. 6, p. 371

I remember being startled by a remark of Mr. Emerson's as we were one day walking beside Walden Pond. . . . As I ventured to comment upon the singular contiguity of the village to what might be termed the fringe of this trackless solitude, the "Sage of Concord" turned to me with a sweet but peculiar smile. "Yes," he said, "we sometimes rang the dinner bell at the lower end of the garden and we were always glad when Henry heard it and came up.

Ralph Waldo Emerson as related by Bret Harte in "A Few
Words about Mr. Lowell" (*The New Review*, September 1891),
pp. 199–200

I have a keen recollection of the first time I met Henry David Thoreau. It was upon a beautiful day in July, 1847, that Mrs. Alcott told us we were to visit Walden. We started merrily a party of seven, Mr. and Mrs. Alcott, the four girls and myself, for the woods of oak and pine that encircled the picturesque little lake called

Walden Pond. We found Thoreau in his cabin, a plain little house of one room containing a wood stove.

He gave us gracious welcome, asking us within. . . . He was talking to Mr. Alcott of the wild flowers in Walden woods when, suddenly stopping, he said: "Keep very still and I will show you my family." Stepping quickly outside the cabin door, he gave a low and curious whistle; immediately a woodchuck came running towards him from a nearby burrow. With varying note, yet still low and strange, a pair of gray squirrels were summoned and approached him fearlessly. With still another note several birds, including two crows, flew towards him, one of the crows nestling upon his shoulder. I remember it was the crow resting close to his head that made the most vivid impression upon me, knowing how fearful of man this bird is. He fed them all from his hand, taking food from his pocket, and petted them gently before our delighted gaze; and then dismissed them by different whistling, always strange and low and short, each little wild thing departing instantly at hearing its special signal.

Then he took us five children upon the Pond in his boat, ceasing his oars after a little distance from the shore and playing the flute he had brought with him, its music echoing over the still and beautifully clear water.

Frederick L. H. Willis in *Alcott Memoirs*, pp. 91–92

He played with much expression on the flute, and in his early years sang in a pleasing voice, although he had no special training in music. After his brother's death he could not be induced to sing. The musical quality of his voice made him a charming reader.

S. E. Rena, February 12, 1896, to the editor of the Boston *Transcript*, as quoted in Kenneth Walter Cameron's *The New England Writers and the Press*, p. 262

Thoreau used to amuse us by gently raising fish out of the water.

Moncure D. Conway in *Life of Nathaniel Hawthorne*, p. 165

Personally, he was odd, in all senses of the term. He was bilious in constitution and in temper, with a disposition somewhat prone to suspicion and jealousy, and defiant, rather than truly independent, in spirit. He had a searching, watchful, unconciliating eye, a long, stealthy tread and an alert but not graceful figure. His heart was neither warm nor large, and he certainly did not share that "enthusiasm for humanity" which was the fashionable profession in his day. His habits were solitary and unsocial; yet secretly he was highly sensitive to the opinion of his fellow-men, and would perhaps have mingled more freely with them, but for a perception that there was no vehement demand for his company. The art of pleasing was not innate in him, and he was too proud to cultivate it. Rather than have it appear that society could do without him, he resolved to make haste and banish society; for a couple of years he actually lived alone in a hut built by himself, on the shores of Walden Pond, near Concord: all his life he kept out of people's way,—you were more apt to see his disappearing coat-tails than his face.

Julian Hawthorne in *American Literature*, p. 146

Thoreau was a good deal of a wag in a quiet humorous way. He once put cloth bandages on the claws of Mrs. Emerson's hens, that good lady having been sorely tried by her fowls invading the family flower patch. I guess Mrs. Emerson invented the notion of gloving her hens, and Thoreau carried out her instructions to the letter, and then went off and had his laugh out.

An "old Concordian" in "Thoreau Gloving Mrs. Emerson's Hens" in *The Minneapolis Tribune*, ca. 1890, as quoted in Walter Harding's *Thoreau: Man of Concord*, p. 72

On a summer morning about fourteen years ago I went with Mr. Emerson and was introduced to Thoreau. I was then connected with Divinity College at Cambridge, and my new acquaintance was interested to know what we were studying there at the time. "Well, the Scriptures." "But *which*?" he asked, not without a certain quiet humor playing about his serious blue eye.... When I went to the house next morning, I found them all (Thoreau was then living in his father's house) in a state of excitement by reason of the arrival of a fugitive negro from the South, who had come fainting to their door about daybreak and thrown himself on their mercy. Thoreau took me in to see the poor wretch, whom I found to be a man with whose face as that of a slave in the South I was familiar. The negro was much terrified at seeing me, supposing that I was

one of his pursuers. Having quieted his fears by the assurance that I too, though in a different sense, was a
refugee from the bondage he was escaping, and at the
same time been able to attest the negro's genuineness, I
sat and watched the singularly tender and lowly devotion of the scholar to the slave. He must be fed, his
swollen feet bathed, and he must think of nothing but
rest. Again and again this coolest and calmest of men
drew near to the trembling negro, and bade him feel at
home, and have no fear that any power should again
wrong him. He could not walk that day, but must
mount guard over the fugitive, for slave-hunters were
not extinct in those days; and so I went away after a
while, much impressed by many little traits that I had
seen as they had appeared in this emergency, and not
much disposed to cavil at their source, whether Bible
or Bhaghavat.

Moncure D. Conway in "Thoreau" (*Fraser's Magazine for Town
and Country*, April 1866), pp. 460–461

He was a man of rare courage, physically and intellectually. In the way of the former, he arrested two young
fellows with horse and wagon on the lonely road leading to his hermitage at Walden pond, who were endeavoring to entrap a young woman on her way home,
and took them to the village; whether they were
brought to court I do not remember, and may not have
given an exact account of the affair, but it is circum-
stantially correct.

Daniel Ricketson in *Daniel Ricketson and His Friends*,
pp. 252–253

Death

As long he could possibly sit up, he insisted on his chair at the family-table, and said, "It would not be social to take my meals alone."

William Ellery Channing in *Thoreau: The Poet-Naturalist*, p. 323

You ask for some particulars relating to Henry's illness. I feel like saying that Henry was never affected, never reached by it. I never before saw such a manifestation of the power of spirit over matter. Very often I have heard him tell his visitors that he enjoyed existence as well as ever. He remarked to me that there was as much comfort in perfect disease as in perfect health, the mind always conforming to the condition of the body. The thought of death, he said, could not begin to trouble him. His thoughts had entertained him all his life, and did still.

When he had wakeful nights, he would ask me to arrange the furniture so as to make fantastic shadows on the wall, and he wished his bed was in the form of a shell, that he might curl up in it. He considered occupation as necessary for the sick as for those in health, and has accomplished a vast amount of labor during the past few months in preparing some papers for the press. He did not cease to call for his manuscripts till the last day of his life.

During his long illness I never heard a murmur escape him, or the slightest wish expressed to remain with us; his perfect contentment was truly wonderful. None of his friends seemed to realize how very ill he was, so full of life and good cheer did he seem. One friend, as if by way of consolation, said to him, "Well, Mr. Thoreau, we must all go." Henry replied, "When I was a very little boy I learned that I must die, and I set that down, so of course I am not disappointed now. Death is as near to you as it is to me."

There is very much that I should like to write you about my precious brother, had I time and strength. I wish you to know how very gentle, lovely, and submissive he was in all his ways. His little study bed was brought down into our front parlor, when he could no longer walk with our assistance, and every arrangement pleased him. The devotion of his friends was most rare and touching; his room was made fragrant by the gift of flowers from young and old; fruit of every kind which the season afforded, and game of all sorts was sent him. It was really pathetic, the way in which the town was moved to minister to his comfort. Total strangers sent grateful messages, remembering the good he had done them. All this attention was fully appreciated and very gratifying to Henry; he would sometimes say, "I should be ashamed to stay in this world after so much had been done for me, I could never repay my friends." And they so remembered him to the last. Only about two hours before he left us, Judge Hoar called with a bouquet of hyacinths fresh from his garden, which Henry smelled and said he liked, and a few minutes after he was gone, another friend came with a dish of his favorite jelly. I can never be grateful enough for the gentle, easy exit which was granted him. At seven o'clock Tuesday morning he became restless and desired to be moved; dear mother,

Aunt Louisa, and myself were with him; his self-possession did not forsake him. A little after eight he asked to be raised quite up, his breathing grew fainter and fainter, and without the slightest struggle, he left us at nine o'clock.

Sophia Thoreau to Daniel Ricketson, May 20, 1862, as quoted by Daniel Ricketson in *Daniel Ricketson and His Friends*, pp. 141–143

It may interest you to hear of the last visit which I with Blake made at his (Thoreau's) house a short time before he died. . . . We found him pretty low, but well enough to be up in his chair. He seemed glad to see us. Said we had not come much too soon. We spent some hours with him in his mother's parlor, which overlooks the river that runs all through his life. There was a beautiful snowstorm going on the while which I fancy inspired him, and his talk was up to the best I ever heard from him,—the same depth of earnestness and the same infinite depth of fun going on at the same time.

I wish I could recall some of the things he said. I do remember some few answers he made to questions from Blake. Blake asked him how the future seemed to him. "Just as uninteresting as ever," was his characteristic answer. A little while after he said, "You have been skating on this river; perhaps I am going to skate on some other." And again, "Perhaps I am going up country." He stuck to nature to the last.

Theo Brown to Daniel Ricketson, January 19, 1868, as quoted in Daniel Ricketson's *Daniel Ricketson and His Friends*, pp. 213–214

Sam Staples yesterday had been to see Henry Thoreau. "Never spent an hour with more satisfaction. Never saw a man dying with so much pleasure and peace." Thinks that very few men in Concord know Mr. Thoreau; finds him serene and happy.

> Sam Staples, as reported by Ralph Waldo Emerson on March 24, 1862, in *The Journals of Ralph Waldo Emerson*, vol. 9, p. 413

Some boys of the vicinity were in the habit of bringing game for him to eat, presenting it at the kitchen door, and then gently withdrawing so as not to disturb the sick man. On one occasion he was told of it soon after their leaving, when he earnestly inquired: "Why did you not invite them in? I want to thank them for so much that they are bringing me." And then adding, thoughtfully: "Well, I declare; I don't believe they are going to let me go after all."

> Sophia Thoreau in 1863 as related by Calvin Greene in "Memories of Thoreau: Unpublished Anecdotes of New England's Anti-Puritan Author and Naturalist" (*The Truth Seeker*, November 20, 1897), p. 144

Some Final Assessments

Why should any one wish to have a sentence of Henry Thoreau's put in print?"

> George Frisbie Hoar, when asked by Thomas Wentworth Higginson to intercede with Sophia Thoreau in getting some of Thoreau's unpublished writings posthumously printed, as reported in Thomas Wentworth Higginson's "George Frisbie Hoar" (*Proceedings of the American Academy of Arts and Sciences*, vol. 40, 1905), p. 762

I loved to hear him talk, but I did not like his books so well, though I often read them and took what I liked. They do not do him justice. I liked to see Thoreau rather in his life. . . . He loved to talk, like all his family, but not to gossip: he kept the talk on a high plane. He was cheerful and pleasant.

> Mrs. Minot Pratt as reported in Edward Emerson's *Henry Thoreau as Remembered by a Young Friend*, p. 80

Henry Thoreau we all remember as a man of genius, and of marked character, known to our farmers as the most skilful of surveyors, and indeed better acquainted with their forests and meadows and trees than themselves, but more widely known as the writer of some of the best books which have been written in this country, and which, I am persuaded, have not yet gathered half their fame.

> Ralph Waldo Emerson, at the opening of the Concord Free Public Library, 1873, in *Miscellanies*, p. 500

I read his books & manuscripts always with a new surprise at the range of his topics & the novelty & depth of his thought. A man of large reading, of quick perception, of great practical courage & ability,—who grew greater every day, &, had his short life been prolonged would have found few equals to the power & wealth of his mind.

> Ralph Waldo Emerson to George Stewart, Jr., January 22, 1877, in *The Letters of Ralph Waldo Emerson*, vol. 6, p. 303

His soul was made for the noblest society; he had in a short life exhausted the capabilities of this world; wherever there is knowledge, wherever there is virtue, wherever there is beauty, he will find a home.

Ralph Waldo Emerson in "Thoreau" (*Atlantic Monthly*, August 1862), p. 249

FIG. 20. Ambrotype by Edward Sidney Dunshee taken on August 21, 1861, in New Bedford, Massachusetts. Photographic copy by Alfred W. Hosmer. The Lewis C. Dawes Collection at the Thoreau Institute at Walden Woods. Courtesy of the Walden Woods Project.

Misquotations and Misattributions

"In wilderness is the preservation of the world."

MISQUOTATION: correct quotation, from "Walking": "In Wildness is the preservation of the World."

Although this appeared in a few minor publications in the first half of the twentieth century, it was Perry Miller's 1957 anthology, *The American Transcendentalists, Their Prose and Poetry*, used in innumerable colleges and universities, that propagated the error.

"Use what talent you possess: the woods would be very silent if no birds sang except those that sang best."

MISATTRIBUTION: correct attribution unknown, although it has also been erroneously and extensively attributed to Henry Van Dyke (1852–1933). The first known use was in *The Ladies Repository: A Monthly Periodical, Devoted to Literature, Arts, and Religion* (September 1874), without attribution.

"Friends are kind to each other's hopes, they cherish each other's dreams."

MISQUOTATION: correct quotation, from the "Wednesday" chapter of *A Week on the Concord and Merrimack Rivers*: "The Friend asks no return but that his Friend will religiously accept and wear and not disgrace his apotheosis of him. They cherish each other's hopes. They are kind to each other's dreams."

"Go confidently in the direction of your dreams. Live the life you have imagined. As you simplify your life, the laws of the universe will be simpler."

MISQUOTATION: correct quotation from *Walden*: "I learned this, at least, by my experiment; that if one advances confidently in the direction of his dreams, and endeavors to live the life which he has imagined, he will meet with a success unexpected in common hours."

"It is not enough to be busy. The question is: what are we busy about?"

VARIANT: "It is not enough to be busy. So are the ants. The question is: What are we busy about?"

MISQUOTATION: correct quotation from Thoreau's letter to H.G.O. Blake, November 16, 1857: "It is not enough to be industrious; so are the ants. What are you industrious about?"

"Many men fish all their lives without ever realizing that it is not the fish they are after."

VARIANT: "Many go fishing all their lives without knowing that it is not fish they are after."

MISQUOTATION: the closest parallel in a non-Thoreau text is from E.T. Brown's *Not without Prejudice: Essays on Assorted Subjects* (Melbourne: Cheshire, 1955), p. 142: "When they go fishing, it is not really fish they are after. It is a philosophic meditation." The actual misquotation in relation to Thoreau can be attributed to Michael Baughman's *A River Seen Right* (Lyons Press, 1995) p. 156, in which he wrote, clearly paraphrasing and not quoting: "I think it was in *Walden* where he wrote that a lot of men fish all their lives without ever realizing that fish isn't really what they're after."

Baughman may have been paraphrasing from Thoreau's Journal, January 26, 1853:

> It is remarkable that many men will go with eagerness to Walden Pond in the winter to fish for pickerel and yet not seem to care for the landscape. Of course it cannot be *merely* for the pickerel they may catch; there is some adventure in it; but any love of nature which they may feel is certainly very slight and indefinite. They call it going a-fishing, and so indeed it is, though perchance, their natures know better. Now I go a-fishing and a-hunting every day, but omit the fish and the game, which are the least important part. I have learned to do without them. They were indispensable only as long as I was a boy. I am encouraged when I see a dozen villagers drawn to Walden Pond to spend a day in fishing through the ice, and suspect that I have more fellows than I knew, but I am disappointed and surprised to find that they lay so much stress on the fish which they catch or fail to catch, and on nothing else, as if there were nothing else to be caught.

"Most men lead lives of quiet desperation and go to the grave with the song still in them."

Misquotation: the first half of this quotation is a misquotation from Thoreau's *Walden*: "The mass of men lead lives of quiet desperation."

Misattribution: the second half is misattributed to Thoreau and may be a misremembering of Oliver Wendell Holmes's (1809–1894) "The Voiceless":

> Alas for those that never sing,
> But die with all their music in them.

"Be true to your work, your word, and your friend."

Misattribution: correct attribution is the poet, novelist, and editor John Boyle O'Reilly (1844–1890), although the words from his poem "Rules of the Road" should more correctly be quoted as: "Be true to your word and your work and your friend."

"If you would find yourself, look to the land from which you came and to which you go."

Misattribution: correct attribution is Stewart Udall, who wrote in *The Quiet Crisis* (New York: Holt, Rinehart and Winston, 1963), p. 190, regarding Thoreau: "To those who complain of the complexity of modern life, he might reply, 'If you want inner peace find it in solitude, not speed, and if you would find yourself, look to the land from which you came and to which you go.'"

"There is no value in life except what you choose to place upon it, and no happiness in any place except what you bring to it yourself."

Misattribution: correct attribution is Lin Yutang (1895–1976) who wrote in *On the Wisdom of America* (New York: John Day, 1950) p. 446: "Thoreau once thought the moon was larger over the United States than over the Old World, the sky bluer, the stars brighter, the thunder louder, the rivers longer, the mountains higher, the prairies vaster, and he mystically concluded that the spirit of man in America should be larger and more expansive 'else why was America discovered?' Thoreau was wrong, and Thoreau was right. There is no value in life except what you choose to place upon it, and no happiness in any place except what you bring to it yourself."

"What lies behind us and what lies before us are tiny matters compared to what lies within us."
MISATTRIBUTION: correct attribution is Henry Stanley Haskins (1875–1957) from his anonymously published *Meditations in Wall Street* (New York: William Morrow & Co., 1940), p. 131.

"You cannot dream yourself into a character; you must hammer and forge yourself one. Go out into life, you will find your chance there, and only there."
MISATTRIBUTION: correct attribution is the English historian James Anthony Froude (1818–1894) from his book *The Nemesis of Faith* (1849). The first line of this quotation appeared in Anna Cabot Lowell's *Seed-Grain for Thought and Discussion: A Compilation* (Boston: Ticknor and Fields, 1856), in which the quotation preceding this was by Thoreau.

"Libraries will get you through times of no money better than money will get you through times of no libraries."

VARIANT: "Books will get you through times of no money better than money will get you through times of no books."

MISATTRIBUTION: this misattribution is an adaption from a Gilbert Shelton *Fabulous Furry Freak Brothers* cartoon ("The Freaks Pull a Heist!"): "Dope will get you through times of no money better than money will get you through times of no dope." The "Libraries will get you through" version first appeared in *The Whole Earth Catalog* (1980 edition). The "Books will get you through" version was published by the American Library Association in the early 1980s.

BIBLIOGRAPHY

WORKS CITED

Works by Thoreau

Cape Cod. Edited by Joseph J. Moldenhauer. Princeton, NJ: Princeton University Press, 1988.

Collected Poems of Henry Thoreau. Enlarged ed. Edited by Carl Bode. Baltimore: Johns Hopkins University Press, 1965.

The Correspondence of Henry David Thoreau. Edited by Walter Harding and Carl Bode. New York: New York University Press, 1958.

Early Essays and Miscellanies. Edited by Joseph J. Moldenhauer and Edwin Moser, with Alexander Kern. Princeton, NJ: Princeton University Press, 1975.

Excursions. Edited by Joseph J. Moldenhauer. Princeton, NJ: Princeton University Press, 2007.

Faith in a Seed: The Dispersion of Seeds and Other Late Natural History Writings. Edited by Bradley P. Dean. Washington, DC: Island Press/Shearwater Books, 1993.

Familiar Letters: Enlarged Edition. Edited by F. B. Sanborn. Boston: Houghton Mifflin, 1906.

Huckleberries. Edited, with an introduction, by Leo Stoller. Iowa City: Windhover Press of the University of Iowa, 1970.

Journal. Edited by John C. Broderick et al. Princeton, NJ: Princeton University Press, 1981– .

The Journal of Henry D. Thoreau. Edited by Bradford Torrey and Francis H. Allen. Boston: Houghton Mifflin, 1906.

The Maine Woods. Edited by Joseph J. Moldenhauer. Princeton, NJ: Princeton University Press, 1972.

Reform Papers. Edited by Wendell Glick. Princeton, NJ: Princeton University Press, 1973.

"Sir Walter Raleigh," second draft manuscript, The Walden Woods Project Collection at the Thoreau Institute at Walden Woods.

Walden. Edited by J. Lyndon Shanley. Princeton, NJ: Princeton University Press, 1971.

Wild Fruits: Thoreau's Rediscovered Last Manuscript. Edited and introduced by Bradley P. Dean. New York: W. W. Norton, 1999.

The Writings of Henry D. Thoreau. Walden ed. Boston: Houghton Mifflin, 1906.

Works by Others

"An account of an evening passed with Thoreau more than 30 years ago, at the house of a common friend." *Leominster (Mass.) Daily Enterprise*, December 28, 1899.

Albee, John. *Remembrances of Emerson*. New York: Cooke, 1903.

Alcott, Louisa May. "Merry's Monthly Chat with his Friends." *Merry's Museum*, vol. 2, no. 3 (March 1869).

Brown, Mary Hosmer. *Memories of Concord*. Boston: Four Seas, 1926.

Cameron, Kenneth Walter. *The New England Writers and the Press*. Hartford: Transcendental Books, 1980.

———. "Thoreau's Schoolmate, Alfred Munroe, Remembers Concord." *American Transcendental Quarterly* 36 (1977).

Canby, Henry Seidel. *Thoreau*. Boston: Houghton Mifflin, 1939.

Channing, William Ellery. *Thoreau: The Poet-Naturalist. With Memorial Verses*. Boston: Roberts Brothers, 1873.

Conway, Moncure D. *Autobiography: Memoirs and Experiences*. Boston: Houghton Mifflin, 1904.

———. *Life of Nathaniel Hawthorne*. New York: A. Lovell, 1890.

———. "Thoreau." *Fraser's Magazine for Town and Country*, April 1866.

Emerson, Edward. *Henry Thoreau as Remembered by a Young Friend*. Boston: Houghton Mifflin, 1917.

Emerson, Ralph Waldo. *The Journals of Ralph Waldo Emerson: With Annotations*. Edited by Edward Waldo Emerson and Waldo Emerson Forbes. Boston: Houghton Mifflin, 1909–1914.

———. *The Letters of Ralph Waldo Emerson*. Edited by Ralph L. Rusk. New York: Columbia University Press, 1939.

———. *Miscellanies*. Boston: Houghton, Mifflin, 1878.

———. "Thoreau." *Atlantic Monthly*, August 1862.

"An Evening with Thoreau." *Concord High School Voice*, November 15, 1895.

Fields, Annie Adams. *James T. Fields: Biographical Notes and Personal Sketches*. London: Sampson Low, Marston, Searle & Rivington, 1881.

Fuller, Margaret. *The Letters of Margaret Fuller*. Edited by Robert N. Hudspeth. Ithaca, NY: Cornell University Press, 1983–1994.

Gilchrist, Anne. *Anne Gilchrist: Her Life and Writings*. Edited by Herbert Harlakenden Gilchrist. New York: Scribner and Wellford, 1887.

Greene, Calvin. "Memories of Thoreau: Unpublished Anecdotes of New England's Anti-Puritan Author and Naturalist." *The Truth Seeker*, November 20, 1897.

Harding, Walter. *The Days of Henry Thoreau*. Princeton, New Jersey: Princeton University Press, 1992.

——. *Thoreau: Man of Concord*. New York: Holt, Rinehart and Winston, 1960.

Harte, Bret. "A Few Words about Mr. Lowell." *New Review*, September 1891.

Haskins, David Green. *Ralph Waldo Emerson: His Maternal Ancestors with Some Reminiscences of Him*. Boston: Cupples, Upham and Co., 1887.

Hawthorne, Julian. *The Memoirs of Julian Hawthorne*. Edited by his wife Edith Garrigues Hawthorne. New York: Macmillan, 1938.

Hawthorne, Julian, and Leonard Lemmon. *American Literature: A Text-Book for the Use of Schools and Colleges*. Boston: D. C. Heath, 1891.

Hawthorne, Nathaniel. *The American Notebooks*. Edited by Charles M. Simpson. Columbus: Ohio State University Press, 1972.

Higginson, Thomas Wentworth. "George Frisbie Hoar." *Proceedings of the American Academy of Arts and Sciences*, vol. 40 (1905).

Howells, William Dean. *Literary Friends and Acquaintance: A Personal Retrospect of American Authorship*. New York: Harper, 1902.

Johnson, Linck C. *Thoreau's Complex Weave: The Writing of A Week on the Concord and Merrimack Rivers, with the Text of the First Draft*. Charlottesville: Published for the Bibliographical Society of the University of Virginia, by the University Press of Virginia, 1986.

Jordan, David Starr. "Thoreau and John Brown." *The Current*, vol. 7, no. 173 (April 9, 1887).

Longfellow, Henry Wadsworth. *Final Memorials of Henry Wadsworth Longfellow*. Edited by Samuel Longfellow. Boston: Ticknor, 1887.

Lyman, Emil R. *Thoreau*. Concord, MA: Privately printed, 1902.

Marble, Annie R. *Thoreau: His Home, Friends and Books*. New York: Crowell, 1902.

"Memories of Thoreau: Unpublished Anecdotes of New England's Anti-Puritan Author and Naturalist." *The Truth Seeker*, November 20, 1897.

Randall, John Witt. *Poems of Nature and Life*. Edited by Francis Ellingwood Abbot, with an introduction on the Randall family. Boston: Ellis, 1899.

Rena, S. E. "Thoreau's Voice." *Boston Transcript*, (February 18, 1896).

Ricketson, Daniel. *Daniel Ricketson and His Friends: Letters, Poems, Sketches, etc.* Edited by his daughter and son, Anna and Walton Ricketson. Boston: Houghton, Mifflin, 1902.

Sanborn, F. B. *Henry D. Thoreau*. Boston: Houghton Mifflin, 1882.

———. *The Personality of Thoreau*. Boston: Goodspeed, 1901.

Todd, Mabel Loomis. *The Thoreau Family Two Generations Ago*. Foreword and footnotes by Millicent Todd Bingham. Berkeley Heights, NJ: Printed for the Thoreau Society by the Oriole Press, 1958.

Traubel, Horace. *With Walt Whitman in Camden (March 28–July 14, 1888)*. Boston: Small, Maynard, 1906.

Weiss, John. "Thoreau." *Christian Examiner*, July 1865.

Waylen, Hector. "A Visit to Walden Pond." *Natural Food*, July 1895.

Willis, Frederick L. H. *Alcott Memoirs posthumously compiled from papers, journals and memoranda of the late Dr. Frederick L. H. Willis* by E. W. L. & H. B. Boston: Badger, 1915.

FURTHER READING

Borst, Raymond. *The Thoreau Log: A Documentary Life of Henry David Thoreau, 1817–1862*. New York: G. K. Hall, 1992.

Howarth, William L. *The Book of Concord: Thoreau's Life as a Writer*. New York: Viking, 1982.

Meltzer, Milton, and Walter Harding. *A Thoreau Profile*. New York: Crowell, 1962.

Miller, Perry, ed. *The Transcendentalists: An Anthology*. Cambridge, MA: Harvard University Press, 1950.

Mott, Wes, ed. *Biographical Dictionary of Transcendentalism*. Westport, CT: Greenwood Press, 1996.

———. *Encyclopedia of Transcendentalism*. Westport, CT: Greenwood Press, 1996.

Myerson, Joel, ed. *Transcendentalism: A Reader*. New York: Oxford University Press, 2001.

Paul, Sherman. *The Shores of America: Thoreau's Inward Exploration*. Urbana: University of Illinois Press, 1958.

Richardson, Robert D., Jr. *Henry Thoreau: A Life of the Mind.* Berkeley and Los Angeles: University of California Press, 1986.

Thoreau, Henry D. *Collected Essays and Poems.* [Edited by] Elizabeth Hall Witherell. New York: The Library of America, 2001.

———. *Consciousness in Concord: The Text of Thoreau's Hitherto "Lost Journal," 1840–1841.* Together with notes and a commentary by Perry Miller. Boston: Houghton Mifflin, 1958.

———. *I to Myself: An Annotated Selection from the Journal of Henry D. Thoreau.* Edited by Jeffrey S. Cramer. New Haven, CT: Yale University Press, 2007.

———. *Thoreau on Freedom: Attending to Man: Selected Writings from Henry David Thoreau.* Edited by Jeffrey S. Cramer. Foreword by Arun Gandhi. Golden, CO: Fulcrum, 2003.

INDEX